Paul's Theology of Preaching

National Association of Baptist Professors of Religion

JOURNAL

Perspectives in Religious Studies
Editor: Watson E. Mills
       Mercer University

SERIES

Special Studies Series
Editor: Edgar McKnight
       Furman University

Dissertation Series
Editor: James Wm. McClendon, Jr.
       Church Divinity School
       of the Pacific

Bibliographic Series
Editor: David M. Scholer
       North Park College
       and Theological Seminary

PAUL'S THEOLOGY
OF PREACHING

NABPR Dissertation Series, Number 6

by
John William Beaudean, Jr.

MP MERCER UNIVERSITY PRESS, Macon, Georgia 31207

ISBN 0-86554-341-0

The paper used in this publication meets the minimum requirements
of American National Standard for Information Sciences—Permanence
of Paper for Printed Library Materials, ANSI Z39.48-1984. ∞

Library of Congress Cataloging-in-Publication Data
Beaudean, John William.
      Paul's theology of preaching.
     (NABPR dissertation series ; no. 6)
     Bibliography: p. 211
     1. Preaching—Biblical teaching.   2. Bible. N.T.
Epistles of Paul—Criticism, Interpretation, etc.
I. Title.   II. Series.
BS2655.P8B43   227'.06   88-27378
ISBN 0-86554-341-0 (alk. paper)

TABLE OF CONTENTS

To my father and mother,
John W. and Elsie M. Beaudean

ACKNOWLEDGMENTS

The completion of a doctoral dissertation is the culmination of a long, arduous process, as anyone knows who has ever tried his or her hand at it. And although it is the work of a single individual, in the final analysis the project cannot be completed successfully without the cooperation, support and assistance of many people. It is only fitting that some of those who have helped the present writer be recognized and thanked for their support.

First and foremost, I must express my profound gratitude to the members of the congregation which I serve as pastor, Holy Faith Lutheran Church in Oak Ridge, N. J. It was not only with their consent, but with their encouragement, that I began my graduate work seven years ago. The leaders of the congregation then and since are to be praised for recognizing that, although it would take me beyond the strict confines of the parish, the congregation would benefit from their pastor's continuing education. I can only hope that what I have learned and tried to put into practice in my preaching and teaching has compensated them for their faith in me.

In particular I need to acknowledge several members of Holy Faith. First, I owe a debt I cannot repay to Doug and Diane Stelling and their two young sons, Lucas and Jonathan. Not only did they do me the great favor of allowing me to "baby sit" their IBM Personal Computer while they are away on business assignments in Japan and the Netherlands, but during the hectic days right before they were to leave Diane took the time to teach me the altogether new experience of working with a word processor. Their generosity and good grace saved me time and effort that is beyond calculation.

Second, my thanks go to Clarence Smith. He was most kind in offering me the use of his copier, and he never flinched at the many times I imposed on his work day, even during the height of the tax season. He has saved me considerable expense and inconvenience.

I am also profoundly thankful to the Rev. Dr. Walter L. Zeile, who, until his recent retirement, has served as President of the New Jersey District of the Lutheran Church—Missouri Synod. Through the years I have been in New Jersey, President Zeile has befriended me in more ways than I can possibly name. Not the least of his kindnesses has been the enthusiasm with which he has supported my doctoral program and the assistance which he provided me on numerous occasions.

Since this was my first experience in working with a computer, I was in continual need of assistance and advice in making the system work. In this respect I must thank my advisor, Dr. Darrell Doughty, who first encouraged me to use a computer and who always offered me his considerable knowledge of the field. In addition, I am grateful to Mark Branton, our nephew, and his friend Bob Toy, who provided technical assistance in handling the machine and keeping it running properly.

I am also most appreciative of the help provided by the members of my Dissertation Committee, Dr. Darrell Doughty, my advisor, Dr. Charles Rice, and Dr. William Stroker. They believed in the importance of the topic, treated all of my work with great respect, took the time to do careful evaluation, and always received me congenially. They have confirmed in me a conviction I have long held, namely, that the best research is collegial research.

My father and mother deserve mention. Besides their support and encouragement throughout the program, they also helped immeasurably with loans that, in a large part, made possible the financing of my graduate work.

Finally, most important of all, I am deeply grateful to my wife, Lynn, and our two daughters, Jenifer and Elizabeth. No amount of praise can compensate the sacrifices they have made for me over the last seven years, and particularly the last two. They have had to bear the burden of a husband and father whose mind was preoccupied and whose time with them was limited by the double obligation of a full-time parish ministry and graduate education. They have also had to put up with countless repairs around the house that have been left until "this is over." I am humbled by the extent and depth of their love. I count myself richly blessed.

Fall, 1985

ACKNOWLEDGMENT TO PUBLISHED EDITION

I wish to acknowledge with thanks two persons who assisted me in meeting my part of the costs for publishing my dissertation. Dean Thomas Ogletree of Drew University Theological School, where I am Adjunct Instructor in New Testament Greek, was kind enough to provide a grant. Also the Rev. Dr. Donald W. Sandmann, President of the New Jersey District of the Lutheran Church—Missouri Synod, assisted through his President's Discretionary Fund. Their support is certainly appreciated.

Fall, 1988

CHAPTER ONE

INTRODUCTION

In his recent book, *Building the Word,* J. Randall Nichols relates how Clement Welsh, Warden of the College of Preachers in Washington, D. C., finds that among the hundreds of Episcopal preachers with whom he deals in continuing education the most difficult question for most of them to answer is, "What do you want to accomplish in preaching?"[1] That question simply rephrases for contemporary preachers of the gospel the concern raised by Karl Barth in the early part of this century, namely, what is preaching supposed to do? *Why* preach? It is surely a question of fundamental importance, for until one has answered that question, preaching misses the essential ingredient of a clear sense of purpose. Thus the observation by Welsh reopens the vital matter of the theology of preaching.

In some respects it is surprising that contemporary preachers have diffi-culty articulating a theology of preaching. One might expect that the issue of a theology of preaching would have become a central concern of modern preachers and contemporary scholarship on preaching. Yet, despite H. H. Farmer's announcement a generation ago that a "rediscovery of the signifi-cance of preaching" was taking place,[2] works concerned with the theology of preaching are few. In the forty-odd years since Farmer's book, *The Ser-vant of the Word,* appeared, there has been a host of works dealing with var-ious aspects of the preaching task. Some treat the method of preaching,[3] others

---

[1] J. Randall Nichols, *Building the Word* (San Francisco: Harper & Row, 1980).

[2] Herbert H. Farmer, *The Servant of the Word,* Preacher's Paperback Library (Philadelphia: Fortress Press, 1964), 1.

[3] As examples, see Fred B. Craddock, *As One Without Authority* (Enid, OK: Phillips University Press, 1971) and Clyde E. Fant, *Preaching for Today* (New York: Harper & Row, 1975). An older work, still in use and still important today, is H. Grady Davis, *Design for Preaching* (Philadelphia: Muhlenberg, 1958).

PAUL'S THEOLOGY OF PREACHING

treat the context of preaching,[4] and still others have related preaching to imagination[5] and the arts.[6] More recently much interest has been generated in the narrative character of preaching and the nature of preaching as story-telling.[7] Many of these have proven helpful and bear eloquent testimony to the fact that preaching still enjoys the resurgence of which Farmer spoke. If, however, that resurgence is to continue, then it would seem vital that the question about a theology of preaching be explored anew. For if preachers have trouble answering Welsh's question about the aim of their preaching, then the entire enterprise is in danger of collapse.

The present work intends to address this question of the theology of preaching, making a biblically based contribution to the contemporary discussion. More specifically, the present writer aims to construct a theology of preaching based on the letters of Paul.

Two questions arise. Why biblically based? And why Paul? The first question is answered by pointing to the fact that at the present there appears to be a renewed interest in biblical preaching.[8] At the same time, as we shall see, most thought devoted to the theology of preaching has come from the field of systematic theology rather than biblical exegesis. It would, therefore, seem appropriate to address the subject from a biblical perspective. The second question, Why a theology of preaching based on *Paul*?, can be answered by observing that the renewed interest in biblically-oriented preaching mentioned above has turned attention primarily to the Gospels (particularly the synoptic Gospels, and especially the parables). Paul's letters have been left largely out of account, a regrettable oversight considering the high regard the apostle had for preaching. Even a cursory reading of the chief letters of Paul reveals how central Paul regarded the task of preaching. And since Paul is the earliest contributor included in the New Testament canonical literature, it is all the more appropriate that we begin with his letters. If, therefore, Paul's theology of preaching could be discovered, his insights might very well illuminate this essential task, to the benefit of both preachers and their congregations.

---

[4]Valuable recent works include Elizabeth Achtemeier, *Creative Preaching* (Nashville: Abingdon Press, 1981) and William H. Willimon, *Worship as Pastoral Care* (Nashville: Abingdon Press, 1979).

[5]See Charles L. Rice, *Interpretation and Imagination: The Preacher and Contemporary Literature* (Philadelphia: Fortress Press, 1970).

[6]R[obert] E. C. Browne, *The Ministry of the Word* (London: S. C. M. Press, 1958) and Frederick Buechner, *Telling the Truth: The Gospel as Tragedy, Comedy and Fairy Tale* (San Francisco: Harper & Row, 1977) are very much recommended to the interested reader.

[7]See Edmund Steimle, Morris J. Niedenthal and Charles L. Rice, *Preaching the Story* (Philadelphia: Fortress Press, 1980).

[8]Charles L. Rice, "Just Church Bells? One Man's View of Preaching Today," *Drew Gateway* (Spring, 1979): 21-27.

The present investigation thus brings together two fields, that of contemporary study related to the theology of preaching and that of New Testament biblical study of the theology of Paul. It is the belief of this writer that these two areas can be brought into fruitful dialogue and that the ensuing discussion will prove helpful as well as timely.

The first step in this task is to examine where matters currently stand in scholarship. We turn our attention, therefore, to a review of the work of leading scholars in these two fields in relation to the question of a theology of preaching.

We begin with a group of theologians who have given serious thought to the theology of preaching. They represent one stream of theological reflection, that stream which can be called "word of God" theology. While there are other traditions which might merit our consideration, this group of theologians makes an appropriate point of departure partly because they are recognized scholars whose influence continues to the present, partly because their thought has had a broad appeal both in mainstream Protestantism and in Roman Catholicism, and partly because they found the letters of Paul a vital resource for their theological endeavor. As we consider what these theologians have to say about the theology of preaching, we will want to keep in mind several key concerns which guide our inquiry. We will ask, What is the theological origin and definition of preaching? How does preaching function? What is its nature and character? And what are its results?

THEOLOGY OF PREACHING BEGINNING WITH BARTH

The discussion of a theology of preaching begins with Karl Barth. Few would dispute that for twentieth century Protestant preachers it was he, more than any other, who first brought the terms "theology" and "preaching" into dynamic relationship. In fact, he himself claimed that his entire theological enterprise was only a "marginal note, a gloss" which arose out of his concern for the "need and promise of preaching."[9]

Barth's theology is a theology of the word of God, which he defined by saying, "God's Word means that God speaks."[10] To clarify what he means by this and other similar expressions Barth takes as his starting point "the fact that God wills to reveal himself."[11] And this revelation is supremely accom-

---

[9]Karl Barth, *The Word of God and the Word of Man* (New York: Harper & Brothers, 1957), 98, 100.

[10]Karl Barth, *Church Dogmatics,* Vol. 1, Part One, second edition (Edinburgh: Clark, 1975), 132. Barth's theology became known as dialectical theology. He understood the Bible as "through and through dialectic," by which he meant that it calls a human being into conversation with God, a God who is the "Wholly Other" (*Word of God,* 73-74).

[11]Karl Barth, *The Preaching of the Gospel* (Philadelphia: Westminster Press, 1963), 16.

plished in Jesus Christ, who is himself the "word become flesh."[12] The heart of this revelation, of all biblical theology, says Barth, is the cross. It is through the cross that redemption comes. In Christ's crucifixion and resurrection God has brought "life to light out of death."[13]

Such a word of God, powerful and redemptive, confronts human beings, calling for a response. According to Barth the word of God "has the simple spiritual power of truth" and the "character of address."[14] And what is the response that is called for? Barth replies, Simply the humility and joy which constitute faith.[15]

Barth's theology of preaching is directly related to his theology of the word of God. Preaching is therefore nothing other than "the word of God which he himself has spoken," using as his medium a human voice.[16] In practical terms this means for Barth that the preacher's task is to "proclaim to his fellowmen what God himself has to say to them by explaining, in his own words, a passage from Scripture which concerns them personally."[17] This definition alerts us to the specific nature of Barth's theology of preaching. For Barth understands the word of God as existing in a three-fold form. First, there is the actual revelation of God, which he describes as "God's own word spoken by God himself," the event of God's grace.[18] Second, this past revelation appears in the Holy Scripture, which "is itself the deposit of what was once proclamation by human lips."[19] Thus Scripture is the secondary level of revelation, the witness to God's primary revelation.[20] It is God's word "to the extent that God causes it to be his word, to the extent that he speaks through it."[21] Preaching is the third form of the word of God. It is in continuity with the actual revelation of God through the instrumentality of the Holy Scripture.[22] This explains why Barth's description of the preaching task is understood in terms of an explanation of a passage of Scripture. In this succession from event of God's actual revelation in Christ to Scripture to proclamation "present-day preaching [is] the continuation of one and the same event."[23]

This understanding of preaching alerts us further to what Barth sees as the essential miracle of proclamation, namely, that the word of God and human

---

[12]Ibid., 18.
[13]Barth, *Word of God*, 77.
[14]Barth, *Church Dogmatics*, 1:One, 136, 140.
[15]Barth, *Word of God*, 25.
[16]Barth, *The Preaching of the Gospel*, 9.
[17]Ibid.
[18]Barth, *Church Dogmatics*, 1:One, 113.
[19]Ibid., 102.
[20]Ibid., 102, 107-11.
[21]Ibid., 109.
[22]Ibid., 102-104.
[23]Ibid., 102.

speech become indissolubly linked. Barth understands this relationship between word of God and human speech as existing along the lines of the analogy of the two natures of Christ, so that what is divine comes through on the human level.[24] Barth can also refer to the event of preaching by saying, "The Word of God means . . . man's talk about God in which and through which God speaks about himself."[25] On the other hand, by its very nature this is an impossible task, since, according to Barth, humanly speaking God is not an object.[26] But if we cannot in fact talk about God, how can preaching occur? Barth answers by explaining that this is the miracle of God's grace, "a divine victory concealed in human failure."[27] Or, as he also succinctly puts it, "God then makes good what we do badly."[28]

Barth also sees preaching as intimately connected to the church. The church is the assembly of believers, and preaching is bound up in its mission and existence. Preaching both constitutes the church and is carried on under apostolic authority only in the context of the church.[29] This means that God has commissioned the church to speak about him, so that "the Word of God is God himself in the proclamation of the church of Jesus Christ."[30] The church exists to carry out this mission, to be God's witness in whom "God declares his revelation."[31]

In the final analysis, therefore, for Barth preaching is an *event*. It is the "exercise of sovereign power on the part of God and obedience on the part of man."[32] Or, as Barth also summarizes it, preaching is a matter of "reproducing in thought that one unique event, the gift of God's grace."[33] Such preaching as event has "one unique end: the fulfillment of Revelation, the redemption which awaits us."[34]

Barth's dialectical theology, which first appeared in his commentary on Romans in 1918, generated a vigorous debate in German scholarly circles. James Robinson notes that his views were widely rejected by many respected scholars as evidencing a lack of mastery of critical historical details and as being "merely practical and edifying, i.e., of no further interest to scholar-

---

[24]Ibid., 94.

[25]Ibid., 95.

[26]Karl Barth, *Church Dogmatics,* Vol. 1, Part Two, second edition (Edinburgh: Clark, 1975), 750.

[27]Ibid., 751.

[28]Ibid.

[29]Barth, *The Preaching of the Gospel,* 33.

[30]Barth, *Church Dogmatics,* 1:Two, 743.

[31]Ibid.

[32]Barth, *The Preaching of the Gospel,* 16.

[33]Ibid., 21.

[34]Ibid., 18.

ship.''[35] But one scholar who found himself in basic sympathy with Barth was the young Marburg professor Rudolf Bultmann. He, like Barth, was seriously concerned about the nature of preaching in the post-war period and keenly aware of the failure of previous liberal theology. Bultmann too sought to rethink Christian theology, but whereas Barth returned to the categories of classical Christian dogma in order to restructure the foundations of Christian theology, and therefore of preaching, Bultmann instead was drawn to the philosophy of Martin Heidegger for his terms of reference.[36] In Heidegger's analysis of human experience, or phenomenology of existence, Bultmann thought he had found a way to express Christian theology in terms understandable to modern people.[37]

The basic starting point for Heidegger's thinking was his belief that all human beings are concerned with existence.[38] His term for the individual human is *Dasein*, a ''being-there,'' which implies that as a ''being'' a person is constantly developing and changing and that also one has one's being ''there,'' in the concrete world. The goal and possibility for such creatures is ''authentic existence,'' an existence which is to be found in confronting certain fundamental questions, the most intense being those of care and death.[39] Heidegger argues that these threats to existence must be faced in order for authentic existence to emerge. The temptation is to surrender to the cares that constantly surround us and to flee from the fact of death. Such surrender results in inauthentic existence. But another possibility exists. That possibility

---

[35]James M. Robinson and John Cobb, eds., *The New Hermeneutic* (New York: Harper & Row, 1964), 28.

[36]The editor's preface to *Church Dogmatics* notes that Barth directs modern theology back to its patristic foundations in the dogma of the Holy Trinity (1:One, viii.).

[37]Stephen Neill, *The Interpretation of the New Testament 1861-1961* (New York: Oxford University Press, 1966), 229. Neill observes, ''This is a familiar procedure. The theologian takes that form of philosophy which is dominant in his day and reinterprets the Christian faith in the terms and categories of that philosophy. This is what Thomas Aquinas did with the Aristotelian system of his time'' (Ibid.).

[38]Heidegger's philosophy began with a fundamental dissatisfaction with metaphysics as the foundation for conceptualizing life, based as it was upon a subject-object split which objectivized reality on the basis of one's prior categories. This he regarded as a distortion, and thus he began to seek a more fundamental ontology, an understanding of human existence from *within* life. For a detailed description and evaluation of Heidegger's thought see Richard E. Palmer, *Hermeneutics* (Evanston, Illinois: Northwestern University Press, 1969), 124ff. See also Paul Achtemeier, *An Introduction to the New Hermeneutic* (Philadelphia: Westminster Press, 1969), 28-29. Norman Perrin, *The Promise of Bultmann* (Philadelphia and New York: J. B. Lippincott Co., 1969), 28ff., serves as the basis for the description that follows. For a fuller treatment of Heidegger's philosophy in relation to Bultmann's theology see Walter Schmithals, *An Introduction to the Theology of Rudolf Bultmann* (Minneapolis: Augsburg Publishing House, 1968).

[39]By ''care'' Heidegger means that we face daily concerns about immediacies of life, such as providing for ouselves, etc. And by ''death'' he means the end of being; thus the human being is a ''being-unto-death.''

comes by way of a *decision* to accept one's death and one's "being-there." Such a decision, according to Heidegger, results in authentic existence.

Bultmann adopts Heidegger's analysis of human existence, but he rejects Heidegger's solution as a "resolution of despair."[40] Instead, on the basis of his theology, Bultmann claims that authentic existence is made possible for us in relation to God. It is a gift received by faith. In Bultmann's view the problem facing humanity is sin, which is understood as our attempt to secure our own existence.[41] Faith is the freedom from sin, which is also described as forgiveness.[42] It is the foundation and living out of authentic existence.

But by what means do faith and authentic existence arise? Bultmann contends that they come through the word of God, which he characterizes as proclamation addressed to the hearer, a call to genuine freedom.[43] This word of God is located in the canonical Scriptures, for to Bultmann, in the words of Walter Schmithals, "the New Testament has the character of Word, . . . *kerygma*, the Word of God."[44] At this point Bultmann is clearly in step with the dialectical theology of Barth. But Bultmann's development of the concept of word of God takes a different direction, partly because he is more keenly aware than Barth of the hermeneutical problems of human understanding and partly because his description is framed in terms of existentialist categories.

Bultmann sees that hermeneutically the connection between the reader/hearer and the text is the question about the possibilities of existence. For both the author and the interpreter have a " 'life-relationship to the *matter* which is . . . expressed in the text.' "[45] In dialogue with the text one's previous self-understanding is tested, challenged, there is an encounter with a claim that calls for decision, and from that decision a new, authentic self-understanding emerges.[46] It is at this point that Bultmann goes beyond Barth in treating the text. For Bultmann's criticism of Barth's *Römerbrief,* in part, was centered in what he regarded as Barth's having identified too closely the "subject matter" (*Sache*) with the text. That is to say, he faulted Barth for the incompleteness of his translation of the subject matter of Paul's theology because Barth framed his exposition in terms of the myth and dogma resident in the

[40]Perrin, *The Promise of Bultmann,* 64f.

[41]Rudolf Bultmann, *Faith and Understanding,* ed. Robert Funk, Vol. 1 (New York: Harper, 1969), 228.

[42]Schmithals, *Introduction to Bultmann,* 112ff. See also Rudolf Bultmann, *Jesus Christ and Mythology* (New York: Charles Scribner's Sons, 1958), 38-41.

[43]Bultmann, *Jesus Christ and Mythology,* 43. See also Schmithals, *Introduction to Bultmann,* 179.

[44]Schmithals, *Introduction to Bultmann,* 222.

[45]Rudolf Bultmann, *Glauben und Verstehen,* Vol. 2, (Tübingen: J. C. B. Mohr [Paul Siebeck], 1952), 217, quoted in Schmithals, *Introduction to Bultmann,* 234.

[46]Schmithals, *Introduction to Bultmann,* 232.

text.[47] Instead, Bultmann believes the subject matter goes beyond the text, beyond the interpreting word, even beyond Paul.[48] This is due, according to Bultmann, to the fact that both language and human conceptualization are inadequate for the subject matter, which is human existence.[49] Thus Bultmann understands the meaning of the text not in terms of its mythical cosmology or dogma, but in terms of an existentialist frame of reference. For this reason, and for purposes of explicating the concern for human existence implicit in the text, Bultmann develops an approach to Scripture which he refers to as *Sachkritik* ("content criticism") and defines as a criticism " 'which distinguishes between what is said and what is meant and measures what is said by what is meant.' "[50]

A further distinction between Bultmann and Barth in interpreting the Scriptures is related to the foregoing. It arises from Bultmann's concern about language. Bultmann sees that the New Testament uses mythological terms in order to express its theology. By this he does not mean merely mythological language, but mythological thinking, both of which are incomprehensible to modern people because people no longer operate with such an obsolete worldview. By myth Bultmann means " 'a way of representing the otherworldly in terms of this world, the divine in terms of human life, the "beyond" in terms of this side.' "[51] Thus, Bultmann, as a part of his *Sachkritik,* calls for "demythologizing" the text, which for him does not mean excluding or eliminating myth, but means interpreting the mythical elements of the text in existentialist categories.[52] The myth's meaning must be adequately expressed.[53] Such interpretation he sees as essential in order to "make clear the call of the Word of God."[54] For kerygma as event does not exist, Bultmann claims, apart from its matrix, which in the case of the Scripture is framed in mythological

---

[47]Robinson, *New Hermeneutic,* 29.

[48]Ibid., 30f. It is on this basis that Bultmann can fault Paul for contradicting himself in his discussion of wisdom in 1 Cor. 1:18-3:2 and of resurrection in 1 Cor. 15 (Bultmann, "Karl Barth, *The Resurrection of the Dead,*" in *Faith and Understanding,* 71f., 83f.).

[49]Robinson, *New Hermeneutic,* 32f. See also Schmithals, *Introduction to Bultmann,* 233ff.

[50]Rudolf Bultmann, *Glauben und Verstehen,* Vol. 3 (Tübingen: J. C. B. Mohr [Paul Siebeck], 1960), 34, quoted in Schmithals, 245. Important to Bultmann's *Sachkritik* is the conception of the hermeneutical circle, which means that one starts from a pre-understanding of human existence which guides the question that is addressed to the text. This interaction with the text moves one to the point of having one's understanding clarified by the text so that a new pre-understanding emerges.

[51]Rudolf Bultmann, *Kerygma and Myth* (London: S. P. C. K., 1953), 10, quoted in Schmithals, *Introduction to Bultmann,* 251. As an example Bultmann points to the fact that in the Scriptures God's transcendence is described in *spatial* terms. See further Bultmann, *Jesus Christ and Mythology,* 18ff.

[52]Schmithals, *Introduction to Bultmann,* 260.

[53]Robinson, *New Hermeneutic,* 34.

[54]Bultmann, *Jesus Christ and Mythology,* 43.

categories, with the result that existentialist interpretation is necessary in order that the kerygma may be recovered and heard anew.[55]

Bultmann's theology of preaching, therefore, emerges from his existentialist understanding of life and of text. For Bultmann preaching is the means by which the hearer is brought to a decision for faith and authentic existence on the basis of the biblical text. For preaching is the word of God spoken in the present, the living voice of the gospel.[56]

For Bultmann preaching is always proclamation, kerygma, announcement.[57] It is "not addressed to theoretical reason, but to the self."[58] It is not a case of communicating information.[59] Instead, the proclamation of the word is a "call for faith;" it constitutes a "challenge to give up one's previous self-understanding."[60] Thus preaching is an eschatological event, a salvation occurrence which is "nowhere present except in the proclaiming, accosting, demanding, and promising word of preaching."[61]

The content of preaching, according to Bultmann, is the death and resurrection of Christ. For the cross is judgment on our self-security, and accepting as our Lord the crucified means relinquishing all boasts and receiving an entirely new identity. At the same time preaching the cross means preaching the resurrection, which signifies that God has raised up the crucified one as Lord of the world and criterion of human existence. According to Bultmann, the existentialist meaning of the resurrection of Christ is that "a historical person and his fate are raised to the rank of an eschatological event."[63] Or, as he further explains, "The meaning of the resurrection is not that he is translated into the beyond, but that he is exalted to the status of Lord (Phil. 2:11)."[63] This is not a fact open to objective scrutiny, but instead it means the risen Christ is present in the proclaimed word.[64] Thus in the cross and resurrection all self-security is ended, and the hearer is called to accept authentic existence as gift of God.[65] For this reason Bultmann can say that Jesus Christ confronts us in the kerygma, that he *is* the word of God.[66] The event of the cross "becomes contemporary in the address itself."[67]

---

[55]Schmithals, *Introduction to Bultmann*, 264. Robinson, *New Hermeneutic*, 34.
[56]Schmithals, *Introduction to Bultmann*, 178.
[57]Ibid., 177.
[58]Bultmann, *Jesus Christ and Mythology*, 36.
[59]Bultmann, *Faith and Understanding*, 241.
[60]Rudolf Bultmann, *Theology of the New Testament*, Vol. 1, (New York: Scribner, 1951-55), 301.
[61]Ibid., 302.
[62]Ibid., 305f.
[63]Ibid., 306.
[64]Ibid., 305.
[65]Schmithals, *Introduction to Bultmann*, 130ff.
[66]Bultmann, *Faith and Understanding*, 308.

It is probably safe to say that the theologies of preaching articulated by Barth and Bultmann not only continue to have influence today, but that almost every respected scholar since their time has been compelled to deal with their work. While the influence of these two theologians has been felt both in Europe and the United States, Barth's influence has been greatest among preachers in the English speaking world, while Bultmann's has been most pronounced in Germany.

Though World War II interrupted the discussion of dialectical theology and its movement into the English speaking world, already in the late 1920s Barth's work was beginning to be recognized in England. E. C. Hoskyns translated Barth's commentary on Romans into English in 1933, and since his lectures became important in the return from liberalism to a more conservative, orthodox posture among British theologians, the influence of Barth in the English-speaking world might very well be dated from that point.[68] It fell to Herbert H. Farmer, however, to develop the theology of Barth into a new theology of preaching on British soil. This Farmer accomplished in the 1940s with his book entitled *The Servant of the Word*, a volume influential out of all proportion to its diminutive size and one which brought the fruits of Barth's theology of preaching to a new generation of American Protestant preachers as well.[69]

For the shaping of his theology of preaching Farmer lays hold of several key Barthian themes. Farmer accepts as his point of departure Barth's insight that preaching and the message form an indissoluble link, one "organic whole."[70] This Farmer illustrates by noting how Barth's emphasis on the objective, historical *givenness* of the event of God's self-revelation in Jesus Christ requires that the event be witnessed to, proclaimed.[71] Also, both Farmer's emphasis on the Christian church as a part of the saving event, an eschatological fellowship, and his reminder that the Gospel is both "claim and succour" are derived from Barth.[72]

This does not mean, however, that Farmer's work is merely a summary of Barth, as is essentially the case with Dietrich Ritschl's work some twenty years later.[73] Instead, Farmer carries the discussion further by addressing

---

[67]Ibid., 241. As a further explanation of what Bultmann means by this Perrin says, "The proclamation of the cross repeats the event of the cross in that it makes it a reality in the present of the hearer" (Perrin, *The Promise of Bultmann*, 69).

[68]Neill, *Interpretation*, 213ff.

[69]Farmer consciously begins with Barth as his prime example of the church's rediscovery of the "indissoluble oneness of preaching and the Christian faith." (Farmer, *Servant of the Word*, 7ff.).

[70]Ibid., 5.

[71]Ibid., 11.

[72]Ibid., 11, 44ff.

[73]Dietrich Ritschl, *A Theology of Preaching* (Richmond: John Knox, 1960).

himself to the question of why preaching should be a part of the saving activity of God. This question is answered, Farmer believes, in Martin Buber's "I-Thou" relationship.[74] On the basis of Buber's insight, Farmer believes our eyes have been reopened to the central truth that "the necessity of preaching resides in the fact that when God saves a man through Christ he insists on a living, personal encounter with him here and now in the sphere of present personal relationships."[75] Preaching is, therefore, God's activity, his address to each of us personally.[76]

Farmer next explores the "I-Thou" relationship in connection with word. He proposes at the outset that God's purpose is such that "He never enters into *personal* relationship with a man apart from other human persons."[77] This is traceable, Farmer claims, to the fact of God's creation, his having ordained that human beings should be distinctively human precisely within this relational structure with God and others. What he means exactly by such a relational structure Farmer spells out by saying, "The heart of the matter is in the relationship of self-conscious, self-directing wills to one another in a situation which is important and significant to both."[78] This is accomplished, insists Farmer, without a violation of the freedom of either person, through an "inescapable claim" on each other within a "community of insight and understanding," or "shared meaning."[79] And this finally is supremely accomplished through the medium of speech.[80] On this basis, then, Farmer calls for preaching which is concrete in its relation to the lives of the hearers and which takes the nature of "spontaneous directness of serious private conversation."[81]

In the United States, during the early 1960s, Paul Scherer identified closely with the message of both Barth and Farmer. Scherer's concern is that of getting the gospel heard, for he agrees with Theodore Wedel that there is "a whole generation . . . which has never heard the Christian Gospel, only the *Reader's Digest* version, the success-story rendition."[82] In the face of this and other hazards in preaching Scherer finds consolation in the fact that the word of God has a power of its own, for it "lays hold on the stuff of human existence and reshapes it."[83] With Barth, Scherer believes that this Word of God is an

---

[74]See Farmer, *Servant of the Word,* 13ff., for a fuller overview of Buber's insights.
[75]Ibid., 15.
[76]Ibid.
[77]Ibid., 22.
[78]Ibid., 26.
[79]Ibid., 27-28.
[80]Ibid., 33.
[81]Ibid., 39.
[82]Paul Scherer, *The Word God Sent* (Grand Rapids: Baker Book House, 1977), 5.
[83]Ibid., 19.

event of revelation, that "it is himself [God] wants to bestow."[84] Further, Scherer regards God's revelatory Word as arising in the Scriptures, and therefore he contends that biblical preaching serves to "reconstitute in every separate and believing life, by means of that very deed which the Bible is, the saving fact of God's redemption."[85] Therefore, preaching is always preaching of the gospel, which Scherer describes as a "radical transformation."[86]

What makes Scherer's theology of preaching distinctive, however, is his conviction that the aim of preaching is a "massive and profound *identity* [emphasis mine]. . . . In what is past God speaks to what is deeply present."[87] According to Scherer, God's speaking to our present has a "sense of immediacy;" it has "the authority of One who stands at the door and knocks."[88] It is this immediacy of the gospel which constitutes its disturbing character, for, as Scherer insists, "Nothing can do [people] good unless it disturbs them. And nothing will disturb them to any lasting effect unless it disturbs them deeply."[89] Thus, Scherer's theology of preaching is supremely conscious of the scandal of the gospel, that the gospel is a word of God that disturbingly gets at the roots of our "sense of bewilderment, alienation and anxiety"[90] and calls us to "ceaseless participation in [God's] eternal and redemptive purposes."[91]

On the European continent the theology of preaching also continued to be rethought. Most notable is Helmut Thielecke, respected theologian and preacher who faced squarely the problem of the credibility of the gospel in post-World War II Germany. In many respects his theology of preaching is not new; his concern for textual preaching and his emphasis that in preaching the "Word becomes flesh again" to serve as a "divider of spirits" resonate deeply with Barth.[92] What is distinctive, however, is his conviction that preaching does not begin with the preacher, or even with theology, but rather with the hearer. Thielecke is highly critical of preachers who from the pulpit transmit unintelligible language from the Christian tradition, language which they themselves do not use in daily living. It is such preachers, Thielecke claims, who have created the problem of credibility. Thielecke's book constitutes a "class action suit" on behalf of those who still listen to sermons. He therefore calls for preaching which translates the gospel into contempo-

---

[84]Ibid., 24.

[85]Ibid., 29.

[86]Ibid., 69.

[87]Ibid., 39.

[88]Ibid., 34.

[89]Ibid., 70.

[90]Ibid.

[91]Ibid., 87.

[92]Helmut Thielecke, *The Trouble with the Church: A Call for Renewal* (New York: Harper & Row, 1965), 40.

rary idiom so that it can be heard again. For in this way there occurs a ''transvaluation of all values,'' which he describes by saying, ''We will smile in the face of what before made us lose our nerve, and we will learn to fear things which hitherto we desired or considered harmless.''[93] Thus, Thielecke succeeds in reintroducing the question of language into the discussion of a theology of preaching.

Not all those who were engaged in the theology of preaching, though, felt so directly the impact of Barth. In this country Richard Caemmerer was articulating a highly respected theology of preaching based on biblical texts and systematized according to the categories of Lutheran confessional theology. For Caemmerer preaching is ''the Word of God to man and the power of God at work in man.''[94] It is essentially a message from God which not only tells of God's gift of life in the cross and resurrection of Jesus Christ but itself gives that gift of life.[95] Its fruits are repentance, faith, and obedience.[96] So high a view of preaching is Caemmerer's that he can refer to it as ''the Sacrament of Holy Preaching,'' having its ''words of institution'' in the commission of the risen Christ in Luke 24: 45-49, its effective power in the imparting of God's grace, and its visible element in the person of the preacher who is witness.[97] His summary of the power and purpose of preaching is a remarkable parody on the description of the power of baptism in Luther's Small Catechism:

> How can words do such great things? It is not the words indeed that do them, but the Word of God which is in and with the words, and faith which trusts such Word of God in the words. For without the Word of God the words are simple words, and no preaching; but with the Word of God the words are preaching, that is, a precious Word of life and the power of God to salvation, as St. Paul says, Rom. 1:16; 1 Thess, 2:13.[98]

In Great Britain Robert E. C. Browne was engaged in recasting the theology of preaching along lines suggested by the arts. Based on his view that the biblical writers were not simply transcribers of divine dictation but rather ''free agents who used their imagination and intelligence in obedience to the divine promptings,'' Browne concluded that the preacher must regard his own work similarly.[99] Browne views preaching as an art, whose correct practice requires form, understatement, and a certain ambiguity.[100] What, then, does preaching accomplish? Browne answers, ''[It is] the communication of an at-

---

[93]Ibid., 38.

[94]Richard R. Caemmerer, *Preaching for the Church* (St. Louis: Concordia Publishing House, 1959), 1.

[95]Ibid.

[96]Ibid., 15ff.

[97]Richard Caemmerer, ''In Many Much,'' *Concordia Theological Monthly* (November, 1968): 654.

[98]Ibid.

[99]R[obert] E. C. Browne, *The Ministry of the Word* (London: S. C. M., 1958), 8.

[100]See Browne, 17-29, for a full explanation of what he means by these terms.

titude, a sense of confidence that will prevent [people] from being lost in the major human experiences of love, hate, treachery, betrayal and death."[101] Therefore, Browne envisions the ministry of the word as having a three-fold aim:

> First, to release people from all tautness of mind; secondly, to free them from the dominance of others and so deliver them from the burden of false obligation; thirdly, to prevent or break their dependence on him. In order to do this his language needs to be as evocative through its imagery as it is stimulating in the variety of its forms.[102]

The emergence of the new hermeneutic in Germany during the 1960s brought fresh impetus toward reconceptualizing the task of preaching. Two leading figures in this movement were Gerhard Ebeling, a systematic theologian, and Ernst Fuchs, a biblical scholar. Both theologians continued the Bultmannian program, with its Heideggerian presuppositions. However, Ebeling and Fuchs evidence more concern with language and the linguisticality of existence, in conformity with the philosophy of the "later" Heidegger.

Heidegger's work is often divided into two periods. The first, referred to as his "anthropological" period, focuses on the human being as the *Dasein*. In his second period Heidegger is more concerned with "Being" itself.[103] This latter period is referred to as his "linguistic" period since, according to his analysis, Being confronts the human being with the necessity of response, and that response is language. According to Heidegger, this language response is traceable to the fact that Being is nameable. And since Being is prior to individual beings, Being is foundational for language. This means language is not the creation of human beings; rather, human beings are the creation of language. That is to say, Being reveals itself to human beings through language. As a result, Heidegger can refer to language as the "house of Being." This emphasis on the linguisticality of existence has had a profound influence on Ebeling and Fuchs with respect to their understanding of language in the Scriptures and in preaching.

Ebeling begins by asserting that there is little certainty in preaching today.[104] This is due, he thinks, to a gap between scientific theology and proclamation, a condition which is in turn traceable to the altered situation of the modern world in which traditional metaphysical categories have given way to a historical understanding of reality.[105] The effects are felt particularly in the area of the critical study of Scriptures, which has served to undermine the

---

[101]Ibid., 64.

[102]Ibid., 81

[103]Our description here follows the analysis done by Achtemeier (*Introduction to the New Hermeneutic*, especially 41-54).

[104]Gerhard Ebeling, *Theology and Proclamation* (Philadelphia: Fortress Press, 1966), 13.

[105]Ibid. 15.

orthodox conception of the authority of the Bible. It is precisely at this point that Ebeling believes hermeneutics serves as the road to bring together again historical theology and authoritative proclamation.[106]

Ebeling understands the task of dogmatic theology to be a reflective one, a matter of exposition.[107] He contends that today this important task is necessary to help resolve a key problem in Christian proclamation, the problem of Christology. For the changed situation, noted above, has eroded the world view which previously served as the structure for Christological thinking.[108] Therefore Ebeling finds value in adopting Bultmann's notion that the essential thing is the kerygma, understood as the word of address in Jesus Christ, which calls for a decisive response. However, Ebeling adopts this term with reservation, for he believes Bultmann his shortchanged the historical nature of that kerygma by focusing too heavily on the "that" of Jesus' historical existence.[109] Instead, Ebeling believes the kerygma not only is something, but also that in its Christological formulation it *was* something, which has as its vital task to "ratify and purify actual kerygma."[110]

As a result, Ebeling sees that we are left to deal with, rather than dismiss, the traditional Christological formulae, which raises the problem of interpretation, for "it seems that precisely those formulae which ought to give most cogent expression to the faith, do, in fact, make it more difficult to understand."[111] One has to interpret the linguistic elements of the tradition, therefore, in order to "show the self-understanding which is expressed in them (by which is meant the comprehensive understanding of the reality they embody)."[112] On the other hand, the preacher has to be clear, Ebeling claims, about the precise nature of that required interpretation. For the key problem is not so much that people lack the understanding of the kerygma as that they no longer regard it as having a claim on them. The task of proclamation, therefore, is to interpret the traditional kerygma, and then, guided by it, to carry out the *kērussein* ("preaching") itself, which means "addressing one's listeners in such a way that they begin to see their situation is determined by the ground of the Christological kerygma."[113]

But how does preaching accomplish this objective? Decisive, for Ebeling, is the question of language. Ebeling has seen that it is not a matter of the

---

[106]Ibid., 25.

[107]Ibid., 20.

[108]Ibid., 35.

[109]Ibid., 36ff., where Ebeling offers a detailed critique of Bultmann's understanding of the "that" of the historical Jesus.

[110]Ibid., 43.

[111]Ibid., 49.

[112]Ibid.

[113]Ibid., 53. It is for this reason that Ebeling, against Bultmann, thinks the question of the historical Jesus is essential for the task of theology and of preaching.

understanding *of* language; rather, the crucial concern is "understanding THROUGH language."[114] Language itself is constitutive of reality. Words achieve understanding by appealing to experience and leading to experience; the very structure of word is that it invites participation, communication.[115] It is a "word-event" (*Wortgeschehen*). Therefore, the word of God cannot be separated from human speech:

> [Man's] existence is, rightly understood, a word-event which has its origin in the Word of God and, in response to that Word, makes openings by a right and salutary use of words. Therein man is the image of God.[116]

The word-event takes place in the gospel, since it "makes man human by making him a believer."[117] This gospel is, finally, rooted in the biblical text, which is past kerygma, and so Ebeling believes the sermon is, following the analogy of legal precedent, "the EXECUTION of the text."[118]

Ebeling's close associate Ernst Fuchs is in essential agreement. His theology of preaching also proceeds from his hermeneutic, a hermeneutic which is very similar to Ebeling's in its emphasis on understanding through language, on the question about one's self as the starting point, and on the language-event character of existence.[119] But whereas Ebeling devotes his thinking to the relationship between preaching and theology, Fuchs is concerned with the relation of preaching to the biblical text, to exegesis.

The key word for Fuchs' concept of preaching, therefore, is "translation," which he describes as letting the living part of the text, its spirit, to be "set over" (*übersetzen*) and expressed anew in our own language.[120] He defines proclamation, then, as the "true translation of the text."[121] The text is, for Fuchs, absolutely essential for preaching; in fact, he insists that "proclamation requires the text, because it only continues what was revealed through Jesus: the event of God's word."[122] And the object of such translation, Fuchs

---

[114]Gerhard Ebeling, *Word and Faith* (London: S. C. M., 1963), 318.

[115]Ibid., 326.

[116]Ibid., 327.

[117]Ibid., 328.

[118]Ibid., 331.

[119]See Robinson, *New Hermeneutic*, 51ff., for an excellent analysis of Fuchs' hermeneutic. Decisive for Fuchs is that the "text interprets us" through the medium of language. More specifically, Fuchs understands such language, in contrast to Heidegger, to be essentially *Christological*. It is in the language of Jesus that it is revealed what space and time are for, namely, "as space for others and time for us." (Ibid., 53).

[120]Ernst Fuchs, *Studies of the Historical Jesus* (London: S. C. M. Press, 1964), 194.

[121]Ibid., 195.

[122]Ibid., 204. This should not be understood as implying that Fuchs makes word and text identical. For him the word is the revelation of God, the "word of love," which calls the hearer to faith. The word precedes the text, for the text "subserves the proclamation of faith and thereby the revelation of love, and delivers to faith as the decisive gift of love the word which was *vicariously portrayed* [emphasis mine] in the text." Thus, says Fuchs, "He who wants to proclaim correctly must then translate the text of love back into the word of love." (Ibid.).

explains, is "[to] allow the life of the text to come to light; translation should create the same sphere, which the text meant to create when the spirit spoke in it."[123] From this analysis it now becomes clear what Fuchs regards as the task of preaching:

> If the word has precedence over the text, because the word intended in the text is God's word, as it was heard and could be said in Jesus as God's 'yes' to man, faith then has to proclaim this word by repeating Jesus. The task of proclamation is to repeat Jesus.[124]

So lofty is his view of preaching that Fuchs can say that proclamation, functioning in this way, "participates in God's omnipotence."[125]

In keeping with this hermeneutical principle, then, Fuchs views the object of preaching to be not God, but the human being. It is not a case either of our interpreting the text; instead, the text interprets us.[126] And on that basis, then, Fuchs can refer to proclamation as a "language-event" (*Sprachereignis*).[127] For language is a giving, a granting, an imparting, especially the Christological language of the gospel; it is a love which creates "space for others and time for us."[128] It is this "assembling function" of the language of the gospel which is the vital aspect of preaching and which creates the church as a community:

> This language-*activity* is the mark of the community. *The language of faith brings into language the gathering of faith and thereby Christ.* It admits Christ into that existence which we ourselves enter upon in the *name* of Jesus. We are then repeatedly able to name Jesus as our Lord, to each other and to the world.[129]

For Fuchs, therefore, the language of preaching is an imparting, a giving.[130]

Our study of Ebeling and Fuchs all but rounds out our review of the theology of preaching. With the exception of the theology of story, which will be treated momentarily, it can be said that in the past two decades the reformulation of a theology of preaching, begun with Barth and continuing through a whole generation, appears to have experienced a decline. Attention has turned to other concerns of preaching, which, though no less important, are not directly related to the task of rethinking the theology of preaching. Robert Duke, for example, has recently reviewed several key movements in contemporary preaching in order to urge a renewal of theology *in* preaching.[131] Rich-

---

[123]Ibid., 195.

[124]Ibid., 200.

[125]Ibid.

[126]Robinson, *New Hermeneutic,* 52ff. Robinson labels this the "positive function" of Bultmann's demythologizing program, pioneered by Fuchs.

[127]Ibid., 57.

[128]Ibid., 53. See further Fuchs, *Studies,* 210.

[129]Fuchs, *Studies,* 209.

[130]Ibid., 210.

[131]Robert W. Duke, *The Sermon as God's Word* (Nashville: Abingdon Press, 1980).

ard Lischer has emphasized the importance of viewing preaching *as* theology.[132] And Leander Keck, who calls for a renewal of biblical preaching, exhibits a greater concern for the preacher who serves as both priestly listener and prophetic witness than for an express theology of preaching.[133]

Recently, however, the thread of the theology of preaching has been picked up in the advent of the theology of story, initiated by Edmund Steimle. This attempt to arrive at a "holistic view of preaching" has generated considerable interest.[134]

Steimle is in sympathy with Barth's definition of preaching as " 'The Word of God which he himself has spoken,' " and he agrees with the description of preaching as "proclamation of the Gospel."[135] On the other hand, he is dissatisfied with these terms as the final description of the preaching task. Steimle regards the expression "word of God" as too abstract and open to confusion, and the word "proclamation," he believes, suggests an activity too formal and distant from people.[136] Steimle's contribution, therefore, is in his development of a new and vital paradigm which embraces the entire activity of preaching. That paradigm is the story-teller.[137]

Steimle reminds us that the primary form of the biblical material is the narrative mode, the story of God's dealing in grace with his people.[138] Even the non-narrative portions of Scripture are derived from the biblical story and are understood in that narrative context.[139] This being the case, Steimle redefines the preacher's task as the interpretation of the biblical story in terms of the hearers' stories.[140] He hastens to add that the word "story" is not to be misunderstood as implying that preaching consists in relating a series of anecdotes; rather, it is the "interweaving of the biblical story with my story, your story, so that new light is shed on both."[141] This means the biblical account of God's faithfulness must be rehearsed, re-enacted so that the story becomes our story, and this takes place within the dynamic constellation of three intersecting stories: the biblical story, the preacher's own story, and the story

---

[132]Richard Lischer, *A Theology of Preaching* (Nashville: Abingdon Press, 1981).

[133]Leander Keck, *The Bible in the Pulpit: The Renewal of Biblical Preaching* (Nashville: Abingdon Press, 1978), 53ff.

[134]Steimle, Niedenthal and Rice, *Preaching the Story*, 8.

[135]Edmund Steimle, "Preaching the Biblical Story of Good and Evil," *Union Seminary Quarterly Review* 31 (Spring, 1976): 199.

[136]Ibid.

[137]Ibid.

[138]Ibid., 200. Steimle's work owes much to the foundational thinking of Amos Wilder, *Early Christian Rhetoric: The Language of the Gospel* (Cambridge, Mass.: Harvard University Press, 1971).

[139]Ibid.

[140]Ibid., 199.

[141]Ibid.

of the listener.[142] In this way the biblical story becomes contemporary and invites the listener to identify with it.[143] Thus the preaching act, as Steimle conceives of it, derives its vitality from the fact that it offers the hearer an opportunity for participation, especially via the imagination.[144] Preaching, therefore, takes its cue from the story-teller's art. Such preaching is dialogical, employs secular language, is lean and spare, but above all is evocative. It evokes faith and trust in God, which makes love possible, is love's precondition.[145] This happens because preaching liberates the hearer from anxiety, which is the precondition of sin.[146] Steimle argues that such an understanding of preaching is especially important for our own times, since it can generate the hope that is so badly needed.[147]

What are the results of our survey? It is evident that much profound thought has been devoted to the theology of preaching in this century. In order for us to make use of this material, it now becomes necessary to compare these theologians, specifying where the areas of consensus lie and where there are yet unresolved differences.

There are important points of agreement among the scholars we investigated, particularly in terms of the theological origin, definition, and results of preaching. As to the origins of preaching, each of them takes the word of God as foundational for life and existence. That word of God is understood as the revelation of God in his saving activity. The emphasis falls on God's word as revelatory. This does not mean, however, that God's word is to be identified with certain words of God, as if there existed a treasury of sacred ciphers. Rather, the word of God is an event, his encountering word of address, which calls for a response. It offers salvation and lays a claim on human beings. This word resides in the Scripture, which puts hearers in touch with it. Given this common foundation, the definition of preaching is also similar among these theologians. Preaching is defined as the proclamation of the gospel, specifically God's gracious, saving act in Christ, for that is the locus of his word. Preaching is not taken by these scholars to refer to moral instruction, religious advice, or opinions; rather, preaching is in the indicative mood. It is the declaration of what God has done in Christ. It is always the preaching of the gospel. And what are the results? These theologians all expect preaching to produce faith in the hearer. As a result, preaching is seen as constituting and supporting a community of believers, the church.

---

[142]Ibid., 201f.

[143]Ibid.

[144]The place of imagination in the preaching endeavor is particularly explored and elaborated by Charles Rice, *Interpretation and Imagination.*

[145]Steimle, "Preaching the Biblical Story," 203f.

[146]Ibid.

[147]Ibid. 204f.

The most noticeable differences among our group of scholars arise in their descriptions of the way preaching functions and in specifying its nature and character. For Barth the event of preaching takes place in the explanation of a passage of Scripture. But Bultmann, while he affirms that the word of God arises in the Scripture, thinks preaching involves interpretation in existentialist categories so as to recover and release the kerygma. For Bultmann preaching is the means by which the hearer is ever anew brought to a decision for faith and authentic existence. Farmer sees preaching as functioning relationally, so that shared meaning comes through the directness of human speech. Scherer conceives preaching as reconstituting the fact of redemption, as a call to transformation through a profound identity. Thielecke is satisfied that preaching involves the translation of biblical and dogmatic language into modern idiom. Caemmerer believes that in the word of the preacher God's power is present so that in the telling of God's grace God imparts it to believers. Browne thinks preaching functions in the communicating of an attitude of confidence evoked through the preaching art. Ebeling regards preaching as the execution of the text, an act of interpretation by which understanding comes through language. Fuchs is impressed with preaching as the translation of the text, which allows the life of the text to create anew its own sphere of influence. And Steimle is persuaded preaching functions in an evocative manner by the rehearsal of God's story in a dynamic moment in which it intersects the stories of preacher and hearers. To be sure, these are not all mutually exclusive conceptualizations, but they demonstrate the range of diversity in describing the way preaching functions.

Since the way preaching is understood to function influences the way its character and nature are conceived, it is no surprise that there are wide differences also among these scholars in their characterizations of preaching. Just a brief look at the models they propose is illustrative. For Barth the preacher's paradigm is a combination of witness and expositor, for Bultmann a combination of herald and existentialist interpreter, for Farmer a personal relationship, for Scherer an agent of transformation. In the cases of Thielecke and Fuchs the key word is translator, while for Ebeling the preacher's model is a legal executor. Caemmerer thinks in terms of a priestly witness, Browne an artist, Steimle a story-teller. Given the range of choices, is it any wonder that there is confusion among contemporary preachers in articulating what they expect their preaching to accomplish?

It should be clear from our survey that a rethinking of the theology of preaching is in order. It would be helpful if there were a greater degree of clarity, especially with respect to the function and character of preaching. At the same time, we must observe that all the theologians we considered addressed the theology of preaching either from the perspective of systematic theology or, in the case of the Bultmannians, from specific and limited concerns that arise out of philosophical presuppositions. And although each in its own way has its basis in biblical theology, none of these theologies of preaching emerges directly from an exegesis of biblical texts. The way is therefore open to explore further the question of the theology of preaching and to do so from an exegetical basis.

THEOLOGY OF PREACHING IN THE CONTEXT OF CONTEMPORARY PAULINE SCHOLARSHIP

While the direction of this study intersects with pathways of contemporary scholarship related to preaching, outlined above, it also coincides with current movements in the field of critical New Testament studies. The concern we address here is how Paul's conception of preaching has been treated among leading Pauline scholars.

Ever since the turn of the century, when Albert Schweitzer reopened the question about the essential nature of Pauline theology, a major aspect of critical investigation has concerned the theological center of Paul's thought.[148] Reformation theology had located that center in the doctrine of justification by faith, understood in a forensic sense, a position still defended by such scholars as Martin Dibelius and Hans Conzelmann.[149] Rudolf Bultmann and Ernst Käsemann also belong to this group, although they interpret the concept of justification somewhat differently. Bultmann interprets justification from the perspective of his existentialist interpretation.[150] His starting point for Paul's theology, therefore, is his anthropology.[151] By contrast, Käsemann understands justification cosmically, as referring not to individuals, but to God's sovereignty as creator over against his creation.[152] Others, however, have looked elsewhere for the center, or key, to Paul's theology. Schweitzer argued that the Pauline center was located in his "in Christ" formula, which he understood as a type of mysticism.[153] In somewhat similar fashion, E. P. Sanders thinks the center lies in Paul's notion of participation in Christ, while J. Christiaan Beker looks for the key in the apocalyptic structure of Paul's thought.[154] H. N. Ridderbos, in sympathy with Oscar Cullmann, regards the

---

[148]Albert Schweitzer, *Paul and His Interpreters* (London: Adam & Charles Black, 1912).

[149]Martin Dibelius and Werner Georg Kümmel, *Paul* (London: Longmans, Green, 1953). Hans Conzelmann, *An Outline of the Theology of the New Testament* (London: S. C. M. Press, 1969).

[150]Bultmann, *Theology,* 1:270-89.

[151]Ibid., 191-269.

[152]Ernst Käsemann, "The Saving Significance of the Death of Jesus in Paul," in *Perspectives on Paul* (Philadelphia: Fortress Press, 1969).

[153]Albert Schweitzer, *The Mysticism of Paul the Apostle* (New York: Seabury Press, 1968).

[154]E. P. Sanders, *Paul and Palestinian Judaism* (London: S. C. M., 1977). J. Christiaan Beker, *Paul the Apostle: The Triumph of God in Life and Thought* (Philadelphia: Fortress Press, 1980).

center of Paul's theology as salvation history.[155] And Peter Stuhlmacher has devoted his interest to Paul's gospel.[156] All these have in common the fact that they focus on the content of Paul's preaching or on the horizon of his preaching, but none has specifically addressed his theology of preaching. As useful as these scholarly works have been, they leave unanswered the prior question, Why preach? What does Paul regard preaching as accomplishing?

Aside from the circles of leading critical scholarship, however, there have been a few attempts made to deal with Paul's concept of preaching. Perhaps the most notable scholar is C. H. Dodd, although he did not treat Paul's theology of preaching specifically or directly. Dodd was concerned with the question of the nature of the earliest Christian proclamation, and in the 1930s he formulated a description of that basic message, which he called "the Kerygma," drawing on the evidence from the letters of Paul, the speeches attributed to the apostles in Acts, and other portions of the New Testament.[157] Dodd presupposes a high degree of unity among the earliest Christian preachers, and into this framework he places Paul. He believes Paul's preaching, like the other apostles, would have appealed to would-be converts by a recital or rehearsal of the mighty works of God, specifically in Christ.

Although Dodd does not treat Paul's theology of preaching or try to describe in any way the distinctive features of his preaching, his work is important because of his influence on those who made later attempts. The first such attempt is that of A. C. Chamberlin, whose dissertation in the late 1950s treats Paul primarily as a model of Christian preaching.[158] Chamberlin is interested in a description of Paul the preacher, and for his work he takes Dodd's analysis as his starting point. This means that he too regards the Book of Acts as providing essentially accurate information with respect to Paul's message

---

[155]H. N. Ridderbos, *Paul. An Outline of His Theology* (Grand Rapids: Eerdmanns, 1975).

[156]Peter Stuhlmacher, *Das Paulinische Evangelium. I: Vorgeschichte* (Göttingen: Vandenhoeck & Rupprecht, 1968).

[157]C. H. Dodd, *The Apostolic Preaching and Its Developments,* second edition (New York: Harper, 1944). Dodd contends that throughout the New Testament there is a clear distinction between that preaching of the early church aimed at converting the non-believers, called *kerygma,* and that preaching (or teaching) which is aimed at the ethical instruction of believing Christians, termed *didache.* The chief elements of the "Jerusalem" kerygma, which Dodd regards as the earliest, he thinks can be isolated on the basis of the speeches attributed to Peter in Acts. These elements are as follows: the age of fulfillment, spoken of by the prophets, has dawned; this has taken place in the ministry, death and resurrection of Jesus, descendent of David; by virtue of his resurrection he has been exalted at the right hand of God, as Messianic head of the new Israel; the Holy Spirit in the Church is the sign of Christ's present power and glory; the Messianic Age will shortly reach its consummation in the return of Christ; and finally, a call to repentance, the offer of forgiveness and the Holy Spirit, and the promise of salvation. (Ibid., 20-23).

[158]Charles A. Chamberlin, "The Preaching of the Apostle Paul, Based on a Study of Acts of the Apostles and Paul's Letters, with Special Reference to the First and Second Corinthians" (Ph.D. Dissertation, Temple University, 1959).

and mode of communication. By combining the information found in Acts, references in Paul's letters, and a word study of characteristic Greek terms used for preaching, Chamberlin describes Paul's preaching as evangelistic, Christological and biblical. Chamberlin defines the content of Paul's proclamation as God's grace revealed in Christ, but other than this very general description he has little that is distinctive to add. Finally, he understands Paul's purpose in preaching as aimed at "lifting others to the same level of vision where he himself stood, that level which enabled him to know the fellowship of Christ, his Lord."[159] By this Chamberlin means that the hearer should share the experience of the apostle manifest at his conversion.

Chamberlin is to be credited for seeing that something is to be gained by a description of preaching that begins with the apostle Paul. However, his work is so methodologically flawed as to be of very limited usefulness. Chamberlin is not conversant with exegetical scholarship. This manifests itself in his failure to justify the use of Acts as a source for Paul's preaching, other than to appeal to Dodd, and his innocence regarding the distinction between Paul's authentic and disputed letters. Aside from his word studies, any serious contextual exegesis is conspicuously absent.

More sophisticated and recent is the treatment of Paul and preaching carried out by the Roman Catholic scholar Jerome Murphy-O'Connor. He aims "to share St. Paul's insight into the structure of a key element in the life of the church, the proclamation of the word of God."[160] To accomplish this he proposes to bring Paul's description of preaching to the surface by means of a systematization based on Pauline texts, which for him include all the canonical books attributed to the apostle. In line with Dodd, upon whose analysis he relies, Murphy-O'Connor limits himself to that preaching which has as its object the conversion of the non-believer.

Murphy-O'Connor first attempts to place preaching within the framework of God's "plan of salvation," which he finds explained in Ephesians:

> The preaching of the Gospel is the instrument whereby the Gentiles are admitted to the heritage of the Jews and, through Christ, have access in one Spirit to the Father (Eph. 2:11-18). The plan of salvation is not merely revealed in preaching, it is thereby actuated and brought to fulfillment.[161]

Preaching, then, forms a "bridge between the objective and subjective orders for redemption."[162] To this he adds that preaching, understood in this way, constitutes a call and that the model for preaching is the prophet of the Old Testament. He believes that Paul is reflective of this pattern, and he devotes

---

[159]Ibid., 65.

[160]Jerome Murphy-O'Connor, *Paul on Preaching* (New York: Sheed & Ward, 1963), xiii.

[161]Ibid., 2.

[162]Ibid., 3. Note the categories of Catholic dogmatic theology reflected in this distinction, terms characteristic of his work as a whole.

considerable space to a description of the prophetic ministry and the terms
Paul uses to describe preaching, terms that connect closely with that prophetic ministry.[163]

The treatment given by Murphy-O'Connor amounts to a step taken in the
right direction. Though by contemporary standards his work is methodologically suspect, he does manage to surface an important issue, namely, the
conceptualization of the structure of preaching as understood by Paul. He is
to be applauded for having undertaken his work in conversation with exegetical scholarship, though aside from Dodd and Bultmann most other references are to Catholic scholars. He also sees that Paul's concept of preaching
must be gained from his letters and thus avoids the pitfall of relying on the
Book of Acts. On the other hand, his reliance on Catholic dogmatic theology
for the categories of his discussion, his use of deutero-pauline material, and
his failure to provide a rationale for taking Ephesians as his starting point limit
the value of his work.

The best work to date which deals with Paul and preaching is that of another Catholic scholar, Paul Bormann. His book, based on his doctoral dissertation, attempts to describe the "salvation effectiveness"
(Heilswirksamkeit) of Paul's preaching.[164] What Bormann is really after is the
restoration of preaching to its rightful place alongside the sacraments in Catholic practice. Having heard the complaint of Karl Rahner that there is no
"Ezekiel" to gather up the dry bones of a Catholic theology of preaching,
Bormann sets himself to this task, which he characterizes as a "gathering
work" (Sammelarbeit).[165] He takes Paul as his starting point because he regards the apostle as foundational to Christian thought, and his investigation
seeks to inquire into Paul's view of preaching and the nature of its effectiveness.

Bormann is convinced an important clue to Paul's understanding of
preaching lies in his formula euaggelizesthai to euaggelion found in Gal. 1:11,
1 Cor. 15:11ff and 2 Cor. 11:7. This expression, which would have to be
translated woodenly "to gospelize the gospel" or "to gospel the gospel,"
Bormann sees as revealing the intrinsic connection between the message and
its communication. Having completed his examination of the three texts, he
concludes:

---

[163]Ibid., 28-76. He treats eight such titles, five from 1 Cor. 3-4: diakonos ("servant"),
synergos theou ("co-worker of God"), hyperetes ("helper"), oikonomos ("steward"), and
apostolos ("apostle"); two from 1 Tim. 2:7 and 2 Tim. 1:11: keryx ("herald") and didaskalos
("teacher"); and one from Philippians: douloi Christou ("slaves of Christ").

[164]Paul Bormann, Die Heilswirksamkeit der Verkündigung nach dem Apostel Paulus; Ein
Beitrag zur Theologie der Verkündigung (Paderborn: Bonfacius Druckerei, 1965).

[165]Ibid., 15.

[These three texts] express the connection between the content of the gospel and its delivery in the message, in the activity of preaching, especially in so far as with *euaggelizesthai* is indicated the activity which corresponds to the *euaggelion*. For Paul his preaching belongs to the gospel, since there can be no preaching without "the gospel." In preaching the gospel comes to speech, to expression and reaches to man.[166]

This *euaggelion* Bormann regards as Paul's key term in his theology of preaching, for "in it he summarizes everything which God has done in and through Christ for the salvation of sinful, lost humanity and the world."[167] Borman points out that the apostle even employs the term as constituting the basis of his own apostolic commission.[168]

Bormann understands the gospel as having two aspects, a specific content and the necessity of its being spoken. The content is Jesus Christ, God's reconciling work through him. But this gospel requires proclamation. It cannot be reduced to silence. Since it intends to open an access to God, it must have voice. Bormann insists, "Gospel is the oral [*mündliche*], actual spoken word, is in the most distinctive sense a speaking out [*Aus-Sage*]."[169] Thus, despite his largely negative appraisal of Bultmann, he finds the Marburg scholar's insights most useful at this point, since Bormann concludes that the verbalization of the message of Christ results in the representation of the reconciling work of Christ which addresses each hearer and calls for faith. This takes place, he explains, because Christ's presence in the preaching of the gospel "happens by means of word as sign [*Bezeichnung*]," a word that is filled with the power of the Spirit.[170] Thus preaching is an effective power, producing salvation in those who heed its call. Or, as he expresses it, "Reception of the gospel is reception of Jesus Christ himself, is faith in him, obedience to him, trust in him."[171]

Bormann has advanced the discussion of Paul's theology of preaching. He has based the first part of his work on serious exegesis. He is in conversation with critical scholarship, though not with the most recent figures. And for the most part he deals with Paul's undisputed letters, though he does include the deutero-pauline correspondence to a lesser extent. Moreover, Bormann has seen that a key element in Paul's theology of preaching is his understanding of the gospel.

But there are also serious weaknesses in Bormann's work. Most important is methodology. His procedure is, like that of Murphy-O'Connor, based on philological exegesis rather than the program of contextual exegesis fol-

---

[166]Ibid., 36.
[167]Ibid., 201.
[168]Ibid.
[169]Ibid.
[170]Ibid., 202.
[171]Ibid.

lowed by contemporary historical critics. Thus his exegesis does not take account of the circumstantial framework of the discussion between Paul and his addressees. Furthermore, although he begins with exegesis, a major portion of his work is more representative of Roman dogma, albeit to a lesser extent than Murphy-O'Connor's. Finally, the scope of his work is not broad enough. By limiting himself to the effectiveness of the preaching of the gospel in producing salvation he has left out of account what Paul felt preaching means to those who are already Christians. This becomes particularly important when one reflects on the fact that Paul's letters are written to Christian congregations, upon whom he expects that his preaching still has effect. Bormann does seem to be conscious of this himself, for at the end he appends a comment that the person who already has received salvation "needs always anew the preaching of the gospel; for he always needs anew the power, the presence of Jesus Christ is his life on the way towards the complete lordship of God."[172]

In addition to these studies of Paul's perspective on preaching there have been several devoted to specific aspects of that preaching. Early in this century Albrecht Oepke focused on the missionary preaching of Paul.[173] More recently Claus Bussmann has taken this project forward by seeking to discover themes of pauline missionary preaching on the basis of comparison with Hellenistic-Jewish mission literature.[174] Otherwise, Gerhard Delling has explored the death of Jesus in the preaching of Paul, although like most others he regards the letters of Paul as being identical with the preaching of the apostle.[175] And finally Georg Braumann mines Paul's letters in search of elements of baptismal preaching from Christian tradition taken up by the apostle.[176] In each case, attention is again given to describing the content of Paul's preaching.

The results of this survey indicate that previous studies of Paul's preaching have focused almost exclusively on its content. There has been no attempt made to discover Paul's theology of preaching. In addition, most prior work has not been informed by the tools and insights of modern historical criticism. Thus the discussion of Paul's understanding of preaching is left unexplored in the depth which the matter requires.

---

[172]Ibid., 203.

[173]Albrecht Oepke, *Die Missionspredigt des Apostels Paulus* (Leipzig: J. C. Hinrichs'sche Buchhandlung, 1920).

[174]Claus Bussmann, *Themen der paulinischen Missionspredigt auf dem Hintergrund der spätjüdischenhellenistischen Missionsliteratur* (Bern: Herbert Lang, 1971).

[175]Gerhard Delling, "Der Tod Jesu in der Verkündigung des Paulus," in *Studien zum Neuen Testament und zum hellenistischen Judentum* (Göttingen: Vandenhoeck & Rupprecht, 1970).

[176]Georg Braumann, *Vorpaulinische christliche Taufverkündigung bei Paulus* (Stuttgart: W. Kohlhammer Verlag, 1962).

THE INTENT AND SCOPE OF THE INVESTIGATION

The aim of this work is to arrive at an understanding of Paul's theology of preaching. That is to say, in contrast to previous scholarship, the purpose is not to describe the content of Paul's preaching nor his understanding of the gospel. It is rather to ask and answer the question, Why does the gospel require preaching? The nature of our concern can be made all the clearer by reminding ourselves that Paul did have other alternatives, the most obvious being his letters. And yet, as we shall notice, Paul does not regard his letters as being an adequate substitute for his preaching. Thus the question, Why preach? What is it about preaching that, for Paul, makes it indispensable to the gospel? What does preaching do?

This research intends to be an exegetical study of selected texts from the letters of Paul. The tools and perspective for the investigation are those of contemporary historical-critical New Testament scholarship. That implies certain limitations. It means that the reports of Paul's activity and preaching recorded in the Book of Acts will not be included, since the consensus among critical scholars is that Acts presents Luke's uniformly stylized version of early Christian preaching and therefore does not reflect Paul himself. Nor will the study embrace all of the thirteen canonical books commonly attributed to Paul. Instead, the investigation will treat only those letters whose Pauline authorship is currently regarded as undisputed and which offer texts important for the discussion. These letters are 1 Thessalonians, Galatians, 1 and 2 Corinthians, and Romans.

METHODOLOGY

It must be noted at the outset that there is a methodological problem. If we leave the Book of Acts out of account, then we have no extant examples of Paul's preaching; in Paul's letters, which address concrete issues in the life situation of particular congregations, his preaching is for the most part presupposed. While this presents an obstacle, however, it does not render the task impossible, precisely because we are primarily concerned not with the content of Paul's preaching, but with his theological understanding of preaching. In his letters Paul speaks about preaching at a number of points and often at length. We will, therefore, use as our basis for this study those texts in which he does so, centering our attention in each letter on those texts which appear most central to his discussion of preaching. At the same time, the exegetical study of each text will be carried out in dialogue with other Pauline texts which relate to the subject, especially those within the same letter. Those texts will be favored in which Paul treats the subject of preaching at length or in special depth. Key texts are to be found in 1 Thessalonians 1:2-

2:14; Galatians 1:6-17; 1 Corinthians 1:17-2:5, 9:14-18 and 15:1-14; 2 Corinthians 4:1-6; and Romans 1:1-17 and 10:14-17. They will be treated in that order, in conformity with the chronology of Paul's activity and letters generally observed within the critical scholarly community.

The procedure and resources for research will be those of biblical criticism. This means the study of the passages will be conducted on the basis of the original Greek text, paying particularly close attention to the word usage which Paul employs. It means also taking into account the context, both the context of the literary character of each book and the context in the life of the congregation to whom Paul is writing. Here we will expect some additional help from the recent sociological studies on the background of Paul's work, particularly the studies of Gerd Theissen, Bengt Holmberg, John Howard Schütz, and Wayne Meeks. Further, a critical analysis of each text will be conducted in order to distinguish Paul's theology from that of his opponents and from that of the early church traditions, both of which he regularly quotes. This will serve to set Paul's own work in contrast to both opponents and tradition, a procedure which modern scholarship regards as crucial for understanding Paul.

Once we have clarified Paul's theology of preaching, the results of this thematic exegetical investigation will be brought into conversation with modern scholarship on the subject of preaching. Distinctive accents in Paul's theology of preaching will be noted, and an attempt will be made to show how these can contribute to more effective proclamation of the gospel in our own time.

CHAPTER TWO

GOSPEL, WORD OF GOD, AND COMMUNITY: THEOLOGY OF PREACHING IN FIRST THESSALONIANS

The congregation in Thessalonica represents one of the earliest churches established by the Apostle Paul on Greek soil. According to both the Book of Acts and the letter which we know as 1 Thessalonians Paul arrived in this capital city of the Roman province of Macedonia soon after his initial missionary activity in Philippi. Evidently the apostle succeeded in founding in Thessalonica a thriving community of Christians. The general tone of 1 Thessalonians is that of joy and deep satisfaction on the part of Paul as he recalls the circumstances of their reception of the Gospel. Kümmel aptly characterizes the letter as a "personal testimony of Pauline missionary work."[1]

THE HISTORICAL SITUATION

The letter of 1 Thessalonians is widely regarded as the first of Paul's epistles and, in fact, the earliest New Testament witness of early Christianity. It seems likely that the congregation was established about 49 A.D., and since there is nothing in the letter to indicate a long period of time between the apostle's departure and its composition, most recognized scholars date the

---

[1]Werner G. Kümmel, *Introduction to the New Testament* (Nashville: Abingdon Press, 1975), 260.

work about 50 A.D.[2] In addition, it is probable that Paul wrote the letter from Corinth, where he had come after brief stays in Berea and Athens.[3]

From the letter we learn that the immediate impetus for its composition is the return of Timothy. Paul had dispatched him from Athens to the congregation to strengthen the recent converts (3:1-6). The congregation seems to have been made up largely, or even exclusively, of gentiles, since the content of the missionary message uses terms from the standard Hellenistic Jewish appeal to non-Jews (1:9).[4] Paul appears to have left Thessalonica under duress, before his work there was complete, for he reports that he had tried repeatedly to return, but was prevented from doing so (2:17f.). Instead, he has had to send Timothy in his own place. His deep anxiety is understandable (3:5). In the absence of their apostle-founder, and in the face of the persecution which they had had to withstand, the fledgling congregation could easily have collapsed.

But at the time of Paul's writing of 1 Thessalonians Timothy had returned with the good news that the church was standing firm in its new-found faith, to the apostle's great relief (3:8). Evidently he has also brought with him, either in oral form or possibly in the form of a letter, certain questions which troubled the Thessalonian faithful. The fact of persecution needed to be interpreted, and the incidences of death among the members produced confusion and uncertainty about the Parousia of the Lord. As Marxsen notes, both these concerns stem from the same root, a ''lack of faith'' (3:l0).[5] Since Paul is still

---

[2]Kümmel, *Introduction,* 257. See also Ernest Best, *A Commentary on the First and Second Epistles to the Thessalonians* (New York: Harper and Row, 1972), 7-13; Günther Bornkamm, *Paul* (New York: Harper, 1971), 62; Willi Marxsen, *Introduction to the New Testament* (Philadelphia: Fortress, 1968), 33-34; and Willi Marxsen, *Der erste Brief an die Thessalonicher* (Zürich: Theologischer Verlag Zürich, 1979), 13-15. Among those who disagree with this reconstruction of the time and circumstances of composition the most significant challenge comes from Walter Schmithals, *Paul and the Gnostics* (Nashville: Abingdon, 1972), 123-95, who argues that the letter arose at a later period when Paul was confronted by the gnostic heresy. On balance, however, the evidence does not favor his view. Extensive reviews and critiques of Schmithals' hypothesis appear in Best (*Commentary,* 8-11 and 16-22) and Kümmel (*Introduction,* 257-262).

[3]Marxsen is not satisfied with the itinerary set forth here and generally recognized among scholars. He is very skeptical of the reliability of Acts 17, and so on the basis of 1 Thessalonians alone he believes there is evidence to suppose that Paul's route was not to the south but west to the coast of Greece, from which he intended to go to Rome. But then, Marxsen hypothesizes, he was forced to abandon the attempt and make his way to Corinth when confronted with the edict of Claudius. See Marxsen, *An die Thessalonicher,* 15f.

[4]There are significant differences between the description of the founding and early experience of the Thessalonian congregation as recorded in Acts 17 and the evidence that comes from 1 Thessalonians. Attempts to harmonize the two, such as that of A. L. Moore, *1 and 2 Thessalonians* (London: Nelson, 1969), 6-10, are not very satisfactory. For our purposes here we followed Best's principle that ''if we have to choose between Luke and Paul the latter is almost always to be preferred'' (*Commentary,* 6).

[5]Marxsen, *An die Thessalonicher,* 25.

unable to return personally, his letter serves as a substitute for his presence and permits him to answer their questions in the meantime (3:10a). It is, therefore, a pastoral letter to the church in Thessalonica addressed to the actual situation in which it finds itself, a situation where it is important to strengthen the first steps in the Christian life against attacks and against doubt (about the fate of those who have died), so that the church, remembering its beginnings, can confidently continue on the road upon which it has set out.[6]

It is within the context of these historical circumstances that Paul, in 1:2-2:14, makes frequent reference to his preaching, the proclamation of the gospel which he brought to them at the start (1:9-10) and which remained in operation while he was present among them. In so doing, Paul alerts us to his understanding of the theological origins, function and results of preaching. Thus 1 Thessalonians makes an advantageous starting point for our study.

FIRST THESSALONIANS 1:2-2:14

A. *The Literary Context*

The letter of 1 Thessalonians falls into two parts, the first, after the greeting in 1:1, extending from 1:2-3:13 and the second from 4:1-5:22. The first section is essentially an extended thanksgiving, recounting experiences common to both the apostle and the congregation, concluding with a prayer of intercession. The second part is parenetic, offering apostolic instruction regarding specific concerns of the congregation and also addressing the matter of Christian ethical conduct generally. The section we are to examine falls within the first part, that is, within the framework of Paul's thanksgiving for the founding and life of the Thessalonian congregation.

This first part of the letter may be subdivided into four sections.[7] In 1:2-10 Paul offers a prayer of thanksgiving for the entire congregation. He mentions the founding of the congregation, whose members accepted his message even in the face of affliction (vv. 5-6), thereby becoming an example to other believers (vv. 7f.). He refers to them as "imitators" (*mimētai*, v. 6), thus indicating a "relationship of dependence: Paul—the Thessalonians—other churches: a line which goes back through Paul direct to the Lord."[8] As to the content of his preaching he mentions the call to turn from idolatry to serve the true, living God and the promise of final deliverance which they await (vv. 9-10).

---

[6]Marxsen, *Introduction*, 36.
[7]We are following the outline proposed by Marxsen, *Introduction*, 30-31.
[8]Ibid., 30.

In the second section, 2:1-12, the apostle refers to the character of his past work and conduct among the Thessalonians. He reminds them that he arrived as one who had himself recently known the meaning of affliction and persecution in Philippi (v. 2). Paul then launches into a lengthy description of his apostolic conduct, often referred to as an "apology" (vv. 3-12), which pictures the apostle ministering to his congregation with selfless devotion.

In the third section, 2:13-16, the prayer of thanksgiving for their reception of the gospel is extended to include the fact that they received his word "not as the word of men, but as what it really is, the word of God" (v. 13). Paul points to the parallel between their experience of persecution at the hands of their own fellow citizens and that of the church in Judea at the hands of fellow Jews (v. 14). The pericope concludes with a description of the wrath-filled fate of those who oppose God (vv. 15-16).

The final section of the first part, 2:17-3:13, deals with Paul's relationship to the congregation during the period since he has left them. He reveals his desire and intention more than once to return, but "Satan hindered us" (vv. 17-20). He tells them of his anxiety about them and of his sending Timothy to strengthen them (3:1-5). He concludes with an account of the joy he experienced when Timothy returned with such good news of their loyalty in the gospel. This report has made him all the more eager to see them again. He therefore prays that he may be able to visit them and intercedes with God on their behalf that in the meantime they may be strengthened and made firm in love and holiness (vv. 6-13).

As we take up our investigation of Paul's references to preaching, it is important to bear in mind this literary and historical context. His descriptions of preaching will not emerge in isolation as pure theological constructs. They are directly related to the experience of the Thessalonian Christians. Preaching, as Paul treats it here, is part of the life of an existing congregation, and his conception of it revolves around his closely related conceptions of the gospel and the word of God.

B. Exegesis of 1:2-10

Paul begins his letter to the Thessalonian congregation with a prayer of thanksgiving, in which he makes specific mention of the effect which his mission activity in the gospel has had upon them. The passage forms an integrated whole, but for purposes of our analysis it can be conveniently broken down into smaller units.

> We offer thanks to God always for you all, constantly making mention of you in our prayers, remembering before our God and Father your practice of faith and labor of love and endurance of hope in our Lord Jesus Christ (vv. 2-3).[9]

---

[9]Translations provided for analysis are my own. Translations for other biblical references are from the RSV unless otherwise indicated.

As is typical of Paul's letters, he begins with a prayer of thanksgiving.[10] In fact, the expression "we offer thanks" is the controlling thought of the entire first chapter.[11] As we would expect, the gratitude which the apostle feels is not directed to the Thessalonians, but to God. What is striking, though, is Paul's use of hyperbole; he "always" prays for "all of you" and makes mention of them "constantly."[12] These expressions serve to introduce the prevailing mood of the letter, that of joyful excitement, a mood that will be reinforced frequently.

Paul next unfolds the content of his thanksgiving prayer (v. 3). The circumstantial participle *mnēmoneuontes* ("remembering") serves to extend the thought of *mneian poioumenoi* ("making mention") in v. 2, thus describing what it is the apostle specifically recalls when he intercedes for the Thessalonians believers.[13] "Remembering," therefore, implies intercession, as it does also in Old Testament thought.[14]

The content of Paul's intercessory prayer is now formulated in a lengthy string of words in the genitive case. At first glance we appear to be confronted with three pairs of words: *ergou tēs pisteōs* ("practice of faith"), *kopou tēs agapēs* ("labor of love") and *hupomonēs tēs elpidos* ("endurance of hope"). These can be taken, as Best does, to be parallel phrases which express "the great worth of their new lives as Christians."[15] Admittedly the structure of thought is parallel in this section, as Marxsen emphasizes, but he is probably more perceptive when he argues that what we have here are not three pairs but two triads.

The faith-love-hope triad is probably a pre-pauline formula and appears at several points in his letters as well as in the New Testament generally.[16] In

---

[10]See Rom. 1:8; 1 Cor. 1:4; Phil. 1:3. An exception is Gal. 1:6, for reasons related to the crisis with which that letter deals.

[11]Marxsen, *An die Thessalonicher*, 34.

[12]*adialeiptōs* ("unceasingly") could be connected with *mneian poioumenoi* ("making mention") in v. 2 or with *mnēmoneuontes* ("remembering") in v. 3. As Moore notes, it does not affect the meaning greatly in either case (*1 and 2 Thessalonians*, 24). However, noting with Best the structure of the three participial phrases, each dependent on *eucharistoumen* ("giving thanks"), we take *adialeiptōs* as rounding off the first phrase and therefore attaching to *mneian poioumenoi* (*Commentary*, 66).

[13]We are here following the Chicago Book of Style in listing the Greek word in italic with its translation immediately following enclosed in quotation marks. The transliteration of the Greek is also based on the Chicago Book of Style, with the exception of the letters Chi, which we will transliterate "ch," and Zeta, which will appear as "z."

[14]Moore, *1 and 2 Thessalonians*, 24.

[15]Best, *Commentary*, 67.

[16]Marxsen, *An die Thessalonicher*, 35. See 1 Cor. 13:13, Rom. 5:1-5, Gal. 5:5f., Col. 1:4f., Eph. 4:2-5, et al. See also Hans Conzelmann, *1 Corinthians* (Philadelphia: Fortress, 1975), 230, note 116; he observes how in 1 Thess. 5:8 the three members of the triad are connected to only *two* pieces of armor in the metaphor, thus suggesting that the triad was already a fixed formula when Paul wrote.

addition, it is important to be aware that the terms faith, love and hope are more than simply descriptions of Christian behavior and spirituality. From the appearance of these terms in Rom. 5:1-5 particularly, where the words are included in a description of access to the power of God, it is clear that Paul understands these key words as referring to transcendent powers which are operative in the Christian life because God has made them available in his grace.[17] In the context of the Thessalonian situation the mention of these transcendent powers is crucially important, since, as far as the Thessalonians are concerned, their subjection to persecution is otherwise obviously evidence of weakness.

This faith-love-hope triad is now interwoven by the practice-labor-endurance triad which, while it appears only in Rev. 2:2 (and there also in the context of persecution), probably also represents an early pre-pauline formula.[18] But the important question is, how are the two triads brought together in v. 3, and what does Paul want the reader to understand by them? Marxsen notes that in Greek the ruling genitive precedes that which is dependent on it. This means that the word *humōn* (''your'' [plural]) serves as the leading edge of the apostle's thought. Paul is not merely recalling certain facts about them, but he is first and foremost remembering the Thessalonians themselves. He is undoubtedly thinking of what they have recently experienced, the successive threats in the form of persecution and the deaths of some members, which have not made their practice of faith at all easy. Thus the entire double triad of phrases, bracketed by the *humōn* (''your'') at the beginning and *tou kuriou hēmōn Iēsou Christou* (''of our Lord Jesus Christ'') at the end, form a unified description of the Thessalonian congregation on their path of Christian experience.[19] The words of v. 3 provide a compact summary of their loyalty to the gospel and simultaneously a witness to the power of the divinely ordained gift of faith, love and hope.[20]

The thrust of what Paul is saying is reflected not only in the unified structure of v. 3, but in the grammatical construction. Each member of the practice-labor-endurance triad is linked to a corresponding member of the faith-

---

[17]Thus it can be seen that his conceptualization of Christian existence in 1 Thess. 1:3 conforms to his broader theology, by which the believer's salvation consists in being incorporated into the sphere of Christ's power. For an in-depth analysis of the structure of Paul's soteriology on the basis of its accompanying metaphorical language see Gerd Theissen, ''Soteriologische Symbolik in den paulinischen Schriften,'' *KD* 20 (1974): 282-304.

[18]Marxsen, *An die Thessalonicher,* 35.

[19]Marxsen, *An die Thessalonicher,* 35ff. In view of this we are best advised not to press the meaning of each individual term. Faith-love-hope provides the standard Christian description of devotion to God, brotherly care, and expectation for the future, out of which flow practice-effort-endurance (see note 18). Although *ergon* literally means ''work,'' we have chosen to translate it ''practice'' in order to reflect the fact that it denotes faith in action.

[20]See 1 Thess. 3:6, 9.

love-hope triad, each of the latter being a subjective genitive. Thus the first triad flows from the second. The transcendent realities that are faith, love and hope produce earthly results in the form of practice, labor and endurance. As Moore explains, "Paul means work prompted and characterized by faith, labour prompted and characterized by love, and steadfastness prompted and characterized by hope."[21] In view of the fact that the Thessalonians' adversities have arisen precisely because they are Christians, it is particularly gratifying to the apostle that they have displayed such loyalty and devotion.[22]

The thought concludes with the words *tou kuriou hēmōn Iēsou Christou* ("in [literally "of"] our Lord Jesus Christ"). Should these words be taken with the last phrase *hupomonēs tēs elpidos* ("endurance of hope"), or do they refer to the entire preceding verse? The words clearly form an objective genitive, meaning that Jesus Christ is the object of hope.[23] In view of the closely unified thought we have discovered in v. 3, however, it is probably best to regard Christ as being the object also of faith and love.[24] Or, even better, rather than isolate faith-love-hope, it is preferable to understand "practice of faith and labor of love and endurance of hope" as a totality which has as its object Christ. The exercise of loyalty and love in the face of opposition, therefore, is oriented toward and demonstrative of their devotion to Christ.

Thus Paul has employed the compact phrases in this verse to serve as an over-arching description of the church at Thessalonica. The meaning is to be understood broadly and supplies a theme note for the rest of the chapter. Taken together with the key word at the beginning, "we offer thanks," v. 3 provides a framework for the entire first part, which concludes at 3:13.

> since we know, brothers beloved of God, your election, for our gospel did not take place among you in speech alone but also with power and holy spirit and full conviction, just as you know what sort of persons we were among you for your sakes (vv. 4-5).

Paul continues his prayer of thanks by using the third of the participles, *eidotes* ("knowing"), in order to make more specific what he has stated broadly in v. 3. The object of his knowledge is their *eklogēn* ("election"). This is, of course, not to be understood in the speculative sense of later controversies. Rather, Paul is referring to the Thessalonians being a part of God's

---

[21]Moore, *1 and 2 Thessalonians*, 25.

[22]Marxsen, *An die Thessalonicher*, 36.

[23]Best, *Commentary*, 69f. As he notes, in view of the fact that *elpidos* ("hope") in the preceding phrase is a subjective genitive, the likelihood is very strong that the next should be taken as an objective genitive, since in Greek it would be quite awkward to have two subjective genitives in succession. Cf. *BDF*, 90, 93.

[24]Moore, *1 and 2 Thessalonians*, 26. Cf. Best (*Commentary*, 69ff.), who argues against this on the basis of the fact that elsewhere in the Pauline letters neither Christ nor God is ever the object of love.

pre-existent plan. As Marxsen explains, Paul thinks of the present situation and of the Thessalonian congregation having proven the genuineness of their faithfulness in the gospel and then reaches back in thought to the eternal counsel of God.[25] As a result, Paul can address them warmly as *adelphoi ēgapēmenoi hupo tou theou* ("brothers beloved of God").

The next verse can be taken as either causal or explanatory, since *hoti* can be understood in the context as either "because" or "that." In either case the sense of the statement is clear enough. It reveals the specific event by which Paul knows that their election has taken place; namely, *to euaggelion hēmōn egenēthē eis humas* ("our gospel happened among you"). Here we are confronted with one of Paul's key concepts and one which is crucial for understanding his theology of preaching. The gospel is conceived of as an event. It is something that happens. And though the word obviously refers to a message, since it literally means "good news," it is not merely a matter of relating certain information. Instead, the gospel comes not only *en logōi* ("in speech"), but also *en dunamei kai en pneumati hagiōi kai en plērophoriai pollēi* ("with power and holy spirit and full assurance"). Thus the gospel is a dynamic, foundational for the election of the Christians at Thessalonica.[26]

But the word *euaggelion,* as used by Paul, carries even further connotations. The apostle personalizes it; it is *hēmōn* ("our") gospel.[27] This is not to be regarded as "loosely possessive," as Moore puts it, referring simply to what Paul and his co-workers preached.[28] Paul does not use his terms so casually. Nor on the other hand should we imagine that Paul regards his gospel as being so unique that it should be understood as his exclusive possession,

---

[25]Marxsen, *An die Thessalonicher,* 36. Best notes that election is a strong element in early Christianity, a concept which is an aspect of and a way of emphasizing the grace of God; further, he reminds the reader that the basic feature of election in both the Old and New Testaments is the call to service (*Commentary,* 71f.).

[26]The majority of references to *euaggelizesthai* and *euaggelion* which occur in the New Testament are found in the Pauline corpus. Paul's usage is derived from the Old Testament, especially from Deutero-Isaiah, where the two terms connote not only a message of good news but an effective power (note that Isaiah 52:7 is quoted in Paul's important discussion of the gospel in Rom. 10:15). The content of the gospel is the saving event that has occurred in Jesus Christ, particularly his suffering, death and resurrection (See Rom. 1:1ff.; 1 Cor. 15:1ff.). Thus Paul can speak of the gospel of Christ or of God. But often he uses the term in an absolute sense. The gospel is proclaimed, as can be seen from the variety of different verbs of speaking which are connected with it. And in its very proclamation is the power of salvation (Rom. 1:16). See G. Friedrich, *TDNT,* 2 (Grand Rapids: Eerdmanns, 1964), 707-37. See also Joseph A. Fitzmyer, "The Gospel in the Theology of Paul," *Int,* 33 (4, 1979) 339-50; John Howard Schütz, *Paul and the Anatomy of Apostolic Authority* (Cambridge: Cambridge University Press, 1975), 35-83; and Stuhlmacher, *Das paulinische Evangelium,* 56-63.

[27]The use of the plural could refer to Paul's companions Silvanus and Timothy, who are mentioned in 1:1, but it is also characteristic of Paul to use the plural editorially to refer to himself. See, for example, 2 Cor. 4:3.

[28]Moore, *1 and 2 Thessalonians,* 26.

in competition and conflict with the message of other apostles.[29] Instead, our clue to understanding this striking expression is found partly in 2:4, where Paul describes the gospel as having been *pisteuthēnai* ("entrusted") to him, and partly by the peculiar reference in v. 5, *kathōs oidate hoioi egenēthēmen en humin di humas* ("just as you know what kind of persons we were among you for your sakes"). The gospel is an effective word, the apostle himself being its foremost example. The gospel has had effect in his own life and ministry. And the way this gospel ministry has taken shape among the Thessalonians is what makes it "his" gospel.[30] Schütz is correct in saying, "It is 'his' gospel because it comes to expression not merely through, but in the Thessalonians."[31] Paul's gospel is qualitatively personal.

We have called attention to the effective power of the gospel, the fact that the gospel is a dynamic. But the question arises, can we further specify the nature of its power? What exactly does Paul have in mind by describing the gospel's happening "with power and holy spirit and full assurance?" It would be tempting to conclude that Paul is referring to signs and demonstrations of a miraculous nature, and as an apostle Paul does lay claim to such power.[32] And it is possible that the apostle has such events partly in mind. But that cannot exhaust the meaning of the statement, as can be seen from the context. Verse 5 is preceded by the encomium of vv. 2-4, which celebrates the solid loyalty of the congregation in the face of adversity, and it is followed by Paul's reference to "what sort of persons we were among you for your sakes," from which Paul will go on to describe the Thessalonians as "imitators" of himself in receiving the word "in affliction." The context, then, suggests not a set of external miraculous phenomena, but rather supernatural forces at work internally within the congregation. The emphasis is on existence. Paul notes in v. 5b that he "became" something, and in vv. 7-8 he will go on to say the Thessalonians have imitated him in also becoming something.[33] Beker is doubtless correct in regarding v. 5 as belonging to a series of Pauline texts which refer to the fact that first and foremost "the power of the gospel is evident in the existence of the churches."[34]

That this interpretation of the triad power-spirit-assurance is accurate can be confirmed by a closer examination of the language employed. As is the case in

---

[29]Thus F. C. Baur and others took this expression in a polemical sense. See Schütz (*Anatomy,* 71-78) for a critique of the arguments. Paul understands his gospel as being in concert with that of the other apostles. See 1 Cor. 15:1ff. See also J. Christiaan Beker, *Paul the Apostle* (Philadelphia: Fortress, 1980), 115-25.

[30]Marxsen, *An die Thessalonicher,* 37.

[31]Schütz, *Anatomy,* 74.

[32]2 Cor. 12:12; 1 Cor. 2:2-4; Rom. 15:19.

[33]Schütz, *Anatomy,* 73.

[34]Beker, *Paul the Apostle,* 34. See also 1 Thess. 2:19-20, 3:8.

the Old Testament, the first two terms, *dunamei* and *pneumati,* are closely related in Paul's thought.[35] In fact, Paul joins the two together in Rom. 15:19, where
he reports that his work is done *en dunamei pneumatos* ("with power of the
spirit").[36] Moore is right, therefore, when he draws attention to the fact that for
Paul "power" is generally used to refer to divine energy and that here it is reinforced by the second term "with divine spirit."[37] The overlapping of these first
two terms, then, only render the third term *plērophoriai pollēi* ("full assurance") all the more conspicuous. The expression seems to stand in isolation.
Perhaps we would not be too far off the mark to suppose that Paul, as he often
does, is taking two terms common to Christian tradition, "power" and "spirit,"
and interpreting them by means of the third, "full assurance." This suggestion
is reinforced by Schütz's observation that elsewhere in the New Testament *plēr-
ophoria* carries the connotation of "assurance" in the sense of a conviction or
certainty about the future, thereby imparting an "eschatological flavor" to the
passage.[38] In view of the importance of eschatology in the letter (especially in
1:9-10 and the lengthy discussion in 4:13-5:11), this interpretation fits the context well. In addition, the end of v. 5, *kathōs oidate hoioi egenēthēmen en humin*
("just as you know what sort of persons we were among you"), elaborates the
thought of v. 5a in terms of existence. Divine power is evident in both the fact
and quality of Paul's apostolic existence among the Thessalonians, which was
"for your sake" (*di humas*). The result is that by means of the triad power-spirit-
assurance Paul points to the power of the gospel in terms of the *founding and
continued existence* of the congregation. The miracle is that the Thessalonian
Christians still "stand fast in the Lord" despite all temptations to abandon faith
(3:5-8). The gospel has not proved to be "empty" (2:1).

> And you became imitators of us and of the Lord, since you received the word in much
> affliction with joy of the Holy Spirit, with the result that you became a model for all
> the believers in Macedonia and Achaia. For from you the word of the Lord has sounded

---

[35]Best, *Commentary,* 74ff.

[36]Grundmann, *TDNT,* 1 (Grand Rapids: Eerdmanns, 1964), 310-13. Grundmann describes
the relationship between spirit and power by saying, "On the one side *pneuma* expresses the
mode in which the exalted Lord is present and there is identification with Him. On the other
hand, it expresses the corresponding mode of existence of believers. The unity of the two is
to be seen in the synonymous use of *en pneumati* and *en christo.* When we grasp this, it is
evident that in the combination of *dunamis* and *pneuma* there is expressed the power with which
the risen Lord is present to His people as *pneuma*" (Ibid., 311-12). See also Schütz, *Anatomy,*
252f.

[37]We translate the expression without the article because in the Greek text it is anarthrous.
All of Paul's references in the undisputed letters appear that way, except in two instances in
which he is probably quoting tradition. He uses the article when he refers to the Spirit as being
"of God" or when he uses it in the absolute sense. In this way Paul seems to understand holy
spirit as a divine power or force available to believers, directly related to but not identical with
the Spirit of God. See also note 36 above.

[38]Schütz, *Anatomy,* 73.

forth not only in Macedonia and Achaia, but in every place your faith toward God has gone forth, so that there is no need for us to say anything (vv. 6-8);

The *kai* (''and'') in v. 6 continues the thought of v. 4, further unfolding the nature of their election.[39] The connection with v. 5 is also clear from the repeated use of the root word *ginesthai* (''to become'') in vv. 4-7. The gospel has occurred among them. And since Paul's life was noticeably conformed to it, the Thessalonian congregation is said to have become *mimētai* (''imitators'') of the apostle and of the Lord. What it is that characterizes their imitation is stated by means of the participial clause in v. 6b, *dexamenoi ton logon en thlipsei pollēi meta charas pneumatos hagiou* (''since you received the word in affliction with joy of the Holy Spirit'').

The word *mimētai* first appears in this verse, but Paul will make frequent reference to the idea in his subsequent letters.[40] The customary translation ''imitators'' is actually a rather weak English equivalent. Paul means far more than mimicry. In his major study of *mimētēs/mimeisthai* (''imitator/imitate'') Betz has shown that Paul's use of the terminology has a ''parallel intention,'' in its theological content, to the concept of discipleship which appears in the Gospels. By this he means that Paul understands *mimēsis* (''imitation'') not as following or mirroring the historical Jesus, as if he were a role model, but rather as living out one's existence ''bound up in destiny with the exalted Lord.''[41]

This conceptualization of *mimēsis* is important for our understanding of v. 6, especially when taken together with two other clues. The first is that Paul's usage of *mimētai* here in v. 6 and at 2:14 is ''distinctive from all the rest of the New Testament by virtue of the fact that Paul does not issue a call *mimētēn einai* (''to be an imitator'') but establishes a fact: *humeis . . . mimētai egenēthēte, adelphoi* (''you are imitators, brothers'').''[42] Here again Paul is describing a state of existence.

Our other clue to the correct understanding of this verse comes, as Marxsen points out, from the use of *tupon* (''model'') in v. 7.[43] This term originates from the minting of coins in ancient times; a coin-stamp, a *tupos*, is stamped to serve as a pattern for the subsequent stamping of coins in the same image, the *mimētai*. Thus ''Paul under stands himself as having been stamped by the Lord'' so that he can in turn be the means by which others are so ''stamped.''[44] When Paul uses the term *mimētai*, therefore, one can observe a chain-link

---

[39]Best, *Commentary*, 76.

[40]Ibid., 76ff., for a list of references and a description of usage.

[41]H. D. Betz, *Nachfolge und Nachahmung Jesu Christi im Neuen Testament* (Tübingen: Mohr, 1967), 42.

[42]Betz, *Nachfolge*, 143.

[43]Marxsen, *An die Thessalonicher*, 39. *Mimētai* and *tupos* are also connected in Phil. 3:17.

[44]Ibid.

effect: Christ is the *tupos* for Paul, Paul for his imitators/congregations, and the congregation at Thessalonica, v. 7, for other congregations.[45] Christian existence, therefore, is a co-extensive relationship between Christ and his church.

The remainder of v. 6 intends to clarify the exact nature of what is meant by *mimētai*. The sentence is not without some exegetical problems, however. Paul designates the Thessalonians "imitators" of himself *kai tou kuriou* ("and of the Lord"). Is this a reference to the earthly Jesus or to the risen Lord? And further, is the imitation conceived of as "receiving the word" or "receiving the word in much affliction?" The answers to both questions are connected. On the one hand, as Best notes, if the reference is to his suffering and death, we would expect the designation "Jesus." On the other hand, the risen Christ does not receive the word. This leads us to place the emphasis on the words *en thlipsei pollēi* ("in much affliction"). Therefore, says Best, "the emphasis in imitation must be placed on the way in which they received the word."[46] In "much affliction," yet with "joy of the Holy Spirit," the Thessalonians welcomed the word.

That this is a correct understanding of the verse finds support in the analysis by Betz. He argues that the connection between *egenēthēte* ("you became") in v. 6 and *egenēthēmen* ("we were") in v. 5 is to be found in the fact that Paul first preached to them *en pollōi agōni* ("in much adversity") 2:2, which is parallel to *en thlipsei pollēi meta charas pneumatos hagiou* ("in much affliction with joy of the Holy Spirit"), v. 6b. Thus "the Thessalonians have experienced in their own existence as a congregation exactly that which they have experienced at the time of their founding. . . . They are *mimētai tou Paulou* ("imitators of Paul") in a profound sense because they, just as he, preach *to euaggelion tou theou* ("the gospel of God"), 2:2, *en thlipsei pollēi meta charas pneumatos hagiou*."[47] Marxsen believes it is this tension between distress and joy that characterizes the Christology of Paul, a way of lordship in humiliation; Christians are stamped with this image so that in their lives they reflect the apostle and the apostle the Lord.[48]

Although the emphasis in v. 6 falls on affliction, still the importance of *dexamenoi ton logon* ("having received the word") must not be overlooked. "Receiving" clearly means accepting the word in faith.[49] The expression *ton*

---

[45]Ibid.

[46]Best, *Commentary*, 77f. The nature of *thlipsis* ("affliction") is left unspecified here, but its context is persecution and eschatology. This does not adequately explain the Christological reference in the verse, however. Thus Marxsen goes on to explain that the reference to *kurios* ("Lord") here is a lordship in humiliation. The Lord remains "the crucified" (*An die Thessalonicher*, 39).

[47]Betz, *Nachfolge*, 143.

[48]Marxsen, *An die Thessalonicher*, 39.

[49]Moore, *1 and 2 Thessalonians*, 28.

logon introduces a key concept of Pauline theology, one that is closely connected with preaching the gospel. The *logos* is Paul's code word for the gospel, the message which he proclaims in the hearing of the congregation. Whether he uses it in the absolute sense, as he does here, or makes it the word "of God" or "of Christ," the import is the same. The *logos* designates the gospel message as originating in God.

Paul's use of *logos* is closely related to the conception of "word" in the Old Testament. There the word carries both a dianoetic and dynamic connotation, meaning that it always contains a thought and also that it is filled with power. As a result, creation is described as happening by means of the word of God. This dual significance finds its greatest development in the prophets, particularly Isaiah and Jeremiah. They understand themselves as speaking under divine compulsion, delivering a message that comes to pass in its very proclamation. Their speaking a "Thus says the Lord" releases a dynamic force, which can be either creative or destructive. The word of God is a historical event. As a result, when Paul speaks of the *logos,* he proceeds from a prophetic consciousness in which his proclamation of the message of Christ is recognized as divinely empowered. The phrase *logos tou theou* ("word of God") is therefore closely related to *euaggelion* ("gospel"), and its usage already appears in fixed form in 1 Thessalonians.[50]

That the Thessalonians are said to have "received the word," therefore, coincides with the dynamic understanding of the gospel we encountered in v. 5. There has been released among them, through the gospel, a divine creative energy. If the gospel is an event, a power structure foundational for the Thessalonian church and a sphere of authentic existence, then that dynamic is traceable to the fact that it is the word of God. It is no surprise, then, when Paul refers to Christian existence as a "new creation" (Gal. 6:15; 2 Cor. 5:17). The gospel is the way the word of God finds expression in the human realm.[51]

The fact that the Thessalonians have been stamped with the image of the apostle and of Christ, in their accepting the divine word in the face of affliction, now has an important consequence. This is briefly summarized in the result clause of v. 7. The Thessalonian congregation has become the *tupon* ("model") for "all the believers in Macedonia and Achaia."[52]

---

[50]O. Procksch and G. Kittel, *TDNT*, 3 (Grand Rapids: Eerdmanns, 1965), 91-117. The explanation of the term *logos* ("word") in this paragraph is based on this article. That Paul's understanding of the word is prophetic finds further confirmation in Gal. 1:15f., where Paul describes his apostolic call in prophetic terms.

[51]I am indebted to Dr. Darrell Doughty for this insight. He has also brought to my attention the fact that while "word" is an Old Testament term for the power of God, it does not have any specific content. In distinction, "gospel" appears to be a specifically pauline Christian term and does have a definite content, the Christ event.

[52]Bartholomäus Henneken, *Verkündigung und Prophetie im Ersten Thessalonicherbrief* (Stuttgart: Katholisches Bibelwerk, 1969), 64. He notes that the word *tupon* is singular, meaning that it refers to the congregation as a whole.

The basis for this far-reaching statement is indicated in v. 8 with the words *aph humōn gar exēchētai ho logos tou kuriou* ("for from you the word of the Lord has sounded forth").[53] Paul amplifies this by saying that the word has reached not only to the regions of Macedonia and Achaia, but beyond, "in every place" (*en panti topōi*). The apostle does not stop at this point, however, but uses this latter phrase to introduce a new sentence. Though grammatically awkward, the expression *hē pistis humōn . . . exelēluthen* ("your faith . . . has gone forth") serves with *aph humōn gar exēchētai ho logos tou kuriou* to emphasize the unlimited range of the word's activity and at the same time to characterize the specific nature of that word. The content of the *logos* ("word") is at this point the *pistis* ("faith" or, perhaps better in this context, "faithfulness") of the Thessalonians toward God. That is why the word has sounded forth from *them*.

From the new turn of expression which Paul introduced with *hē pistis* ("faith") he now draws a further consequence, namely, that he himself does not have to say anything. And this in turn is explained by vv. 9-10.

> For they themselves report concerning you what kind of arrival we had before you, and how you turned to God from idols, to serve a living and true God, and to await his son from the heavens, whom he raised from the dead, Jesus who rescues us from the coming wrath vv. 9-10).

These verses bring to a climax the first part of Paul's prayer of thanksgiving, in which he has described the current standing in faith on the part of the Thessalonians. Verses 9-10 are a summary of the conversion of the Thessalonians and disclose the content of the faith to which they are remaining loyal. Paul reports that he himself does not need to mention this fact, "for they themselves report" (*autoi gar peri hēmōn apaggellousin*) the news about the apostle's arrival among the Thessalonians and their subsequent conversion. This is undoubtedly what is meant by the term *eisodon* ("entrance").[54] Who "they" are is not specified, but probably it refers generally to the people of Macedonia and Achaia.[55]

The rest of vv. 9-10 has the appearance of a traditional Christian credal formulation.[56] As Marxsen observes, v. 9b represents a missionary appeal typical of both Judaism and Christianity, the call to abandon idolatry and turn to the true God.[57] It is v. 10 that expresses the specifically Christian content

---

[53]Literally *exēchētai* means "echo forth;" or it could possibly be translated "ring out." See BAG, 275. Note also that *humon* ("you") is in an emphatic position.

[54]Best, *Commentary*, 81. Cf. 2:1.

[55]Ibid.

[56]Marxsen, *An die Thessalonicher*, 40f.; Best, *Commentary*, 84f.

[57]Marxsen, *An die Thessalonicher*, 41. From this Marxsen concludes that the Thessalonian congregation was made up primarily of god-fearers who had previously been associated with the synagogue.

of their faith. The Thessalonians, like all other Christians, "await" (*anamenein*) the coming of the risen Son of God, for in his coming is their final deliverance.[58] And that from which they are to be rescued is "the coming wrath" (*tēs orgēs tēs erchomenēs*). This expression is typical of apocalyptic thought both in later Judaism and early Christianity, a reference to God's coming intervention into human affairs to punish all who oppose his will and to vindicate those who are faithful to him.[59] It is this strong eschatological note that concludes this part of the argument, and it is doubtless placed here as a reinforcement for their faith. The fact that the Thessalonian Christians have received the word *en thlipsei* ("in affliction") points to the eschatological woes which were expected to precede the Parousia of Christ. In this way the Thessalonians can take heart from knowing they are part of God's final plans of deliverance and also that their affliction points to the nearing of the time of their redemption.

Now that we have analyzed the components of vv. 6-10, it remains for us to clarify their meaning. What does Paul mean when he refers to the word going forth, echoing forth from Thessalonica? Are we to imagine a specific missionary enterprise undertaken by the Thessalonians to spread the gospel into surrounding regions?[60] Probably not. The reference here is to an "indirect mission," as Marxsen calls it, which he explains by saying, "Where the report of the existence of such a congregation is noised abroad, Paul can precisely characterize this knowledge as 'Word of the Lord.' "[61] The reason for this can be understood, Marxsen believes, from the historical situation of the apostle at the time of his writing the letter. Marxsen thinks the description of the Thessalonian congregation is purposely chosen by Paul in view of his mission *in Corinth*. After Timothy's return and the arrival of brothers from Macedonia, the narrative of the conversion of the Thessalonians and their faithfulness, despite persecution, becomes an effective "Word of the Lord" in Corinth. Thus the Thessalonian congregation helps him in his mission. At the same time, his mention of this to the Thessalonians helps them to understand their own situation in the gospel more comprehensively.[62]

Marxsen's solution is persuasive as well as attractive, for it helps to explain why Paul places such emphasis on the Thessalonians as *mimētai* ("im-

---

[58]This waiting does not mean inactivity, as is clearly indicated by 4:11. Instead, their expectation of the Parousia "defines present life," allowing them to face the future in confidence (Marxsen, *An die Thessalonicher*, 41).

[59]Moore, *1 and 2 Thessalonians*, 32; Marxsen, *An die Thessalonicher*, 41; Best, *Commentary*, 84f.

[60]Best thinks we should imagine a general spreading of the gospel from certain centers into surrounding towns and villages (*Commentary*, 79-80).

[61]Marxsen, *An die Thessalonicher*, 37.

[62]Ibid., 37-38.

itators'') through whom the word has gone forth. Marxsen's analysis is given further credence by recent studies in the social setting of early Christianity. Wayne Meeks points out that because of frequent travel on the part of people in the Greco-Roman world, there was a certain "contagion" from new converts that spread into surrounding areas, so that "people in other places are able to describe Paul's arrival in Thessalonica and the conversions that followed."[63] Also, Bengt Holmberg draws attention to the fact that Paul is continually "holding up his churches as examples to one another, . . . thus weaving a net of relations between them."[64] This emerging picture of joint ministry on the part of Paul and his Thessalonian congregation, therefore, has crucial implications for the way in which Paul conceives of the gospel "happening." And it helps us to see why Paul spends so much time in 2:1ff. describing the joint experience of the Thessalonians and himself in the gospel.

C. Exegesis of 2:1-14

Chapter 2:1-14 describes the mutual experience in the gospel which the apostle Paul shared with the Thessalonian congregation. In it the most noticeable feature is the integrity of the apostle. His conduct corresponds to the message he delivers. The pericope has often been referred to as an "apology" on the part of the apostle. Because of the defensive tone of 2:1ff., Schmithals has argued that these verses point to a different letter, from another occasion, dealing with charges from certain opponents.[65] But more convincing is Marxsen's contention that while 2:1-12 may be a defense, it is a defense not of the apostle, but of his gospel, for the discussion is threaded through with repeated references to the gospel and word.[66] The thought sequence is rounded off in vv. 13-14 on the note of the power of the gospel exercised through the personal suffering and weakness of both the apostle and the Thessalonian congregation.[67]

Within the context of the letter, therefore, 2:1-14 functions in two ways. First, on the basis of shared experience it documents the far-reaching claims

---

[63]Wayne Meeks, *The First Urban Christians* (New Haven: Yale University Press, 1983), 27, 231 n. 9.

[64]Bengt Holmberg, *Paul and Power* (Lund: C. W. K. Gleerup, 1978), 56. Holmberg considers Paul's collection for the church in Jerusalem as the foremost example of this. See also 1 Thess. 2:14, 4:10a.

[65]Schmithals, *Paul and the Gnostics,* 135ff.

[66]Marxsen, *An die Thessalonicher,* 43.

[67]Though the Greek text in this section continues through vv. 15-16, the vehemence and hostility of its attack on the Jews, together with terms which do not otherwise appear in Paul (e.g., that the Jews are "opposed to all men," an expression customary of pagan polemic against the Jews), point to a later interpolation. See Meeks, *Urban Christians,* 227 n. 117. Cf. Marxsen (*An die Thessalonicher,* 48-51) for a cogent attempt to prove the verses authentic.

Paul has made for the Thessalonians in the first chapter, confirming their current status in the gospel by reference to the circumstances of their founding. Secondly, the chapter builds up to and prepares for Paul's parenesis in the second part of the letter. Paul uses himself as the model of the conduct to which he will call the Thessalonians in chapters 4-5.

> For you yourselves know, brothers, that our arrival before you was not empty, but even though we had previously suffered and been abused at Philippi, as you know, we were bold in our God to speak to you the gospel of God in much adversity (vv. 1-2).

Verses 1-2 turn the discussion in such a different direction that the reader is left wondering whether there is any connection with the preceding chapter. But a closer examination reveals that *autoi gar* (''for you yourselves'') and *eisodon* (''arrival'') pick up from 1:9, where those exact words appear.[68] And even though 1:9b-10 disrupt the transition, in view of the fact that those verses represent a credal formula which Paul has taken up and quoted to describe the Thessalonian conversion, they should not be understood as breaking the thought sequence. Instead, the apostle moves from a description of the gospel's effect in Thessalonica, confirmed by outside witnesses (1:9a), to the testimony which emerges from within the shared experience of apostle and congregation (2:1). The *autoi gar oidate* (''for you yourselves know'') is in an emphatic position, as if to say that the Thessalonians do not need others to confirm their having ''received the word in affliction'' (1:6), since the best evidence lies within their own recollection.

Paul's introductory term *oidate* (''you know'') has already appeared in 1:5, and it will reappear in 2:5, 9, 10, 11. The apostle is not telling his congregation anything new. Instead, he is tacitly calling them to witness to the power of the gospel at work in himself. He is raising to a conscious level their joint experience in the gospel so that he can interpret it.[69] This becomes clear with the expression *hoti ou kenē gegonen* (''that it was not empty''), which summarizes the effectiveness of his arrival among them. Paul intends to demonstrate that in the circumstances of his arrival there is to be found the clue which opens up the meaning of the gospel as it has worked itself out among the Thessalonians. In v. 1 it is said negatively, that his arrival was *ou kenē* (''not empty'' or ''not fruitless,'' or, with the RSV, ''was not in vain.'').[70]

The positive significance of Paul's work in Thessalonica is now explained in v. 2, beginning with *alla* (''but'').[71] It consists in this, not merely

---

[68]Best (*Commentary,* 89) prefers to connect the verse with 1:2-10 as a whole, especially with a view to 1:5.

[69]Marxsen, *An die Thessalonicher,* 44.

[70]*Kenē* could mean either ''empty-handed'' or ''fruitless.'' Moore (*1 and 2 Thessalonians,* 33) cannot decide between them. But in the context the word undoubtedly means ''ineffective,'' as Best notes (*Commentary,* 89). See 1 Thess. 3:5. See also 1 Cor. 15:10, 14, 58; Gal. 2:2.

[71]Notice the antithetical structure which continues through v. 8.

that Paul delivered the gospel to them and founded their congregation, as we might have been led to expect from 1:9b-10, but that he "was bold to speak the gospel to them" in spite of the previous suffering and abuse he had experienced at Philippi and in spite of the *polloi agōni* ("great adversity" or "conflict") that greeted his preaching in Thessalonica. Here Paul amplifies a crucial theme, a theme which will show up repeatedly in his subsequent correspondence, namely, the power of the gospel through human weakness and suffering.[72] This is the pattern of the gospel, based as it is on a Lord who was crucified, and it is repeated in the lives of the faithful. Paul has already made reference to that pattern in 1:6 and revealed how the Thessalonians have been stamped with it. Now Paul proceeds to document its truth from his own experience and conduct of ministry in the gospel. He has come from an unpleasant situation in Philippi where he has suffered mistreatment. This the Thessalonians *oidate* ("know"), at least from a worldly perspective. His arrival in weakness, therefore, which was openly recognizable to them, was hardly a recommendation for the power of his message. Yet the apostle found the courage to speak the gospel to them in spite of it and even in the face of *polloi agōni* ("great adversity"). The exact nature of this adversity is not specified, but in view of the context most scholars think he refers to external opposition.[73] For Paul the most important thing is the fact that he was bold to speak "in our God" (*en tōi theōi hēmōn*). The gospel is not barren, but fruitful, because the power of God is at work within it. The fact that the gospel comes to them and creates a community by means of a vulnerable messenger simply confirms its divine origin and power.[74]

> For our appeal comes neither out from deception nor impurity nor with craftiness, but just as we have been approved by God to be entrusted with the gospel so we speak, not as those who are pleasing to men but to God, who tests our hearts (vv. 3-4).

Verses 3-4 now introduce an argument which both explains and supports the point Paul has made in the preceding two verses, as is shown by the word *gar* ("for") which appears at the beginning of the sentence. The power of the gospel resident in the preaching of Paul is bare of the customary marks of human power, thereby drawing attention to the truth of the gospel and also confirming the integrity of the apostle.[75]

---

[72]This is especially noticeable in the Corinthians letters, for example 1 Cor. 2:1-4, 2 Cor. 11-12. See also Henneken (*Verkündigung*, 99ff.), who argues the case for "an inner theological connection of suffering and gospel."

[73]Best, *Commentary*, 91f.; Moore, *1 and 2 Thessalonians*, 33f.

[74]See Rom. 1:16; 1 Cor. 1:17.

[75]Henneken, *Verkündigung*, 9-13.

Paul first explains the nature of his preaching by use of *paraklēsis* ("appeal").[76] This is undoubtedly a reference to his attempts to win converts to the faith.[77] More important here, however, is the phrase which modifies the appeal, *ouk ek plānes oude ex akatharsias oude en dolōi* ("not from deception nor impurity nor with craftiness"). Although the verb is missing and must be supplied, the fact that the first two terms are governed by *ek* ("out of, from") and the last by *en* ("with," in the instrumental sense) makes it clear that the verb understood is "come" (from v. 1). Or, perhaps better for translation purposes, we should think of two verbal expressions, "come from" and "come with." Paul's appeal does not come from deception, meaning to mislead someone into error.[78] Nor does his appeal spring from impurity, probably meant in the moral sense of impure motives.[79] And it does not come by means of *dolōi* ("guile") in the sense of cunning deceit.[80]

The fact that Paul engages in emphatic denial of certain motives and practices is what led Schmithals to argue that Paul is defending himself against specific charges. He believes Paul's choice of words reflects a defense against gnostic accusers.[81] Marxsen on the other hand, warns against pressing these terms too hard.[82] His caution is well taken, especially in view of the recent study by Malherbe. Malherbe has discovered a remarkable correspondence between Paul's language in v. 3ff. and that of Cynic apologists used to distinguish the true philosopher from the misguided, the frauds and the charlatans.[83] His findings support the view of most scholars that Paul is dealing here not with a particular set of opponents but with the standard practices of many wandering preachers, philosophers, and wonder-workers who were so in evidence in that day and time. This is not to say that Paul's use of the terms carries the same meaning as that of the Cynics—in fact, the Cynics themselves were not in agreement on their meaning.[84] But Paul seems to have borrowed

---

[76]*Paraklēsis* can mean either "comfort/exhortation" or "appeal." In 2 Cor. 5:20, 6:1 we find the latter meaning in a similar context. The fact that it appears here in the context of verbs of speaking (vv. 2, 4) also supports that meaning. See Best, *Commentary*, 92. See also 2:12.

[77]Moore, *1 and 2 Thessalonians*, 34.

[78]Our translation of *plane* here is influenced by Malherbe, who has shown that this term, along with "impurity" and "craftiness," was a standard rebuke among Cynic philosophers for marketplace preachers who misled their hearers with flattery ("Gentle as a Nurse," *NovT* 12 (1970): 203-17). Note Paul's reference to flattery in 2:5. See also BAG, 671, and Schmithals (*Paul and the Gnostics*, 144f.), who argues that it is a gnostic term, meaning "deception, fraud." But cf. Best, who is not convinced by Malherbe or Schmithals and prefers to abide by a more literal rendering, "error" (*Commentary*, 93-95).

[79]Best, *Commentary*, 93.

[80]Moore, *1 and 2 Thessalonians*, 34.

[81]Schmithals, *Paul and the Gnostics*, 135ff.

[82]Marxsen, *An die Thessalonicher*, 45.

[83]Malherbe, "Gentle," 203-17.

[84]Ibid., 217.

terms which were in general use among Cynic apologists in order to distinguish his apostolic message and conduct from that of the usual itinerant preachers. We are not to imagine that such preachers have produced an immediate crisis, for Paul learns from Timothy that the Thessalonians are standing firm in faith. But in view of the persecution they had experienced, the Thessalonians could easily fall victim to the temptation to look for salvation that was much less costly, and Paul knew there were more than enough itinerant preachers who would be glad to offer it.[85] Thus Paul distinguishes his gospel from fraud and error on the basis of his personal suffering and self-giving for the gospel's sake, thereby suggesting at the same time that the Thessalonians should be on guard in the future, as in the past, against all false claims.

What Paul has said negatively he now states positively. Although the word *paraklēsis* (''appeal'') falls from view in v. 4, it is not far from the apostle's mind. His preaching of the gospel, his appeal, originates in God. And since ''we have been approved'' (*dedokimasmetha*) by God, Paul knows himself ''to be entrusted'' (*pisteuthēnai*) with the gospel.[86] By this he means that just as the truth and power of the message comes from God, so in his preaching and conduct he is answerable to God. What Paul understands this responsibility to entail is indicated by v. 4b, where he claims that he does not speak in order to please men, but God, *dokimazonti tas kardias hēmōn* (''who tests our hearts'').[87] This final relative clause, as Henneken notes, is a quotation from Jer. 11:20 (LXX), which strongly suggests that Paul sees himself in a prophetic role. His preaching is from God and therefore is not acceptable to people in general; this means the prophet must suffer.[88] So at the same time the fact of his suffering is also a truth-claim for the gospel he preaches.

> For we never used a word of flattery, as you know, nor did we appear with pretense that cloaked greed—God is witness—nor seeking glory from men (neither from you nor from others), even though as apostles of Christ we are able to insist on our being treated with importance. But we were gentle among you, as a mother cherishes her children, having such affection for you that we were willing to share with you not only the gospel of God but also our very own selves, because you had become very dear to us (vv. 5-8).

Still using the language of the Cynic apologists Paul now resumes his denial, begun in v. 3, of all means of preaching and conduct which would com-

---

[85]Marxsen, *An die Thessalonicher,* 45.

[86]Note that *dedokimasmetha* is in the perfect tense, thereby denoting an existing state. Best (*Commentary,* 96) believes Paul means by ''approval'' both the fact that he has been chosen by God to be an instrument of the gospel and also that in his carrying out of its ministry he has been tested and found trustworthy.

[87]Best (*Commentary,* 97) points out that *areskontes* (''pleasing'') is not just a matter of intention but of fact. This is borne out in 2:5a. See also Henneken, *Verkündigung,* 101.

[88]Henneken, *Verkündigung,* 98-103. Henneken also finds this theme reflected in the word *dokimazein* (v. 4a), which in LXX means to be ''tested by fire.''

promise the integrity of the gospel of God.[89] And indirectly, of course, he calls the Thessalonians to be on guard against the motives and unethical conduct on the part of the "market-place preachers," as Malherbe calls them.[90] They fit the pattern of standard denials on the part of philosophers and are to be taken in a general sense here.[91] What makes Paul's claims specific to the Thessalonians is his call for witnesses. The Thessalonians themselves are called upon to testify that Paul did not use flattering speech, as he says "you know" (*kathōs oidate*).[92] But since his inner motives cannot be observed by the Thessalonians, he calls God to witness that he was not acting out a charade which disguised motives of greed, v. 4b.[93]

But if Paul is not seeking material gain by means of his preaching, as v. 5 implies, neither is he "seeking glory from men" (*zetountes ex anthrōpōn doxan*), v. 6. What does he mean by *doxan* ("glory")? Best believes he is referring to spiritual pride, and Moore thinks he is talking about some human quality or achievement.[94] But those who argue that financial support is at issue here are most persuasive. In the first place, if the words of v. 7a, *dunamenoi en barei einai* ("able to insist on importance"), are to be taken with the preceding rather than what follows, then they would modify *doxan*. This is probably the case in view of the antithetical structure of thought and the fact that *alla* ("but") does not appear until the next clause. Second, in view of the appearance of the same root *bar-* in v. 9, where the discussion is centered on his means of financial support, it is likely that the expression *en barei einai* ("to be in importance" or, more literally, "weight") should refer to financial support.[95] Thus *en barei* imparts to *doxan* a "concrete, material and figurative sense," to use Henneken's words, which he takes to mean that the central meaning is "importance," though with a secondary allusion to material upkeep.[96] In

---

[89]It is interesting to note how the series of Cynic apologetic terms so clustered in vv. 3-7 is interrupted by v. 4, in which no Cynic terms appear. This suggests that v. 4 is Paul's interpretation of v. 3 and also, because it is clearly a break in the language, that he is following a pattern of set words and phrases.

[90]Malherbe, "Gentle," 214.

[91]Best, *Commentary*, 97.

[92]Moore (*1 and 2 Thessalonians*, 36) describes flattery as here meaning a speech to "curry favor," or "deception by slick eloquence."

[93]*Prophasis pleonexias* literally means "pretext of avarice." Best (*Commentary*, 98) explains that the expression refers to a "a false outward attitude inspired by avarice" and so translates "with a veiled desire to exploit."

[94]Ibid., 99; Moore, *1 and 2 Thessalonians*, 36.

[95]Evidence from recent sociological studies of Paul confirms this. See Ronald Hock, *The Social Context of Paul's Ministry* (Philadelphia: Fortress, 1980), 30. See also Holmberg, *Paul and Power*, 91-93. Holmberg mentions a study by Strelan of the root *bar-* which shows that it has to do with financial support.

[96]Henneken, *Verkündigung*, 14-17.

this context, then, Paul is arguing that his preaching is not for personal advantage; on the one hand he renounces any underhanded ways to gain something at their expense (v. 5), and on the other he refuses to exercise his apostolic rights in order to get something from them (v. 6), whether it means prestige or the financial support which is commensurate with prestige, or, as is likely, both.

Verses 7b-8 now state Paul's case positively. He has been "gentle among you" (*ēpioi en mesōi humōn*).[97] Flowing from what he has just said, this certainly means he did not make demands upon them, financial or otherwise. Instead, rather than his receiving support from them, it was the other way around. He has supported them *hōs ean trophos thalpēi ta heautēs tekna* ("as a nurse might cherish/nurture her children").[98] Though *trophos* is used of a wet-nurse, it is also used for a nursing mother, and in view of the parental images in what follows and the fact that elsewhere Paul pictures himself as a mother, the apostle probably means that he treated them with a mother-love.[99]

With v. 8 Paul completes the picture of gentle care which he exercised over his congregation in Thessalonica. He felt a deep affection toward them, so much so that he was pleased "to share" (*metadounai*) with the congregation not only the gospel of God but "our own selves" (*tas heautōn psuchas*).[100] Here Paul means by *euaggelion* ("gospel") the oral proclamation, in the narrower sense, and by *psuchas* he has in mind his very "life." As Marxsen argues, for Paul gospel and life cannot be separated. The word of the gospel and the life of the preacher become visible together and only in that way become truly effective.[101] Paul's authority among the Thessalonians was and continues to be exercised in terms of his self-giving devotion, based as it is upon the self-giving devotion of Christ.[102]

---

[97]The reading *nēpioi* ("babies") has good support among some of the best witnesses. But it is likely due to a scribal error. In the context the variant reading *ēpioi* ("gentle") makes better sense. See Moore, *1 and 2 Thessalonians*, 38. See also Malherbe, "Gentle," 211, who informs us that *ēpios* was for the Cynics synonymous with *philanthropos* ("benevolent"), meaning that one is not irrascible or harsh. Cf. Bruce Metger, *A Textual Commentary on the Greek New Testament* (New York: United Bible Societies, 1971), 629f.

[98]It is a question whether *hōs ean . . . tekna* should be taken with the preceding or following clause. Best opts for the latter in view of the fact that it would conform better to the "as . . . so" structure of vv. 7c-8a (*Commentary*, 101f.). However, the *houtōs* ("so") clause extends through all of v. 8, meaning that the entire passage of 7c-8 modifies *ēpioi*. Thus we are justified in connecting *hōs ean . . . tekna* with *ēpioi* in v. 7b.

[99]Best, *Commentary*, 101f.; Moore, *1 and 2 Thessalonians*, 38.

[100]Meeks, *Urban Christians*, 85-87, draws our attention to the tenderness and warmth of Paul's language here and goes on to point out how such inclusive language is used to create a sense of belonging within a group.

[101]Marxsen, *An die Thessalonicher*, 46.

[102]Ibid., 45.

For you recall, brothers, our labor and toil; night and day we worked in order not to be a burden to any of you while we proclaimed to you the gospel of God. You and God are witnesses how holy and justly and blamelessly we were among you believers, just as you know how we were to each one of you as a father to his children, appealing to you and encouraging you and charging you to walk worthy of the God who calls us into his own kingdom and glory (vv. 9-12).

Although the thrust of Paul's thought continues in these verses, it is not altogether clear to which element in his train of thought v. 9 is to be connected. The *gar* ("for") usually gives the reasons for a statement, but it hardly makes sense that he is supplying evidence for the fact that they have become beloved, v. 8b. More likely v. 9 continues the assertion of v. 7, since the account of how he earned his own living gives evidence of his renunciation of apostolic right to financial support so as not to burden them.[103] Specifically Paul calls them to remember "our labor and toil" (*ton kopon hēmōn kai ton mochthon*). The reference is not only to the fact that the apostle worked as a tradesman, a leather-worker, but that his life as a tradesman involved long, arduous and exhausting labor.[104] The point is made all the more emphatic by his description of toiling *nuktos kai hēmeras* ("night and day").[105] This description serves as a paradigm for Paul's parenesis of 4:10-12, where he calls the Thessalonians to "work with their own hands" and "be dependent upon no one."

Verses 10-12 pursue the characterization of the apostle's conduct in the gospel by turning to his pastoral care.[106] This time *both* the Thessalonians and God are to serve as witnesses for the fact that his behavior toward the believers was unimpeachable. The three terms Paul uses, *hosiōs kai dikaiōs kai amemptōs* ("holy and justly and blamelessly"), are practically synonymous. They are broad strokes, and, in view of the witness of both God and the Thessalonians, the words mean that his way of life has been conformed to the will of God and has demonstrated the ethic expected of a genuine apostle approved to be entrusted with the gospel.[107]

Paul now carries his general statement of v. 10, that his care of the believers has been faultless before God and the Thessalonians, over into a specific instance, the manner in which he has addressed the gospel to them. Not only has he brought the gospel to them as a group, but he has cared for each

---

[103]The notion of his being "gentle among them" is probably also implied.

[104]Hock's study of the nature of work in the Greco-Roman world shows that this is no exaggeration. Not only that, but working with one's hands was not highly esteemed. Thus Paul's self-supporting labor is a labor of love, an exercise in humility (*Social Context*, 30-36).

[105]This does not mean working all night but probably beginning before day-break and continuing past dark. See Hock, *Social Context*, 30-31.

[106]Best, *Commentary*, 10.

[107]Ibid., 105; Moore, *1 and 2 Thessalonians*, 40.

one individually, v. 11.[108] The verse lacks a verb, but *egenēthēmen* ("we were") at the end of v. 10 is probably understood. Paul's pastoral care is described in terms of the manner of his existence, which takes the form of "a father to his children" (*pāter tekna heautou*). The recourse to parental images, the mother image in v. 7 and the father image here, express Paul's understanding of himself both as the begettor of the congregation and as the one who has continuing responsibility for their education in the faith. As a parent his care is exercised under the authority of love.[109]

Paul's fatherly, individual care of the congregation now receives precise formulation with the three participles *parakalountes humas kai paramuthoumenoi kai marturomenoi* ("appealing to and encouraging you and charging"), v. 12. The first two terms are very similar in meaning, pointing to the use of gentle persuasion.[110] We are not, however, to think of Paul pleading or begging. The third term, *marturomenoi*, connotes a charge laid upon the believers, a call to obedience.[111] And that obedience is characterized in v. 12b as *to peripatein humas axiōs tou theou* ("that you walk worthy of God"). The use of the word "walk" to describe one's way of life is a frequent Old Testament image. Their acceptance of the gospel takes the form of a certain Godward path, a concrete direction in their lives qualified by "worthy of God." This latter phrase means a life that corresponds to the very character of God.[112]

The sequence of thought which began in 2:1 now concludes with a relative clause descriptive of the God in whose paths they are to walk. It is particularly focused on God as the one who issues a saving call. The expression *tou kalountos humas eis tēn heautou basileian kai doxan* ("who calls us into his own kingdom and glory") reads very much like a credal or liturgical fragment. The use of the term *basileian* ("kingdom"), which is rare in Paul, especially suggests a pre-Pauline tradition. Add to this the fact that the first part also concluded with a formula (1:9-10) and the fact that some textual witnesses want to change the participle *kalountos* ("who calls") from present to aorist tense (on the basis that Paul should be describing God's call as something that happened in the past), and one has persuasive evidence that Paul is making use of an existing Christian formula. But what is most important here is not so much the fact as the function of the formula. It is made up of escha-

---

[108]Concern for the individual was one of the characteristics of the ideal Cynics (Malherbe, "Gentle," 209, 216f.). Thus Paul on the one hand avoids the behavior of false preachers and at the same time practices the standards associated with the genuine philosopher.

[109]Holmberg, *Paul and Power*, 75, 79f.

[110]Best, *Commentary*, 106f. Cf. 2 Cor. 4:1ff.

[111]Best prefers the translation "insisting" (*Commentary*, 107).

[112]Marxsen, *An die Thessalonicher*, 46f.

tological terms. On the one hand it is a word of assurance that the God to whom the Thessalonians owe their faithfulness continues to call them into his own sphere. At the same time Paul has linked it up to an ethical expression "to walk worthy" of such a God. As Marxsen says, "Their walk corresponds to living now the future that awaits them."[113]

> And for this reason we also offer thanks to God unceasingly that when you received the word of God which you heard from us, you accepted it not as the word of men but for what it really is, the word of God, which is also working among you who believe. For you became imitators, brothers, of the churches of God in Christ Jesus which are in Judea, because you also suffered the same things at the hands of your fellow citizens as they did at the hands of the Jews (vv. 13-14).

These verses round out this portion of Paul's thanksgiving prayer. At the same time they prepare for his description of the current state of affairs between himself and the Thessalonians in 2:17-3:13.

Verse 13 begins in an awkward way, however. The customary use of the phrase *dia touto* ("for this reason") requires an antecedent, but it is difficult to know exactly what that is. Some, such as Schmithals, have thought the transition so abrupt as to suggest that this is a thanksgiving from another, later epistle which has been inserted by a redactor.[114] Others, such as Pearson and Boers, regard the whole of vv. 13-16 as a later, non-pauline interpolation.[115] But the terminology and themes of v. 13 are clearly pauline. And however awkward the transition, the trend of thought in vv. 13-14 certainly does not represent a sharp change from what Paul has been saying. In fact, as Marxsen observes, the continuation of the persecution theme speaks against any "partition hypothesis." He goes on to say that it is precisely in view of the situation reflected in v. 14 that v. 2 was formulated, and he believes v. 13 is consequent on the whole previous discussion, namely, the danger of the Thessalonians, suffering trials because of the gospel, falling victim to the temptation of regarding Paul's word as

---

[113]Ibid., 47.

[114]Schmithals, *Paul and the Gnostics*, 154. But his argument does not have much evidence to support it. As Best notes, it would be more persuasive if it could be documented that there were a definite, identifiable group of opponents (*Commentary*, 34f.).

[115]Birger Pearson, "1 Thessalonians 2:13-16: A Deutero-pauline Interpolation," *HTR* 64 (1971): 79-94, and Hendrikus Boers, "The Form-Critical Study of Paul's Letters. 1 Thessalonians as a Case Study," *NTS* 22 (1975/76): 140-58. Pearson examines the structure of 2:13-16 as well as the use of traditional and formulaic material. Boers subjects 2:13-16 to a thorough form-critical analysis. Both regard as decisive Funk's argument, on the basis of the structure of the epistolary genre, that the theme of "apostolic parousia" in 2:17-3:13 picks up from 2:11-12, leaving vv. 13-16 isolated as an interpolation. But cf. Karl Donfried, "Paul and Judaism: 1 Thessalonians 2:13-16 as a Test Case," *Int* 38 (July, 1984): 242-53. Donfried contends, on the basis of Beker's thesis that Paul's structure of thought is apocalyptic, that vv. 13-16 are authentic since they fit into that apocalyptic framework (any non-typical features being traceable to Paul's use of traditional and formulaic material).

merely a "word of men."[116] There is good reason, therefore, to regard the words as authentic, even though the exact reference of *dia touto* ("for this reason") is not indicated. It is quite possible, of course, that the expression points forward instead of back, in other words to the *hoti* ("that") clause of v. 13b.

The theme of thanksgiving which sets the tone for the entire first part of the epistle is now consciously resumed in v. 13. But in contrast to 1:2, here *kai hēmeis* ("we also") is in an emphatic position. Who are the "we" that warrant special mention? Marxsen thinks the reference is made in view of Paul's situation, that Paul's words are intended to be inclusive of the Corinthians. The Corinthians enter into the prayer of thanks because the good report from Thessalonica is a "word of the Lord" to them. In this way the "solidarity motif" in v. 14 is prepared for.[117] The content of the thanksgiving is at this point the fact that the Thessalonians have received the word from Paul as *logon theou* ("word of God").[118]

In v. 13 a central thrust of Paul's argument emerges, namely, the effectiveness of the preaching of the gospel, which originates in the word of God. Two aspects of this thrust are most interesting for our investigation. The first is that preaching is positioned between word of God and gospel. The gospel is spoken (2:2), shared (2:8), and preached (2:9). And when it is received, it is recognized as the word of God (2:13). Preaching the gospel is thus the exercise of the word of God. For Paul preaching is the mediating term between word of God and gospel. It is by means of the preaching of the gospel that the word of God comes to light, and it is by hearing the gospel that one receives the word of God.

This is confirmed by the second important aspect of Paul's thrust, namely, that the message which the Thessalonians received is described as *logon akoēs par hēmōn tou theou*, an expression that defies smooth translation. Literally it is "the word of God of hearing from us," which in fluent English is best rendered "the word of God which you heard from us." This translation, however, dilutes the strength of the sentence. To speak of the message which is preached as a *logon akoēs* ("word of hearing") is a pregnant expression. For it points to the fact that the nature of

---

[116]Marxsen, *An die Thessalonicher*, 47. Best connects v. 13 to 2:1, the fact that the gospel is not in vain (*Commentary*, 109).

[117]Marxsen, *An die Thessalonicher*, 47.

[118]The *hoti* could be causal, but probably it is intended to suggest the content of the prayer (Best, *Commentary*, 110). There is a question whether any distinction should be made between the two words for "receiving," *paralambanein* and *dechesthai*. Beker thinks there is a difference in that *paralambanein* refers to receiving the Christian tradition, which he calls a "horizontal" reception, while *dechesthai* denotes the appropriation of the divine word in faith, or a "vertical" reception (*Paul the Apostle*, 122f.).

preaching is essentially *oral*. And reception in faith is essentially aural. It is, as was the case in the Old Testament, a matter of hearing.[119] The fact that it is called a *logon* (''word'') of hearing, a word identified with God, signifies that there is a divine, creative energy released in the act of listening to the orally proclaimed gospel.

The power of the gospel in one's hearing is elaborated by Paul in two ways. The Thessalonians accepted that word as coming from God, even though its medium was the human voice. This implies that divine power was at work within the gospel to create its own acceptance. But the qualifying relative clause *hos kai energeitai en humin tois pisteuousin* (''which is also working among you who believe'') must not be overlooked. Decisive for Paul is the fact that God, through his word, still ''is at work'' (*energeitai*) in them. The basis for this assertion is in v. 14, the fact that the Thessalonian church became imitators of the church in Judea, having similarly suffered at the hands of their fellow countrymen.[120] ''The endurance of the Judean congregations has become as a 'word of the Lord' to the Thessalonians.''[121] Thus the second major section of Paul's prayer of thanksgiving concludes on the same note with which it began in 1:2-3, the theme of faithful endurance.

CONCLUSIONS

Paul's letter of 1 Thessalonians contributes substantially to our understanding of his theology of preaching. His frequent references to his preaching in 1:2-2:14 are surrounded by important key terms which provide a first glimpse of Paul's understanding of the theological origin, function, and expected results of preaching in his ministry.

Several things are conspicuous at the outset. It is clear that the key words ''gospel'' and ''word'' are closely related and that this single sphere of the gospel and the word is the locus of Paul's preaching. For him preaching mediates between the two terms. In addition, it is crucial for Paul's theology of preaching that it creates a community of believers, a congregation, the church.

---

[119]Rom. 10:17; Deut. 6:4. See Henneken, *Verkündigung*, 47-52. Note also how the importance of hearing is reinforced by Paul's reference to his personal presence 3:10-11.

[120]The reference to fellow-countrymen means the citizens of that country. In this case it is fellow gentiles in Thessalonica, despite Acts 17. Best tries to harmonize the evidence with Acts by arguing that the Jews incited the gentiles to attack the congregation (*Commentary*, 114).

[121]Marxsen, *An die Thessalonicher*, 48. He calls attention to the parallel in thought between this verse and 1:6, 8.

It remains for us now to explain precisely what these terms mean within the Thessalonian context. Of primary importance is the fact that, as we noticed in 1:4-5, the gospel is more than a mere message. It signifies an effective force, a power which creates and sustains the Christian community. The density of the power language which surrounds his discussion of the gospel, particularly in 1:5ff., testifies eloquently to that fact. The gospel is something that happens, an event. When the message of good news arrives, it calls forth faith and gathers the believers into its circle. The gospel is therefore something of a saving, dynamic *environment*.[122]

However, what gives the gospel message its dynamic is the fact that it is the word of God (2:14). In contrast to whatever power is at work in the "word of men," the gospel originates in the true, living God (1:9, 2:13).[123] This means it is true and reliable. But above all it signifies that it is the expression of the creative power of God. In the preaching of the gospel God's power is released. When God speaks, as in the Old Testament, new worlds come into being.[124] In this case, within the gospel message there is a creation taking place. A new sphere, a new environment, a new order of human life emerges under the word-gospel influence. The Thessalonians have experienced that in their conversion from idolatry, in the power given them to withstand persecution, and in their having become a model/pattern for other churches.

But the fact that the gospel is charged with the word of God has yet another important consequence. Since it is "word" (*logos*), it requires a voice! In the same way that Paul explains that the preaching of the gospel and living of the gospel must correspond to its message, to Christ (1:6), so also the medium of the gospel must correspond to the fact that it is the word of God. If the word is alive and creative, it requires a means of communication that is alive and creative. And that means is the human voice. The word is oral. The human voice calls forth an audience, and in the audience's hearing it has a direct, personal effect. There is, as Beker observes, an immediacy and directness in oral speech which is not the same in a written text.[125] For Paul, therefore, preaching the gospel is the direct

---

[122]This will become clearer in our examination of 1 Cor. 15:1-11. Stuhlmacher, in his study of Gal. 1 and 2, refers to it as a "material-spatial, temporal area of the word *[Wort-Raum]*" (*Das paulinische Evangelium*, 80).

[123]This, of course, raises the question, What distinguishes the gospel as "word of God" from the "word of men?" How are the Thessalonians to tell the difference? Paul does not say specifically, but the allusions to his apostolic lifestyle provide an important indication.

[124]See 2 Cor. 5:17ff.

[125]Beker, *Paul the Apostle*, 122. This explains why the letter form is not Paul's primary vehicle of the gospel. Notice again his desire to be present among the Thessalonians in order to further instruct them; 3:10.

vocal activity of the creative word of God in time and space. This is the apostle's definition of preaching.

That Paul understands preaching as the living medium of the word of God can be demonstrated and clarified by three important aspects of his preaching which Paul relates in 1 Thessalonians. First, there is the fact that preaching is directly related to the gospel/word. For Paul there is no preaching without the gospel, which is understood both in the sense of the message of Christ and in the sense of the environment it creates. It is this that sets his preaching off from other messengers and messages which are only the "word of men." Of course, Paul recognizes the dynamic quality resident within the human voice generally, since he devotes so much of the second chapter to setting his work off from that of wandering preachers and implying that the Thessalonians should be on the guard against other messengers whose seductive voice misleads people and springs from ulterior motives. But that recognizable human rhetorical power is not to be equated with the living voice whose origin is in God, the living voice of the gospel of Christ.

Secondly, Paul regards the preaching of the gospel as personal. It is *his* gospel. As we have seen, that means his preaching is a matter of both message and quality of life. The nature of the gospel is derived from its Lord, who was victorious through suffering. The apostle reflects that pattern in his own life, and so do the other Christian congregations. It is here that we can see the importance of the oral character of preaching. If the gospel is personal, both in the life of Paul and his congregations, then the living voice is necessary. For the way in which the gospel has shaped the character of preacher and congregation has to be expressed in a way that is uniquely personal, and nothing discloses one's character as much as speech.

This leads us to our third and final point. The preaching of the gospel is clearly understood by Paul as grounded in the Christ event (1:9-10), and the content of preaching proceeds from that. However, Paul's preaching is not confined to the Christ event, in the sense of being delimited to historical events that have occurred in the past. Since the gospel is a dynamic sphere in which Paul and the Thessalonians live, their mutual experience in the gospel becomes part of the gospel itself! The gospel is living and growing. It is *cumulative*. That is why Paul can refer to Timothy's report as "gospel" (3:6). Paul's word *euaggelisamenou* is intentional. It is not just that Timothy brought a favorable report, but "he gospeled to us your faith and your love" (*euaggelisamenou hēmin tēn pistin kai tēn agapēn* (3:6). The faithfulness of the Thessalonians is divinely inspired good news to Paul (and to the Corinthians!). This can also be seen from the repeated use of *oidate* ("you know") in his description of the experience of himself and the Thessalonians in the gospel. Paul employs that term frequently in his letters to designate an authoritative Christian tradition or scriptural text, one that is common to both himself and his readers. He then uses such quotations as the basis for further interpretation. In quite the same way Paul here interprets the joint experience of the Thessalonians and himself, drawing on their common knowledge of the way in which the gospel occurred among them. The Thessalonians themselves, therefore, become the *text* for Paul's further proclamation. But because such experiences are personal and contingent to each situation, they must be witnessed to by the living voice. The cumulative experience in the gospel requires oral proclamation.

CHAPTER THREE

GOSPEL, APOSTOLIC AUTHORITY, AND FREEDOM: THEOLOGY OF PREACHING IN GALATIANS

THE HISTORICAL SITUATION

Paul's letter to the Galatians was composed in the face of a serious crisis. Just how serious the apostle regarded the problem can be seen by his vehement tone and the wide range of arguments he marshals in order to deal with it. From Paul's point of view, the nature of the disturbance is such that the very foundation of his apostolic mission is in jeopardy.

What is not clear, however, is the exact nature of the crisis. For the past century and a half, since the time of F. C. Baur, modern scholarship has been engaged in a vigorous debate about the issues and in attempts at reconstructing the historical situation.[1] The evidence from Paul's letter presents vexing problems, and the attempts to correlate the evidence with the account of Paul's missionary activity in Acts only serves to complicate matters.[2]

---

[1]For a brief, useful description of the history of the investigation in Galatians see George Howard, *Paul: Crisis in Galatia* (London: Cambridge University Press, 1979), 1-7. See also Robert Jewett, ''The Agitators and the Galatian Congregation'' *NTS* 17 (1971): 198-200.

[2]This is most evident in attempts to locate the Galatians geographically. The question is whether Galatia is meant to refer to the territory (the ''North Galatian theory'') or to the Roman province (the ''South Galatian theory''). The latter theory emerges from attempts to identify Paul's addressees with the churches mentioned in Acts 13:14 and 16:1ff., but the attempt

Some of the important questions are answered rather easily. There is, for example, no serious doubt today that Paul is the author of the epistle. Nor is there much serious challenge to the unity or integrity of the letter, as was the case in the latter part of the nineteenth century.[3] As for the question of the date of composition and where Paul might have been located at the time, there is so little evidence that one can only speculate. The best guess, according to most standard introductions, is that Galatians was written about 50-55 A.D., probably from Ephesus or Macedonia, possibly from Corinth.[4]

Much more important for exegetical purposes, however, and much less easily answered, is the question of who Paul's opponents were and what their message was. Since Paul's arguments are arrayed against them, a precise understanding of the opponents' position would contribute immeasurably to clarifying the apostle's theological argument. Unfortunately there is no firm consensus about this at present. But because our exegetical study is oriented toward understanding Paul in terms of his situational context, it is important that we arrive at some working hypothesis about his opponents. In what follows we attempt to do this on the basis of clues derived from the letter as well as analyses provided by current critical scholarship.[5]

It can hardly be doubted that the opponents represent a "judaizing" movement of some kind. Their compelling interest in circumcision (2:3), the Torah (2:15-17; 3:2-5), Abraham (3:6ff.), and Jerusalem (1:18ff.; cf. 4:25-26) all suggests that the key elements of Judaism were regarded as supremely important. On the other hand, they do not seem to exhibit the behavior we might expect of more self-consciously traditional and observant Jews or Jewish Christians. For while Paul pictures them as promoting justification on the basis of "works of the law" (2:15-17), he can also accuse them of not keeping the whole law (6:13; cf. 3:10, 5:3). Somehow circumcision must not have been felt by Paul's opponents to be connected with rigorous adherence to the Torah. It is for this reason, as well as the fact that they seem to regard Torah and circumcision as the "avenue of the Spirit," that Schütz refers to the op-

is forced, since there is no evidence in the letter itself to support it. Thus Galatia probably refers to the territory, though we do not know the exact location of the churches there. See Kümmel (*Introduction*, 296-98) for the arguments and analysis. But cf. Marxsen (*Introduction*, 45-47) for a different conclusion.

[3]Kümmel, *Introduction*, 304.

[4]Ibid. See also Betz, *Galatians*, 12, and Marxsen, *Introduction*, 46.

[5]It should be noted that this is *Paul's* understanding of his opponents. The suggestion by Marxsen that Paul may not have understood them well deserves consideration (*Introduction*, 55-57). However, in view of the fact that Paul seems to have kept close contact with the congregations he started, through use of emissaries, (see Meeks, *Urban Christians*, 107-10), we should be able to assume a reasonable degree of accuracy. Also, it is difficult to believe that Paul would respond with such vehemence and in such detail unless he was confident that he had the facts in hand.

ponents as "syncretistically oriented" and labels them "hellenistic Jewish Christians."[6] On the whole this seems to be the most equitable way to characterize them.

But what is it that Paul's opponents are saying? What is their message that has so "bewitched" the Galatians (3:1) that they are ready to abandon the gospel they received from Paul (1:6) in favor of the opponents' version? In order to answer this question it is useful to distinguish between two closely related aspects of the opponents' argument. On the one hand we must try to formulate what they are saying, negatively, about Paul and his presentation of the gospel, as they understand it. On the other hand, positively, there is the nature of the message which the opponents themselves deliver.

As to the first aspect of this question, it is worth observing that scholars have generally regarded the letter to the Galatians as apologetic. Thus the apostle is pictured as defending himself against specific charges and allegations, such as, for example, "falsifying the gospel and of high-handed presumption in wanting to be an apostle."[7] But it is not necessary to assume that there were such open charges against Paul. As Howard has recently argued, it is possible that the opponents did not know Paul that well and assumed that he belonged essentially to the same stream of theology and practice as they themselves.[8] They may have, as Beker thinks, considered their work as completing or "perfecting" the preliminary missionary work accomplished by Paul.[9] For in their conception of the Christian movement, traceable as it was to Jewish roots, it would have been thought impossible for Christian converts to avoid the essential ingredient of circumcision. The threat which they posed, then, may very well have been an indirect one. Regardless of whether the opponents have leveled charges or not, they have certainly characterized Paul's preaching and practice in such a way that it has become suspect in the minds of the Galatians.

Paul provides several hints as to what he believes his opponents are saying about him. Perhaps most important is his firm insistence that during his

---

[6]Schütz, *Anatomy*, 125f. For an appraisal which confirms Schütz's view see also Helmut Koester, "Gnomai Diaphoroi," in *Trajectories through Early Christianity*, by James M. Robinson and Helmut Koester (Philadelphia: Fortress, 1971), 144-46. But cf. Jewett ("Agitators," 205f.), who believes the opponents are Jewish-Christians from Jerusalem who are circumcizing gentile converts under pressure from Judean zealots, and Schmithals, who thinks they are Jewish-Christian gnostics (*Paul and the Gnostics*, 35ff.). On the other hand, cf. Johannes Munck, *Paul and the Salvation of Mankind* (Atlanta: John Knox, 1977), 89ff., who argues that the opponents are gentiles.

[7]Bornkamm, *Paul*, 18. See also Kümmel (*Introduction*, 300-301) who conceives of the opponents as attacking Paul's apostleship and suggesting that he is guilty of antinomian libertinism. Schmithals, however, insists that they accuse him of dependency (*Paul and the Gnostics*, 25).

[8]Howard, *Crisis*, 7-11.

[9]Beker, *Paul the Apostle*, 42.

meeting with the "pillars" in Jerusalem they "added nothing to me" (2:6; cf. 3:3, where it is implied that the opponents want to "perfect" his work).[10] Quite clearly Paul understands his opponents to be thinking of him as working with an incomplete version of the gospel. They evidently know nothing of his law-free gospel (2:7-10). Paul's version would have been understood by them as an "abbreviated gospel," as Beker terms it.[11] In addition, they appear to have suggested that Paul has made use of this shorter version because he wanted his gospel to be more "pleasing," more attractive, to the would-be Galatian converts (1:10).[12] Furthermore, in view of Paul's statement that he "preaches circumcision" (5:11)—which in the context of the whole epistle can only be understood as the apostle repeating what has been attributed to him by others—it is likely that his opponents think of Paul as being in essential agreement with their position, but as having not mentioned this to the Galatians at the time of their initial reception of the gospel (4:8-9). The opponents may have presupposed that this must be the case, since for them it was inconceivable that any presentation of the gospel would not be in complete conformity with Jerusalem tradition, which they themselves have inherited (1:15-17). Thus, even though it is possible, as some scholars think, that the opponents attack Paul's apostleship because his gospel is out of phase with their own version, thereby discrediting his authority, it is perhaps more probable that the opponents only intend to trim Paul's apostolic authority down to the size of their own, to make him no more than equal to them and thus equally under the jurisdiction of Jerusalem.[13] And finally, in view of Paul's lengthy parenetic section (5:13-6:10), the apostle may also have been said to be promoting a version of the gospel and practice which bordered very close to antinomianism, or at least was its "logical consequence."[14]

---

[10]Ibid.

[11]Ibid., 44.

[12]This need not have been a cynical or harsh judgment. See Beker, *Paul the Apostle*, 44 note. See also Howard for options in the interpretation of the meaning of "pleased" in v. 10, since it is not altogether clear which "men" Paul may have been accused of pleasing (*Crisis*, 8f.).

[13]We are following here the view of Howard (*Crisis*, 7-11) and that of Beker (*Paul the Apostle*, 44). But cf. Peter Stuhlmacher, (*Das paulinische Evangelium*, 67); he thinks Paul is being seen merely as an emissary of Antioch.

[14]Kümmel, *Introduction*, 301. How Paul's ethical section in Galatians is to be correlated to the rest of the letter has been contested at length. Schmithals suggests Paul is dealing with a gnostic licentiousness (*Paul and the Gnostics*, 52ff.). Jewett, in a variation of the hypothesis put forth by Lütgert a half century ago that Paul was dealing on two fronts, argues that, in view of the wavering loyalty of the congregation, Paul is directing his ethics to two dangers, nomism and licentiousness, the former being imported while the latter was native to gentiles everywhere ("Agitators," 209f.). Betz claims that Paul's ethical section is a "manifestation of divine redemption" (*Galatians*, 32-33). More highly nuanced and persuasive is the argument of Howard that Paul uses the ethical argument to show how being under law leads to *sin*, since both are in the realm of the flesh (*Crisis*, 11-14).

But the opponents would also have had a positive message of their own, a competing claim for the loyalty of the Galatians. It may have gone much as follows: Paul, like the rest of us, bears the missionary burden of calling people to the gospel of Christ and its great benefits. Under his ministry you gentiles have made the first step when you gave up idolatry to turn to the true and only God (3:8-9). Thus you have received the gift of faith in Christ. However, this is not the whole story. Paul undoubtedly wanted to spare you the burden of ''too much at once,'' and therefore he did not acquaint you with the rest of your spiritual pilgrimage. Faith puts you in a correct orientation toward God, but it does not yet place you within God's scheme of salvation history. Since Jesus Christ is the messianic fulfillment of the promise to the Jewish patriarch Abraham and is himself a Jew, it is clear that to receive all the blessings of God you must be fully incorporated into God's people of promise, the Jews. This happens when you receive circumcision, which makes you an heir to the seed of Abraham (3:29). Then you take on the yoke of the Torah, and in your observance of it you have access to the full Spirit of God. Now this does not mean you are obligated to practice all the statutes of the law, any more than we do. Instead, the Torah is to be understood as revealing the principles of the meaning of the universe, and therefore when you accept circumcision and its other cultic practices you achieve full status as Christians, receive the full blessings of God, and have the advantage of life with the cosmic powers under your influence (4:10).[15]

It is probably with such a sophisticated and seductive line of reasoning that Paul must deal. Not only that, but, as Betz observes, the apostle is hindered by a double limitation. The first is that he must resort to a letter in place of an oral exchange, which he clearly would have preferred (4:20). Second, he is compelled to use the rhetorical devices of the apologetic genre, which among knowledgeable persons was always suspect.[16] Despite these handicaps, Paul makes a spirited defense. It must be emphasized, however, that his ''defense'' is not of himself, but a defense of the ''truth of the gospel'' (2:5, 14). In fact, though he has employed the apologetic genre, Paul's orientation is not at all apologetic; rather, it is polemical![17] Schütz doubts that there is a ''single, sustained apology in the whole of the letter,'' and he claims

---

[15]The above reconstruction is a modified version of that proposed by Beker (*Paul the Apostle*, 43-44). See also Koester (''Gnomai Diaphoroi,'' 145) who concurs in this, saying the opponents have ''mythologized'' the law. Bornkamm also sees the opponents as combining Jewish conceptions with ideas about cosmic powers and astral worship (*Paul*, 82-83). This seems to be what Betz refers to when he talks about Galatians being used as a ''magical letter'' (*Galatians*, 25).

[16]Betz, *Galatians*, 24.

[17]Schütz, *Anatomy*, 126-28.

that Paul consistently argues the truth of the gospel through polemic.[18] He goes on to say, "Paul is on the offensive in attacking *their* attachment to tradition (i.e., the gospel as the law) and arguing over against this the case of the one gospel which is illustrated through the apostolic person."[19] Thus, confronted with a theology which links into a single chain Abraham and Torah and circumcision and Christ, Paul "drives a radical wedge between Abraham and the Torah on the one hand and between Torah and Christ on the other hand, by arguing that the blessing (= promise) and faith belong together, just as do the curse and the works of the law (3:10-13)."[20] We might add that Paul simultaneously drives a wedge between apostolic authority and Jerusalem (1:15-2:10). As we shall see, for Paul apostolic authority originates in the gospel; the two are inseparable. Paul's essential theme note is the singularity of the gospel (1:7-9), and on the basis of this principle he argues vigorously for the priority of faith and freedom from the law.[21] Paul's accent on the authority of the gospel will deepen our understanding of both the origin and character of his conception of the preaching task.

GALATIANS 1:6-17

A. The Literary Context

Paul's letter to the Galatians consists of a prescript and preamble at the beginning, followed by three major sections, and ending with a conclusion in the apostle's own hand.[22] The prescript (1:1-5) differs from those of other pauline letters in that there is no prayer of thanksgiving or other words of commendation for the congregation he is addressing. Instead, there is an immediate reference to his apostleship as originating "through Jesus Christ and God the Father." The prescript is followed by the preamble (1:6-9), or *exordium*, in which Paul briefly outlines the crisis in Galatia: the readers are in danger of apostasy from the gospel. The apostle addresses the issue of the "other gospel" to which the readers have been attracted and pronounces a curse upon anyone who perverts the gospel of Christ.

---

[18]Ibid., 127. He refers especially to 1 Cor. 15 as a parallel. See also 2 Cor. 10:5-6.

[19]Ibid., 128.

[20]Beker, *Paul the Apostle*, 48.

[21]Schütz, *Anatomy*, 127-28. See also Beker (*Paul the Apostle*, 44-47) and Erich Grässer, "Das eine Evangelium. Hermeneutische Erwägungen zu Gal. 1:6-10," *ZThK* 66 (1969): 306-44.

[22]We are following the outline and description of contents provided by Marxsen (*Introduction*, 47-50) and Kümmel (*Introduction*, 294f.). For a different outline based on the rhetorical categories of the apologetic genre, see Betz, *Galatians*, 14-25.

The first major section (1:10-2:21) discusses the issue of the origin and authority of his apostolate, already brought to the attention of the readers in 1:1. Paul claims to have received his apostolic call directly, through a revelation of Christ (1:12), on the basis of which he claims his gospel is not "according to man." This theme of the autonomy of the gospel and of his own apostleship is documented in a lengthy autobiographical section (1:13-2:21) in which he puts distance between himself and Jerusalem (1:13-24), gives an account of the vindication of his gospel at the time of the apostolic council in Jerusalem (2:1-10), and describes how he defended the truth of the law-free gospel in a confrontation with Peter (2:11-21).

The second major section is the heart of the letter (3:1-5:12). Paul's theme is the freedom of the gospel. It is developed along three lines. First, Abraham becomes for Paul an exemplar of faith, while works of law are shown to result in a curse (3:6-18). Next the status of the law is reviewed. Its subordinate status is underscored by its temporal distance from Abraham and by its having been mediated; the law is powerless to effect salvation and has its place in salvation history only as a temporary guardian (3:19-4:7). Paul's final argument refers to the experience of the Galatians at the time of their conversion and their relation to the apostle, an experiece which is undergirded by Scriptural proof in the form of an allegorical exegesis of the account of Abraham's two sons (4:8-31). The section is concluded with a final appeal and curse on his opponents, the key-note being the emphasis on freedom in Christ (5:1-12).

The last major part deals with ethics. Paul describes the way in which the Christian lives out life in the freedom of the gospel guided by the power of the Spirit (5:13-6:10). By contrast, he argues that being "under the law" puts one in the sphere of the flesh, and he catalogs the vices that pour forth from that sphere (vv 19-21). Paul's argument is that freedom means service in love, which is the fulfillment of the law (vv 13-14).[23]

The letter comes to an abrupt end with Paul himself taking pen in hand to denounce and warn against his opponents, claiming that they only wish to "glory in the flesh," and countering this with his own apostolic posture of "glory in the cross" (6:11-18).

It is important to notice, for purposes of our study, that Paul's references to preaching occur in the opening portion of the letter. In the *exordium* (1:6-9) and the beginning of the first major section (1:10-17) Paul makes important references to the gospel and its implications. Thus he places his understanding of preaching within the framework of his apostolic authority.

---

[23]For a careful, persuasive analysis of the ethical section, particularly on the relationship between law and flesh, see Howard, *Crisis,* 11-14.

B. Exegesis

Since Paul's references to the gospel and preaching follow immediately after his expanded prescript (1:1-5), close attention should be paid to the theology implicit in it. For Paul has expanded his prescript, as Betz observes, at precisely those points which relate to the other parts of his letter (1:1,4).[24] The first expansion is in v. 1, where Paul claims to be an apostle, then immediately defines his apostolic status in both negative and positive terms. His apostolic calling is not "from men or through men;" instead, it is "through Jesus Christ and God the Father," to which he adds the important relative clause, "who raised him from the dead." This theme of apostleship, directly given to him by the resurrected Lord, will be elaborated in 1:12-16. The second expansion occurs in v. 4. There the apostle lays hold of an existing Christological formula, "who gave himself for our sins" (v. 4a), and interprets it soteriologically in v. 4b. Paul understands the sacrificial death of Jesus "for our sins" to mean that humankind has been liberated from enslavement to the present evil age, an interpretation that implies an eschatological structure. Thus Paul's theme of freedom in the gospel is unveiled, to be interpreted in depth in the central section of the epistle (3:23-5:1).[25] The twin emphases on freedom and apostolic authority dominate his letter from the outset and influence our analysis of 1:6-17.

> I am astonished that you are so quickly abandoning your call in grace in favor of another gospel, which is a non-gospel; except that there are some people who are confusing you and trying to subvert the gospel of Christ. But even if we or an angel from heaven should preach a gospel contrary to that which we preached to you, let him be cursed. As we have said before, I also say now again, if anyone preaches a gospel to you contrary to the one you received, let him be cursed. Am I now persuading men or God? Or am I trying to please men? If I were still trying to please men, I would not be a slave of Christ. (vv. 6-10)[26]

Paul comes to terms immediately with the problem in the Galatian congregation. He expresses his amazement (*thaumazō*) that they are "so quickly" *(houtōs tacheōs)* at the point of apostasy. Betz informs us that *thaumazō* and *houtōs tacheōs* are rhetorical devices, originating in the law courts and political arena. They function in an ironic and polemical fashion, a "device of indignant rebuttal."[27] We are therefore ill advised to attach too much importance to these words as revealing Paul's state of mind

---

[24]Betz, *Galatians*, 37.
[25]Our analysis of the prescript is based on Betz, *Galatians*, 37-43.
[26]Whether there is a rounding off of the opening statement after v. 9, v. 10, v. 11, or v. 12 is not easily determined. Actually the thought progression continues, though v. 10 does provide a transitional verse, as Betz notes (*Galatians*, 54f.). For the sake of our study we have divided the section after v. 10.
[27]Betz, *Galatians*, 46-47.

at the time of writing or as suggesting the historical time-frame of the letter. The most we can say is that by *thaumazō* the apostle is on the attack right from the start with a startling accusation.[28] And with the expression *houtōs tacheōs* Paul probably refers simply to the time between the Galatians' acceptance of the gospel and the time of Paul's writing.[29]

With this surprising beginning Paul launches into the statement of the case at issue. Verse 6 is structured in antithetical parallelism, presenting a sharp contrast between that away from which the Galatians are turning and that to which they are now attracted. The Galatians are about to abandon "the one who has called you in grace" (*tou kalesantos humas en chariti*) and turn to a *heteron euaggelion* ("another gospel"). Paul chooses as his term for their apostasy *metatithesthe* ("you are deserting"), a Greek political expression which carries with it a partisan point of view, the connotation that their stability and loyalty have become questionable.[30] The fact that Paul uses the present tense suggests strongly that the apostasy of the Galatians is not a foregone conclusion. It is a crisis in which the "maneuvers are still in progress," and the apostle clearly intends to reverse the process.[31]

Of great significance for our understanding of Paul's argument in Galatians, and for our analysis of his theology of gospel and preaching, is the antithesis in v. 6. The first part of the sentence describes what the Galatians are about to fall away from. It is not a matter of deserting something but someone. They are about to desert *tou kalesantos humas en chariti* ("the one who called you in grace").[32] In view of Paul's general use of the verb *kaleō*, the subject can only be God.[33] This is a serious indictment, especially in view of the fact that later Paul will describe their condition prior to their conversion

---

[28]Jürgen Becker, "Die Brief an die Galater," in *Die Briefe an die Galater, Epheser, Philipper, Kolosser, Thessalonicher, und Philemon*, by Jürgen Becker, Hans Conzelmann and Gerhard Friedrich (Göttingen: Vandenhoeck & Rupprecht, 1976), 10. Becker regards vv. 6-8 as reflecting the style of the Old Testament prophetic oracle; thus v. 6f. is the accusation and v. 8f. the threat of judgment. But compare the view that Paul's astonishment is genuine in Heinrich Schlier, *Die Brief an die Galater* (Göttingen: Vandenhoeck & Rupprecht, 1951), 11.

[29]Ernest Burton, *A Critical and Exegetical Commentary on the Epistle to the Galatians* (New York: Scribner's, 1920), 19; he thinks the expression refers to the "brevity of the interval." However, cf. Betz, *Galatians*, 47. Also cf. Grässer, who thinks it refers to a "rapid process" of apostasy ("Das eine Evangelium," 314f.).

[30]Betz, *Galatians*, 47. See BAG, 515.

[31]Betz, *Galatians*, 47. See also Burton, *Commentary*, 19ff.

[32]The word *Christou* follows *en chariti* in many of the best manuscripts. However, it is omitted by other good witnesses, especially the early P46. It is easier to understand it as a scribal insertion, added to supplement the text, than to suppose that such an important word would have been omitted. Thus we leave it out. See Bruce Metzger, *A Textual Commentary on the Greek New Testament* (New York: United Bible Societies, 1971), 589f. See also Betz, *Galatians*, 48 note 55.

[33]Schlier, *Galater*, 12; Burton, *Commentary*, 19ff.

as a form of slavery in which they "did not know God" (4:8-9). Paul implies that they are throwing away their entire relationship to the true, living God (cf. 1 Thess. 1:9-10).

The call from God is then clarified by *en chariti* ("in grace"). With the mention of *charis* one of Paul's central terms is brought into focus, an expression which Conzelmann characterizes as referring to the "structure of the salvation event."[34] The fact that *charis* is here preceded by *en* should not mislead us into thinking that the term is to be understood instrumentally. Rather, in view of Paul's customary use of language the *en* should be attached not to *charis* but to *kalein*. By means of the expression *kalein en* Paul refers to the state or sphere in which one exists, thus making it almost synonymous with "in Christ" or the "body of Christ."[35] This interpretation fits the context, for the issue is not the instrument of God's call but the condition in which they exist.[36] The analysis which Schütz works out is helpful in clarifying what is at stake for Paul and the Galatians. Schütz reminds us that the soteriological statement of 1:4 is essential for understanding vv 6-9. According to Paul's soteriology we are "bound to this age through sin or freed from it through Christ's death," a distinction between the two possibilities for life which Schütz finds confirmed in Romans 5:20ff., where sin and grace are characterized as powers which reign.[37] Thus there are two spheres, or power structures, for human existence, which means that the apostasy of the Galatians is a "departure from power, from that which marks the proper realm of Christian existence."[38] Is it any wonder that Paul deals with the crisis in Galatia with such vehemence? The heart of the matter is life or death.

Over against his description of what is about to be forfeited by the Galatians Paul now places his description of the lethal instrument of their demise. He calls it a *heteron euaggelion* ("another gospel"), immediately following up this expression, in v. 7b, with a disclaimer, *ho ouk estin allo* ("which there is not another"). This is in turn succeeded by an exceptive clause, which restates the matter in a different form, this time as an accusation against the opponents.[39] With the words *tines eisin* ("there are some") Paul makes reference to the opponents for the first time. Against them he

---

[34]H. Conzelmann, " *TDNT*, 9 (Grand Rapids: Eerdmanns, 1974), 394.

[35]Betz, *Galatians*, 48. See also Burton (*Commentary*, 21), who observes that the absence of an article gives *charis* a qualitative force; Schütz, *Anatomy*, 117; and Schlier, *Galater*, 12. Becker refers to the Jewish antecedents for the idea of grace, describing how Paul makes an either-or, separating grace and law, crucial to the rest of his argument ("Galater," 10-11).

[36]Burton, *Commentary*, 21.

[37]Schütz, *Anatomy*, 116. He finds this parallelism of distinctions confirmed in Rom. 5:20ff., where sin and grace are powers which reign.

[38]Ibid., 117.

[39]Burton, *Commentary*, 22; he translates, "which is not another except in the sense that." See also Betz, *Galatians*, 49, and BAG, 219.

makes two charges. They are "disturbing" (*tarassontes*) the Galatians and they wish *metastrepsai to euaggelion tou Christou* ("to subvert the gospel of Christ"). Betz calls attention to the fact that *tarassein* and *metastrephein* are political terms suggesting destructive agitation of a sort that induces people to revolution.[40] With such connotations Paul characterizes the work of his opponents as having a negative effect both on the Galatians and on the gospel. In fact, *metastrephein* has the sense of " 'transforming something into its opposite.' "[41] The gospel is being stood on its head. More importantly, since for Paul the "gospel of Christ" (*euaggelion tou christou*) refers not merely to the content of preaching, but also to the means through which Christ himself comes to expression (2 Cor. 5:20; 1 Thess. 4:2), for the opponents to overturn the gospel in Galatia "is to attack Christ who is revealed in it."[42]

It remains for us now to clarify what Paul means by referring to "another gospel" which "does not exist."[43] It seems most probable that the adjective "another" (*heteros*) is not a description attributable to the opponents, but rather is Paul's own term, his way of characterizing their failure to remain in the sphere of grace.[44] But otherwise, in view of v. 7b, it is really a non-gospel.[45] We are not by any means to suppose that there can be more than one gospel. As Grässer says, "The coming of Jesus as the fulfillment of promise excludes any other as the way of salvation."[46] Grässer goes on to explain that the nature of the opponents' message, conceived as a non-gospel, is accounted for by the eschatological context of Paul's thinking. With the coming of Christ there has occurred an "eschatological caesura" (1:4; 3:23), an event in which the righteousness of God has been revealed in Christ so that an era of faith has displaced law (3:23). This means that any "other gospel," which returns to the law, would by nature fall back behind this "eschatological caesura," thereby making it a non-gospel.[47] "Another" gospel is therefore a contradiction in terms, as indicated by its contradictory content, the "yoke of slavery" (*zugos douleias*) (5:1) which the Galatians invite upon themselves when they abandon the freedom of Christ in order to be "under law" (*hupo nomon*) (4:21).[48]

---

[40]Betz, *Galatians*, 49-50.

[41]Schütz, *Anatomy*, 120; Schlier, *Galater*, 13.

[42]Schlier, *Galater*, 14.

[43]The distinction between *heteros* and *allo* is insignificant. See Schütz, *Anatomy*, 118; Grässer, "Das eine Evangelium," 315. But cf. Burton, *Commentary*, 421-22.

[44]Schütz, *Anatomy*, 117.

[45]Grässer, "Das eine Evangelium," 315. The expression is otherwise variously characterized as an "absurdity" [Unding] by Becker ("Galater," 10) or "imaginary gospel" by Schlier (*Galater*, 12).

[46]Grässer, "Das eine Evangelium," 317.

[47]Ibid., 316.

[48]Ibid., 317.

Of equal importance is the other term in the expression, *euaggelion* ("gospel"). As Schütz observes, the introduction of the word in 1:6b is striking, since Paul has not mentioned preaching up to this point and doesn't really discuss it until v. 8. Nor does he describe their apostasy as being from the gospel, which we might expect to make the distinction clearer. Instead the contrast is between "the one who called you in grace" and "another gospel." Schütz asks, "What then is the connection between the desertion from God's grace and the allegiance to 'another gospel'?" He answers, "It must be that God's call through grace and to grace is identical with 'the gospel,' so that apostasy from it is thought of as turning to another proclamation."[49]

Having thus characterized the crisis in Galatia in the mutually exclusive terms of the grace of God versus another gospel, Paul now reacts to it. His reaction is in the form of a curse (vv. 8-9), a curse under which he places even himself and "an angel from heaven," thereby indicating with what utter seriousness he regards the crisis.[50] The hypothetical form of the curse in v. 8 is clear from the use of *ean* with the subjunctive mood; it sets down the conditions under which the curse would become effective and also indicates, when taken together with the *alla kai* ("but even"), the "unmistakable degree of improbability" that Paul or a heavenly emissary would depart from the gospel.[51] It is vital to note that it is the gospel that is at the heart of the curse formula. That is emphasized by the double appearance of the verb *euaggelizesthai* ("to gospelize") in v. 8 and the expression *par ho* ("contrary to which").[52] Any "gospel" which is not the authentic one, which subverts the gospel of Christ (v. 7b), is contrary to the gospel that Paul first preached in Galatia and invites condemnation upon the messenger.

For the curse formula Paul employs the expression *anathema estō* ("let him be cursed"). The *anathema* refers in Greek thought to something which is dedicated to a deity, taken out of circulation either as an offering to the god or for divine destruction. The latter is Paul's use of the term here.[53] But the full significance of the term for Paul can be seen, as Stuhlmacher points out, from his usage in 1 Cor. 5:1ff. and also from the Qumran literature. In both cases *anathema* refers to a "fully executed, obligatory decision of dismissal

---

[49]Schütz, *Anatomy*, 117.

[50]Burton, *Commentary*, 25. Paul's reference to an angel here may be due to a claim made by the opponents that they derive their message from angelic revelation. See Betz, *Galatians*, 53.

[51]Schütz, *Anatomy*, 121. The concessive nature of the sentence, he says, makes it probable that *humin* should be omitted in v. 8.

[52]The word *para* can mean either "besides" or "contrary to," but standard usage in both the classical writers and the New Testament suggests the latter (Burton, *Commentary*, 27). See Rom. 1:26. See also Schütz, *Anatomy*, 121.

[53]J. Behm, *TDNT*, 1 (Grand Rapids: Eerdmanns, 1964), 354-55. See also Schlier, *Galater*, 14.

in the name of God toward heretical elements.''[54] Paul's *anathema* thus bears witness to his authority as an apostle in that he not only proclaims the judgment of God, but he inflicts it.[55]

Although v. 8 has in mind a hypothetical case of subverting the one gospel, the following verse shows that Paul is thinking of an actual case. This is clear from the change in the construction of the conditional clause in v. 9. Paul changes to *ei* (''if'') with the indicative mood (a present general condition), signalling that he is applying the curse formula to the present, to a concrete situation.[56]

At first sight it appears that in vv. 8-9 Paul issues a double curse, especially since the language in both verses is closely parallel. However, two factors militate against such an interpretation. One is the fact that in v. 9 the verb *proeirēkamen* (''we have said before'') is in the perfect tense, thereby denoting a completed action in the past. The other factor is that with the expression *arti palin legō* (''now again I say'') Paul changes to the present tense, thus implying a temporal distance. Both factors taken together suggest that v. 9 is the reissue of a curse formula from an earlier occasion.[57] Therefore we are dealing not with a case of repetition, for the sake of emphasis, but rather an exercise of apostolic authority, which amounts to a ban or excommunication.[58]

Two other important aspects of v. 9 are more conspicuous. The first is the appearance of *humas* (''you'' [plural]) in the accusative case (an accusative of the person) as the direct object of the verb *euaggelizetai* (''is preaching''). Thus the verb really means ''to evangelize.'' Or, we might translate ''to gospelize you.'' And though the content of the message is not specified, the distinction between *euaggelizetai* and *par ho parelabete* (''contrary to that which you received'') clearly shows that what Paul refers to is *the* gospel.[59] This word usage once more underscores the event character of the preaching of the gospel of Christ.

The second striking aspect in the verse is the verb *parelabete* (''you received''). It is surprising, as Schütz notes, because we would have expected *par ho eueggelisametha* (''contrary to that which *we preached*''), which would correspond in parallelism to the first verb. Instead, Paul

---

[54]Stuhlmacher, *Das paulinische Evangelium*, 64.

[55]Schlier, *Galater*, 54.

[56]Schütz, *Anatomy*, 122; Betz, *Galatians*, 54; Schlier, *Galater*, 14; Becker, ''Galater,'' 11.

[57]Betz, *Galatians*, 54. See also Burton, *Commentary*, 29. Schlier believes the previous issuing of the curse formula would have been on Paul's second visit recorded in Acts 18:23 (*Galater*, 14).

[58]Betz, *Galatians*, 54.

[59]Schlier, *Galater*, 15.

changes to *paralambanein,* the technical term for receiving a tradition.[60] Schütz believes this is due to the polemical nature of the apostle's intent and calls our attention to 1 Cor. 15:1ff., where *euaggelizesthai* and *paralambanein* also appear in close conjunction. There, Schütz claims, Paul has joined the terms in order to counteract an "undue (and unusual) attention to the tradition process, where he thinks the very reliance on tradition threatens the gospel as a field of power in which the Corinthians stand."[61] Since Paul in Galatians also makes "an eschatological equation with the gospel," Schütz argues that the two passages are parallel, which reveals Paul's polemical intention in Gal. 1:1-9. If our earlier reconstruction of the opponents' position is accurate, then this explanation fits the context. For if the opponents nurture a strong sense of linkage between Christian tradition and Jerusalem, which they understand as legitimizing it, and if Paul intends to separate the two, then the appearance of *paralambanein* in v. 9 functions to connect tradition *directly to the gospel.* That corresponds exactly to Paul's own personal experience related in 1:12, where the same term recurs. This means that tradition is understood by Paul as being normed by the gospel, so that not only his preaching, but their receiving, is subordinated to it.[62]

With the application of the curse formula the *exordium* is brought to a close, rather abruptly as Betz observes. What is needed is a transition, particularly if Paul is following the form of Greek apologetic genre, and this is provided by the next verse.[63] Verse 10 is a curious mixture of elements, however, presenting a number of problems to the interpreter. The first is the force of the *gar* and its connection with the preceding verse. Normally the word is translated "for" and carries a causal or explanatory sense, a justification for what has just been said. On the other hand, it would suit the context better if it indicated an inference to be drawn. Since Paul's usage, like that of the New Testament generally, is usually the former, the *gar* is probably best regarded as explanatory.[64] The strong application of the curse formula is grounded in the fact that Paul is the "slave of Christ." If v. 10 is to be translated so as to bring this out, we should translate *arti gar* as either "now therefore" or "now then."

A second problem, both for interpretation and translation, is the verb *peithō* ("persuade"). If its object were only *anthrōpous* ("men"), there would be little difficulty. But the fact that the verb has a second object, *ton theon*

---

[60]Schütz, *Anatomy,* 122.

[61]Ibid., 123.

[62]Ibid. Schütz also observes that not a word is said about the Galatian congregation being subordinated to *Paul.*

[63]Betz, *Galatians,* 54. He thinks that v. 10 and v. 11 are both transitional.

[64]Burton, *Commentary,* 31.

("God"), makes one think the word must carry here a different meaning from "persuade." What could Paul mean by picturing himself "persuading" God? Yet that is really the only possible meaning for the word, and it is very likely that in using it Paul is answering a reproach against him, as Schlier believes.[65] Furthermore, the expression "to persuade God" has a background in Greek rhetoric, where it refers to "magic and religious quackery."[66] In view of this, Paul in v. 10, having identified the crisis and dealt with it in vv. 6-9, now brings the character of what he has just said into clear focus for the Galatians. His questions are ironic.[67] They are meant to suggest graphically the ridiculous nature of the charge against him. Anyone who delivers solemn curses is hardly cajoling or persuading God. As Becker so succinctly states, "There is no bridge between coaxing and curse."[68]

Nor can one who delivers curses be attempting to "please" (*areskein*) people, as the next rhetorical question implies (v. 10b). This question, like the first, has frequently been understood as suggesting that Paul is taking up a charge made by his opponents, namely, that in trying to win converts among the gentiles Paul has reduced the cost with his concession that the law may be dispensed with.[69] However, as Betz reminds us, since Paul's terminology (*areskein* as well as *peithein*) comes from Greek rhetoric, it is not necessary to conclude that any charge has been made against him.[70] Paul may have regarded the suggestion that he is a man-pleaser as implied, particularly if, in view of 2:5, Paul is supposed to have been offering a scaled-down version of the gospel.[71] The force of both rhetorical questions, taken together, is well summarized by Stuhlmacher:

> Paul's curse in the name of God and from the eschatologically new point of view of the gospel, explains the ironical questions of 1:10. He would be denying the essence of his office were he to risk the message commissioned to him according to human standards or, rather, to alter it according to the measure of the old aeon.[72]

Paul's apostolic anathema not only deals boldly with the opponents, but also demonstrates the integrity of his apostolic office both on the side of God and of humanity.

---

[65]Schlier, *Galater*, 15.

[66]Betz, *Galatians*, 54-55.

[67]Ibid., 55. Schlier prefers "sarcastic" (*Galater*, 15).

[68]Becker, "Galater," 15.

[69]Ibid.

[70]Betz, *Galatians*, 56. Betz cautions, "Not every rhetorical denial is an accusation turned around" (Ibid., note 115). See also Paul's similar rhetorical denials in 1 Thess. 2:4-5. However, in view of the context, it is hard to believe that Paul's choice of words here is attributable strictly to rhetorical considerations.

[71]However, cf. Schütz (*Anatomy*, 129), who believes Paul is "referring more generally to subordinating the gospel to human standards," a viewpoint which he finds confirmed in vv. 11-12 where the claim is made that Paul's gospel is not from human origins.

[72]Stuhlmacher, *Das paulinische Evangelium*, 72.

The apostle's use of the verb "please" in v. 10b leads naturally into the slavery image which dominates the earnest pronouncement of v. 10c, since *areskein* ("please") was closely associated with *douleuein* ("serve") in Greek thought.[73] The claim made by the apostle underscores the negative answer to both questions and points to their meaning. If Paul were "still" (*eti*) trying to please men, he could not be "Christ's slave."[74] To be Christ's "slave" (*doulos*) is the opposite of being a man-pleaser. The word *doulos* is for Paul a synonym for an apostle, and it means that his apostolic office is to represent Christ and that his accountability is to Christ alone.[75] In view of Paul's larger argument in the letter, that to be under law is to be under the sphere of the flesh (the old aeon) and thus a slave to sin (5:13-6:5), his use of the slave motif at this point is not only appropriate but entirely understandable. Paul locates himself within the domain of Christ, as Christ's slave, and the rest of his argument will spell out the consequences of being the slave to anyone or anything else (5:1, 21). The best description of the way Paul understands his slavery to Christ is the words of 2:19-21: the apostle has "died to the law," and now his life in the flesh is lived "by faith in the Son of God."

I make known to you, brothers, that the gospel preached by me is not according to man; for I too neither received it from man, nor was I taught it, but [I received it] through an apocalypse of Jesus Christ (vv. 11-12).

If Betz's rhetorical analysis of Galatians is correct, then v. 11 is introductory to the *narratio*, or statement of facts, which follows in v. 13ff. The verse "announces the argument Paul is going to prove."[76] The first word, *gnōrizō* ("I make known"), is not intended to introduce new information, nor is it ironic, but it really forms a "solemn assertion."[77] In the opening section, 1:6-10, Paul has denounced and cursed the proclamation of "another gospel," and now in v. 11 the apostle states and prepares to elaborate his exalted view of the gospel, a view which has led him to reply with such vehem-

---

[73]Schlier, *Galater*, 16 note 1.

[74]Betz thinks *eti* is probably a reference to Paul's pre-Christian existence (*Galatians*, 56). See also Burton, *Commentary*, 33f., and Schlier, *Galater*, 16. Burton points out that the use of the imperfect tense (*areskon*) carries a conative connotation, "the endeavor to please men" (*Commentary*, 32).

[75]K. Rengstorff, *TDNT*, 2 (Grand Rapids: Eerdmanns, 1964), 261-79.

[76]Betz, *Galatians*, 52.

[77]Burton, *Commentary*, 35. See also Karl Kertelge, "Apokalypsis Jesou Christou (Gal. 1:12)," in *Neues Testament und Kirche*, edited by Joachim Gnilka (Freiburg/Basel: Herder, 1974), 281; Betz, *Galatians*, 56; and Schlier, *Galater*, 17. Stuhlmacher explains it as an expression for "making known an eschatological fact," as in Dan. 2:23 (*Das paulinische Evangelium*, 69).

---

ence to the activities of his opponents.[78] In stating his case Paul addresses his *adelphoi* ("brothers") in Galatia, for they are the ones who must make the final decision as regards the gospel.[79]

It is essential to notice that it is the gospel which occupies center stage in v. 11.[80] This means that his autobiographical references in the rest of the chapter are not intended to focus on himself, even though they document his claim to be an authentic apostle (1:1), but are subordinated to the *euaggelion* ("gospel"). Paul reacts to the Galatian crisis because the gospel is being devalued. His defense is simple: his gospel is not *kata anthrōpon* ("according to man").[81]

The expression *kata anthrōpon* is used by Paul in several places to refer to "something inferior compared with the divine."[82] It therefore has to do with the quality of his preaching; it is a way of saying, negatively, that his is a "divine gospel," a more precise understanding of which the apostle provides in v. 12.[83]

In v. 12 Paul does two things. He substantiates his claim that the gospel he preaches is divine, and he puts forth the premise he will defend in what follows. His gospel is "more than human because of its origin."[84] The assertion is made both negatively and positively. In correlation to *kata anthrōpon* in v.11, he emphasizes that he did not receive the gospel *para anthrōpou* ("from man"), nor was he "taught (it)" (*adidachthēn*).[85] Then, positively, Paul concludes with the climactic point that he received it *di' apokalupseōs Iēsou Christou* ("through a revelation of Jesus Christ").

The verse begins with *oude gar egō*, which presents difficulties in interpretation and translation. Usually *oude gar* ("for neither") introduces an ad-

---

[78]There is a question whether *gar* in v. 11 should be connected with vv. 6-9, as Burton thinks (*Commentary*, 35-36), or with v. 10, as Schütz believes (*Anatomy*, 129). If the latter is the case, it would explain why Paul describes himself as a "slave of Christ," and that interpretation fits better with Betz's rhetorical analysis, in which vv. 10-11 are transitional and thus belong together. But leaving aside the technical argument, Paul appears in vv. 11ff. to be making a statement which climaxes the thought of the entire first section, 1:1-10.

[79]If in the rhetorical style of the apologetic genre the aim of the *narratio* is to influence the judge, then Paul's use of *adelphoi* is surely intentional here. The Galatians are "brothers." Thus Paul not only calls on them to decide, but he lays claim to their allegiance at the outset. See Betz (*Galatians*, 58-62) for a complete description of the rhetorical features.

[80]*euaggelion* is the direct object of *gnorizo*. Note also, with Burton, that *euaggelisthen* ("which was gospeled") is in the aorist tense, meaning the gospel Paul preached initially in Galatia. But in the *hoti* ("that") clause which follows the present tense *estin* ("is") appears, indicating that it is the same gospel (*Commentary*, 37). Cf. 2:12.

[81]Betz, *Galatians*, 52.

[82]Ibid., 56 note 125. See Gal. 3:15; Rom. 3:5; 1 Cor. 2:3, 9:18, 15:32. Cf. 1 Pet. 4:6.

[83]Schlier, *Galater*, 17.

[84]Betz, *Galatians*, 62. See also Schlier, who reminds us that Paul is not referring here to the gospel's content, since the gospel is for him a historical event (*Galater*, 17).

[85]*para anthropou* can be translated "from *a* man," but in the context Paul is not speaking about his relation to specific individuals. The contrast is between the human and the divine.

ditional fact which provides evidence for the previous statement. In that case the evidence introduced in v. 12 would support Paul's statement that his gospel is not *kata anthropōn* ("according to man"). On the other hand, *oude* ("neither") can throw its force on another term, in this case *egō* ("I"), which is by its very appearance emphatic in this verse. The interpretation then would be, " 'Neither did I any more than they receive it . . . , ' " implying that Paul has a comparison in mind, a claim he can make which puts him on an equal footing with others.[86] This second option would appear to be the more preferable, since, as Schlier insists, one cannot really ignore the emphatic *egō* ("I"). In addition, there is the fact that the expression *oude gar* is subordinated to *parelabon* ("I received").[87] But in choosing either of the options we do not want to overlook the fact that these opening words serve to amplify Paul's claim that his gospel is not human. Therefore *oude gar egō* refers just as much to the positive assertion in the second half of the verse as to the negative one in the first half. He is making the claim that he *also* has received his gospel through a "revelation of Jesus Christ."[88]

The appearance of *parelabon* ("I received") in v. 12 is significant. The term *paralambanein* ("to receive") and its correlative *paradidonai* ("to deliver") are, as we have noted, technical terms for the handing on of a tradition.[89] This means that Paul's claim to a divine origin for his gospel is "set over against the traditioning process," and since *parelabon* is the single controlling verb of v. 12, the contrast is between "received from men" and "received through a revelation of Jesus Christ."[90] This does not mean, though, that Paul dissociates himself from the Christian tradition or disparages its authority. In fact, he emphasizes in 1 Cor. 15:1ff. that he is a bearer of tradition and that his gospel corresponds to it. How then are we to understand him here? Beker points to the fact that there is both a vertical and horizontal aspect to Paul's understanding of tradition. He explains:

> Paul never admits that "receiving tradition" marks him as a "dependent" apostle, because the vertical dimension of "receiving" is uppermost in his mind. Therefore, he equates the "receiving" of the tradition with the immediate "revelation" of Gal. 1:12, when he significantly adds the clause "from the Lord" to the traditional terminology (1 Cor. 11:23; cf. also 1 Thess. 4:15). In other words, the risen Lord himself stands behind the tradition as Paul's direct source of the gospel.[91]

---

[86]Burton, *Commentary*, 38-39. He believes the comparison is between Paul and the Twelve.

[87]Schlier, *Galater*, 18.

[88]Kertelge, "Apokalypsis," 281. Kertelege is of the opinion, based on his analysis of *apokalupseōs Iesou Christou*, that the emphasis of *oude gar egō* is placed even more strongly on the positive conclusion of v. 12. See also Stuhlmacher, *Das paulinische Evangelium*, 70f.

[89]Schlier, *Galater*, 18-19. See above pages 71f. and also note 60.

[90]Schütz, *Anatomy*, 129-30.

[91]Beker, *Paul the Apostle*, 123. This is further supported by Holmberg's sociological description of Paul's relationship to Jerusalem. Holmberg shows that Paul very carefully posi-

As a result, Paul's understanding of Christian tradition does not conflict with his claim to a revelation of Christ.

That we are correct in interpreting v. 12 as dealing with Christian tradition is shown by the second term Paul introduces, *oute edidachthēn* ("neither was I taught [it]"). As Schlier informs us, there is a definite established sense to Paul's usage, a reference to an intra-ecclesial function whereby the apostle teaches the members of the church. This puts *didaskein* ("to teach") on the same plane with *paralambanein* ("to receive"); it refers to "the tradition of the Lord which, in its widest sense, is in a learnable form."[92] Thus, just as he has not received the gospel from any human being, neither has he been taught it, meaning that it was not presented to him by other apostles, in whose debt he must now carry on his missionary enterprise. There is a further connotation in that Paul "stands with older traditions according to which truth in the authentic sense cannot be obtained through teaching but only through direct revelation."[93]

With the expression *di' apokalupseōs Iēsou Christou* ("through a revelation of Jesus Christ") we reach the climax of vv. 11-12, the punch line for Paul's previous claims. The phrase is not without difficulties, however. First, we need to know whether *Iēsou Christou* ("of Jesus Christ") is an objective or subjective genitive, that is, whether it is Jesus Christ who has been revealed or whether he is the revealer. The context must help us decide. The expression "through a revelation of Jesus Christ" picks up on the vital theme-note of 1:1b and is further treated in 1:16a. There is, therefore, a natural thematic connection between 1:12 and 1:16. And since in 1:16a it is clearly God who does the revealing, *apokalupseōs Iēsou Christou* cannot very easily refer in 1:12 to a self-revelation of Jesus Christ. Instead, it is Jesus Christ who is revealed, a revelation to be understood as "an appearance of Christ 'in Paul' (1:16a; cf. 2:20a)."[94]

The second problem is how Paul intends the word *apokalupsis* ("revelation") to be understood. The form that this experience took, whether visual

---

tions himself so that he is subordinated to Jerusalem, yet autonomous (*Paul and Power*, 50-57). Cf. also Stuhlmacher, who says, "Paul understands his gospel as revelation itself, that is, he understands it as tradition-affirming, but not as bound to the pre-pauline normative tradition" (*Das paulinische Evangelium*, 70f.).

[92]Schlier, *Galater*, 19.

[93]Betz, *Galatians*, 62-63. This contrasts with the way the majority of Christians received it. See Burton, *Commentary*, 40.

[94]Betz, *Galatians*, 63. He says this revelation is thus "identical with the revelation of the gospel to Paul" (Ibid.). See also Stuhlmacher, *Das paulinische Evangelium*, 71. Cf. Burton, who describes it as a "divinely given revelation of Jesus Christ which carried with it the conviction that he was the Son of God" (*Commentary*, 43). On the other hand, Oepke defends the idea that it is a subjective genitive, referring to the self-revelation of Christ; see A. Oepke, *TDNT*, 3, (Grand Rapids: Eerdmanns, 1965), 583-84.

or verbal, or both, does not contribute much to grasping its meaning.[95] The main point is the contrast between his own experience and that of receiving the gospel by way of human intermediaries.[96]

Oepke provides us with a starting point for understanding *apokalupsis*. The term, he says, has its origin in Old Testament theology. There God is the Lord of history who reveals himself as he wills in history, in creation, and in his holy, gracious activity. Especially important, however, is the future aspect of revelation, the prophetic revealing of that which is to be. Thus the emphasis falls on God revealing himself, and the locus of that revelation is eschatological. The New Testament inherits this Old Testament model (especially Deutero-Isaiah and Jeremiah), where its future aspect is embedded in apocalyptic language.[97]

This general description, however, requires more precision if it is to be helpful in our interpretation. It must be made specific, concrete. The question becomes, How does *Paul* conceive of the "apocalypse" which he claims to have experienced? An examination of key passages shows that for Paul *apokalupsis* is the "object of eschatological expectation," an expectation which has both a negative (the "coming wrath" in Rom. 1:18) and a positive significance (the revelation of the "righteousness of God" in Rom. 3:21, or of the "glory" of the day of salvation in Rom. 8:18 ff).[98] Bultmann is correct, therefore, when he argues that for Paul "revelation" is an event. This is clear also from Gal. 3:23, where *pistis* ("faith") is spoken of as something which "comes" (*elthein*). Therefore, when Paul speaks of an *apokalupsis,* he is not dealing with some "unknown teaching that is being expounded," but a phenomenon that has "become a possibility, . . . a reality," has "become operative."[99]

But neither Oepke's general description of *apokalupsis* nor the more specific description of its dynamic conceptualization in Paul really provides a complete explanation for his use of the term in Gal. 1:12, 16. Kertelge acknowledges this and so offers further illumination by adding, "Paul gives us to understand in Gal. 1:12, 16 that the revelation which came to him is not one among others, but a decisive one, in which Jesus Christ has come to him as the ground and content of his gospel."[100] Kertelge continues by explaining

---

[95]Probably we are to understand both the visual and verbal aspects as occurring simultaneously. See Betz, *Galatians,* 64, and Bornkamm, *Paul,* 21. Stuhlmacher has argued that the various terms used to describe revelatory experiences should not be regarded as mutually exclusive; in fact, they are, according to the pattern of Old Testament apocalyptic since Daniel, interchangeable terms for the same phenomenon (*Das paulinische Evangelium,* 76f.).

[96]Betz, *Galatians,* 65.

[97]A. Oepke, *TDNT,* 3:571-91.

[98]Kertelge, "Apokalypsis," 272. See also Bultmann, *Theology,* 1:275.

[99]Bultmann, *Theology,* 1:275.

[100]Kertelge, "Apokalypsis," 275.

that in view of Rom. 1:17 and 3:21, where the essence of the revelation is the righteousness of God, what Paul refers to here is not a special revelation, but rather "to his call as an extension of the *one* anticipated eschatological self-communication of God in Christ."[101] In other words, Paul is dealing with a proleptical experience of salvation. But how does Paul conceive of this in terms of his own vocation? Kertelge answers:

> The apocalypse of Jesus Christ is the decisive, gripping self-communication of God in Paul's life through which it comes "perceptible" . . . to Paul, as the receiver of revelation that God has raised up salvation through no other than Jesus Christ, who is his Son and who as the ground of salvation has become the content of the gospel which the apostle preaches to the gentiles.[102]

It can be seen from this analysis that Paul understands both his gospel and his vocation as traceable to this apocalyptic experience.[103]

Kertelge finds this interpretation to be confirmed by reference to Matt. 11:25-27, a logion from the Q source, which, in conjunction also with the revelation to Peter in Matt. 16:17, serves to document that for the early church the foundation of the missionary activity and authority of an apostle was an "apocalypse through which God disclosed to them the true significance of Jesus."[104] This concept of the "apostolic apocalypse" also fits into the situational context of Galatians, which Kertelge finds to have close parallels with the situation in 2 Corinthians, where the problem is also Jewish-Christian intruders. In both cases Paul is faulted for displaying a lack of apostolic credentials, for his opponents find missing in him the pneumatic-ecstatic phenomena which, for them, play an important role as criteria of apostleship.[105] The opponents find his gospel to be wanting, to be of only human origin, because they think that, despite his having had a revelatory experience, he has not had the experience of the "apostolic apocalypse." It is hardly surprising, then, that Paul solemnly declares (*gnōrizō*) that he "also" (*gar egō*) has received the "revelation of Jesus Christ" as the foundation and origin of his gospel. His "reference to the origin of his gospel in the 'apocalypse of Jesus Christ' denies his critics their hold on his preaching and thus supports its authentic, eschatological quality."[106] Even more, the fact that his reception of the gospel is from God, direct and unmediated, makes it possible for Paul to put distance between himself and the Jerusalem tradition. This puts Paul in an enviable position. For it means, polemically, that he can disparage

---

[101]Ibid. See also Bornkamm, *Paul*, 22.

[102]Kertelge, "Apokalypsis," 275.

[103]Ibid. See also Stuhlmacher, who defines *apokalupsis* as a "proleptic disclosure of the end-time realities" (*Das paulinische Evangelium*, 71).

[104]Kertelge, "Apokalypsis," 279.

[105]Ibid., 280. Kertelge is following Georgi's reconstruction of the historical situation.

[106]Ibid., 281.

the authority of his opponents, since their Torah tradition and Jerusalem connections mean that they have only a *mediated,* and therefore *inferior,* version
of the gospel (cf. Gal. 3:19b-20!).

> For you heard about my previous conduct in Judaism, that excessively I was perse-
> cuting the church of God and was trying to destroy it. And I was making progress in
> Judaism beyond many contemporaries among my own people, since I was extraordi-
> narily zealous for the traditions of my fathers (vv. 13-14).

Verses 13-14 are intended to support the profound claims Paul has made,
in vv. 11-12, for the gospel he preaches. This is shown by the presence of the
gar ("for") in the opening words of v. 13. The verses are background for
recounting the radical change which took place in Paul and thereby rule out
any possibility of previous preparation or development; rather, "all developments point in the opposite direction."[107] Paul had been deepening his
commitment within Judaism.[108] His conduct, he points out, was extraordinary because of his "excessive" (*kath' huperbolēn*) efforts in trying to stamp
out the Christian church and his "excessive" (*perissoterōs*) zeal in maintaining the Jewish traditions.[109] The presence of the two adverbial expressions
(*kath' huperbolēn* and *perissoterōs*) indicate where his emphasis lies.

Verses 13-14 begin the *narratio* portion of Paul's argument. It is a "biography of reversal," his previous life being the very antithesis of what he
now proclaims on the basis of the "revelation of Jesus Christ."[110] Or, as Beker
states, "Paul's pre-Christian career demonstrates that his Christian apostolate was impossible in terms of his own volition."[111]

> And when it pleased him who set me apart from my mother's womb and called me
> through his grace to reveal his Son in me, so that I might proclaim him to the gentiles,
> I did not immediately confer with flesh and blood, nor did I go up to Jerusalem to those
> who were apostles before me, but I went away into Arabia, and again I returned to
> Damascus. (vv. 15-17).

Verse 15 continues the argument from the previous two verses. Just as his
previous experience cannot be construed as connecting his gospel to human
antecedents, so also after his call he has not "conferred with flesh and

---

[107]Betz, *Galatians,* 66.

[108]Paul's use of the expression "Judaism" is hellenistic-Jewish; see Betz, *Galatians,* 65
note 105.

[109]Betz points out that the imperfect tense reflected in the verbs of v. 13b *(ediōkon* and
eporthoun) are conative (*Galatians,* 67 note 112). Betz also reminds us that the mention of
zeal does not mean Paul was a zealot, but an "ardent observer of Torah," conforming to "contemporary expectations of what a faithful Jew ought to have been" (Ibid., 68).

[110]Schütz, *Anatomy,* 133. However, this does not imply that Paul's former life is seen by
him now as utterly sinful, that he he was "converted" to God. Rather he sees even his former
life as lived under God's sovereignty, as is shown by his reference to being "set apart from
my mother's womb" in 1:15 (Ibid., 133f.). See also Betz, *Galatians,* 69.

[111]Beker, *Paul the Apostle,* 46.

blood.''[112] In making this point Paul offers an important biographical reference to his apostolic call. And it cannot be emphasized too strongly that Paul's "Damascus experience" is, from his own point of view, not a conversion, but a *call*. It is cast in the language of an Old Testament prophetic call, especially those of Deutero-Isaiah (Is. 42:6; 49:1,5-6) and Jeremiah (Jer. 1:5).[113] Paul describes his call in terms similar to that of Jeremiah, who, like himself, was a "prophet to the nations," and he functions like the servant of Deutero-Isaiah, probably even deriving his key term "gospel" from him.[114] It is a call that comes "through his grace" (*dia tēs charitos autou*), a commission traceable directly and exclusively to God.[115]

Paul focuses on two aspects of his call, the fact that he was "set apart" (*aphorisas*) from his mother's womb (cf. Jer. 1:5) and that he was "called" (*kalesas*) through God's grace. He has, therefore, been set aside as holy.[116] His commission is, by virtue of the revelation of God's son, to "preach him to the gentiles." In this way the past, present, and future in Paul's life are all embraced by a divine choice. The remarkable thing, as Becker sees, is that the key word for his appointment, *apostolos* ("apostle"), is not mentioned, but only indirectly referred to in his missionary goal.[117] Why is it missing? Becker answers, "That Paul can do without it shows again that his gospel, not his apostolic office, is in question."[118] That may be overstating the matter, though Becker's instincts are surely correct. More accurately, Paul's apostolic authority is in jeopardy along with the gospel, but the absence of "apostle" in v. 15 demonstrates the subordination of his apostleship to the gospel. The formulation of vv. 15-16a is, as Schlier claims, already influenced by the main thought, "the impossibility of human cooperation in the receiving of the gospel," which at the same time also contains an "indirect reference to the untruthfulness of the opponents' assertion."[119]

Verse 16 describes the manifestation of the choice and call of God in commissioning Paul. It came when God was pleased "to reveal his Son in me" (*apokalupsai ton huion auton en emoi*). As we have already seen, Paul

---

[112]Burton, *Commentary*, 49. He argues that *de* should be translated "and" rather than "but."

[113]Becker, "Galater," 18.

[114]See Is. 52:7, 61:1. See also Beker, *Paul the Apostle*, 10, 115-16. Beker informs us that *doulos* ("slave") in 1:10 is a prophetic title (Ibid., 115).

[115]Schlier explains that *eudokēsen* ("pleased") indicates that Paul was "chosen by divine decision" (*Galater*, 25). Schlier further argues that *dia tēs charitos autou* ("through his grace") goes with *kalesas* ("called") and not with *apokalupsai* ("to reveal"), (Ibid., 26). See also Betz, *Galatians*, 70. Although *ho theos* ("God") is in brackets in the text, it should be deleted as a scribal gloss, as Betz suggests (*Galatians*, 70 note 132); there is no question, of course, that it is God who is meant.

[116]Betz, *Galatians*, 70 note 134.

[117]Becker, "Galater," 18.

[118]Ibid., 19.

[119]Schlier, *Galater*, 24.

means an apostolic apocalypse by which the crucified and risen Lord became a living and present reality for him, the basis of his gospel. That is expressed here by the Christological title *ton huion autou* ("his Son"), which is able to "transcend particularistic Jewish usage, now meaning that salvation is open to all."[120] That this significance is intended here is supported by Betz's observation that while v. 15 uses Jewish categories, v. 16 sees the introduction of "specifically Christian ideas."[121]

Perhaps the most striking thing, however, is that Paul says the revelation of God's Son took place *en emoi* ("in me"). The words could perhaps be taken to have a dative sense, meaning "to me." But that denies the plain meaning of the words. As Burton insists, *en emoi* can only mean "in me," the question then becoming whether Paul means a "subjective revelation in and for the apostle" or an "objective manifestation of Christ in and through him to others."[122] In favor of the former interpretation are three facts: the fact that *apokaluptein* usually refers to a disclosure to an individual, the fact that *hina euaggelizōmai* ("in order to preach him") would be awkward and redundant if the revelation was supposed to be "through" the apostle; and, finally, the important fact that the point of the passage is not how Paul made known his gospel but "how he received it."[123] What exactly does Paul mean that God revealed his Son "in me?" Schlier believes that Paul, with these words, brings to expression the "intensity of the revealing of the Son."[124] But in view of the recurrence of the same phrase in v. 24, where Paul says "they glorified God in me" (*en emoi*), and the context of our passage, in which gospel and apostolic call coincide, it seems probable that the apostle points to himself as the locus of the revelation of God's Son and therefore the "paradigm of the gospel he proclaims."[125] The fact that his is a biography of reversal testifies to the saving grace of God, all the more sharply distinguishing his apostolic gospel from human authorization, especially that of Jerusalem.

Paul refers to his apostolic commission as having its purpose "that I might preach him among the nations" (*hina euaggelizōmai auton en tois ethnesin*). Two things are noteworthy. First, Paul's commission is limited to the gen-

---

[120]Bornkamm, *Paul*, 21-22. Stuhlmacher emphasizes that Paul's call and apostolic autobiography *both* follow the prophetic model. They testify not only to the divine origin and autonomy of his gospel, but also the sovereign *freedom* of God in revealing his Son to Paul (*Das paulinische Evangelium*, 82). We can see, then, the connection between Paul's account of his call and his argument for freedom from the law which appears later.

[121]Betz, *Galatians*, 70.

[122]Burton, *Commentary*, 50.

[123]Ibid., 50-51.

[124]Schlier, *Galater*, 27.

[125]Schütz, *Anatomy*, 134. See also Schütz's discussion of *en emoi* ("in me"), (Ibid., 136f.). See Gal. 2:20, 4:6.

tiles. And secondly, the fact that "preach" has as its object "him" (*auton*), a personal object, emphasizes that the content of the gospel is Christ.[126]

With vv. 16c-17 we arrive at the central point of the argument which Paul inaugurated in 1:11, that his gospel is not of human origin. Here the apostle wants to underscore his immediate reaction to the call. He relates that he did not confer (*ou prosanethemēn*) with "flesh and blood" (*sarki kai haimati*), meaning that he had no conversation with any human beings.[127] Why such an emphatic denial? Is he, as Betz suggests, refuting accounts (such as that in Acts 9) which relate that he received his gospel from a human teacher?[128]

Whatever Paul may be refuting in v. 16c, his immediate intention is made clear by his denial that he has had contact with the Jerusalem authorities (v. 17a). Since for his opponents Jerusalem is important, his disclaimer, "nor did I go up to Jerusalem to those who were apostles before me," underscores his independence. He felt initially no compulsion to go there. In fact, he did not go there *at all,* at least in his early ministry. That is made perfectly clear by his early itinerary, mentioned in the remainder of v. 17. He "went away into Arabia."[129] And after that, when his tour was ended, even then he did not go to Jerusalem, but returned to Damascus. Only later does he go up to Jerusalem to present his gospel before the authorities, and then only by "revelation" (2:2).

As our exegetical analysis now comes to an end, we are in a position to sharpen our understanding of a key element in Paul's theological consciousness, the *apostolos* ("apostle"). "Apostle" is the self-designation with which Paul's letter to the Galatians begins (1:1), and it reappears in 1:17 when he refers to the Jerusalem apostles. So even though the term itself does not appear in the crucial verses where he describes the origin of his gospel and call in the "revelation of Jesus Christ" (1:12,16), it is clearly in his mind. What does the term signify, and why does he insist on identifying himself as *apostolos* (cf. Rom. 1:1, 1 Cor. 1:1, 2 Cor. 1:1)? As Betz reminds us, the origin and conception of the "apostle" is obscure and still under investigation.[130] However, on the basis of what evidence we find in Paul we are able to at least clarify its essential contours.

The word *apostolos* means "sent one" and is probably derived from the Jewish institution of *shaliach* ("messenger"), an authorized representative.

---

[126]Betz, *Galatians,* 72.

[127]Ibid. Stuhlmacher, citing Jeremias, explains that the expression "flesh and blood" also carries the connotation of weak creatureliness over against God (*Das paulinische Evangelium,* 83).

[128]Betz, *Galatians,* 73.

[129]It is not known what Paul did in Arabia, but it is probable that he was there for purposes of his missionary activity. Arabia means the Nabatean kingdom. See Betz, *Galatians,* 73f. See also Becker ("Galater," 19) who thinks his activity may be further reflected in 2 Cor. 11:32.

[130]Betz, *Galatians,* 74.

In Christian usage, this means one sent by the risen Lord. Essentially the apostle is a missionary, a proclaimer of the gospel in whom "the Lord himself encounters men."[131] But perhaps most important within the context of Galatians is the key element of *authority*. The word of the apostle, as Bultmann maintains, is "the word legitimated by the Lord."[132] Paul, as apostle, is not just a preacher of the gospel but "interprets the gospel with an authoritative, unique claim of a resurrection witness and as the founder of the church."[133] This explains Paul's continual effort in Gal. 1 to set himself apart from Jerusalem and the line of legitimacy followed by his opponents.[134] If he is to reclaim the Galatian congregation for the law-free gospel, which he is convinced originates in the prophetic call of God, he must exercise his authority as an autonomous interpreter of gospel and tradition (cf. Paul's bold reinterpretations of the Old Testament in 3:6-4:31). Thus, as Schütz has seen so clearly (based also on his further analysis of 1:18-2:21), Paul *distinguishes* between authority and legitimacy.[135] Authority for Paul is located in the gospel, and it takes precedence over legitimacy, so that, as Schütz explains, "He is not authoritative because he is an apostle, but is an apostle because he is the authoritative, i.e., faithful, commissioned preacher of the gospel."[136] Paul's apostolic commission is subordinated to and arises out of the gospel of Christ. In the faithful exercise of that gospel Paul, as "sent" by Christ, is himself the "apostolic paradigm for the Galatians."[137] In the preaching of the law-free gospel and in the exercise of his care for the congregation the apostle demonstrates what it means to live in the eschatological dominion of the grace of God, to live out, by the Spirit, the freedom in Christ.

CONCLUSIONS

Even though in Galatians Paul's chief concern does not revolve around preaching as such, the fact that his references to preaching in the first chapter are fused to his treatment of the gospel has important consequences for his

---

[131]Bultmann, *Theology*, 2:105. See also K. Rengstorff, *TDNT*, 1 (Grand Rapids: Eerdmanns, 1964), 407-443, and Karl Kertelge, "Das Apostelamt des Paulus, sein Ursprung und seine Bedeutung," *Biblische Zeitschrift* 14 (1970): 100-29. Cf. the excursus on *apostolos* by Betz (*Galatians*, 74-75); he thinks the closest parallels for the understanding of the term are to be found in Syriac gnosticism.

[132]Bultmann, *Theology*, 2:105.

[133]Beker, *Paul the Apostle*, 47.

[134]This should not mislead us into thinking of Paul as completely separate from the rest of the church. In fact, in 1:18-2:14 he documents his connections with the Jerusalem. Rather, as Schütz aptly suggests, the emphasis is on discontinuity within continuity (*Anatomy*, 135). See also Holmberg, *Paul and Power*, 15, 54f.

[135]Schütz, *Anatomy*, 153.

[136]Ibid., 145. He adds, "Parity is achieved not by clarifying Paul's claim to apostolic status but by clarifying Jerusalem's subordination to the gospel's authority and hence the claim of those leaders to Paul's vision of apostolic authority. The Jerusalem leaders meet his standards. Legitimacy has nothing to do with it. Authority has everything to do with it. It is not surprising that Paul stresses that nothing was added to *him*" (Ibid., 145f.).

[137]Beker, *Paul the Apostle*, 47.

theology of preaching. There can be little doubt, based on our exegesis, that for Paul the gospel, and the gospel alone, constitutes the highest authority for the church. Not only does Paul understand himself to be under the gospel's authority, but the thrust of his argument is that all the apostles, even the Jerusalem church, are equally under its charge. As such, the gospel is the authoritative norm for all preaching.

If the gospel is the norm of preaching, it becomes important to recognize the essential authoritative nature of the gospel. On the basis of what Paul relates in Galatians, several characteristic features of the gospel's authority emerge. First, the gospel originates in God's revelation of his Son, Jesus Christ. This eschatological event discloses the true character of the possibilities for life. It is a case of reversal. Since the resurrected Lord is none other than the one who "gave himself for our sins" (1:4), a glorious paradox has been divinely transfused into human life. That paradox consists in the fact that freedom from the power of sin, which is resident in "this age" (1:4), is made available through one who became a victim of its power (see also 1 Cor. 1:17-25). But that freedom does not exist as an independent commodity; instead, it exists in the Christian's being incorporated into the power structure of God, or, as Paul describes himself, in being a "slave of Christ" (1:10). That is to say, the gospel, as understood soteriologically by Paul, is essentially a *relational* context. The gospel "of Christ" (1:7) makes Christ himself present to believers. Christ is present in his authoritative, saving lordship where he is preached as the crucified.

This explains why Grässer is quite correct in emphasizing that the gospel is identical with the *call* of God. A call is a relational term, the issue of an offer which expects a response. The authority of the gospel, then, is intimately connected to the fact that in its sphere the hearer is brought into a direct encounter with God. This also explains why for Paul, in his controversy with the judaizing movement in Galatia, the authority of the gospel stands above any questions about legitimacy. Because his apostleship rests on the gospel, not on human antecedents, Paul can without hesitation exercise its authority in dealing with the opponents and the Galatians.

What implications does this understanding of the gospel have for Paul's theology of preaching? First, if the preaching of the gospel and the call of God are identical, then preaching is also *relational*. It requires as its medium a person, someone to whom the hearer can relate. For, as we have seen, Paul as apostle, and therefore preacher of Christ to the gentiles (1:16), becomes a model for the gospel's power. In the relationship of hearer to preacher the call of God is issued.

That brings us to a second observation. The character of the gospel is such that, as norm, it informs not only the message but the character of the preacher. For Paul that means he is the "slave of Christ." The cues for his whole life are taken from his Lord. In Paul's case this shows up in the sovereign freedom of God, the freedom from the works of Torah and thus the new creation (6:15), which informs his own biography (1:13-16a). Paul has himself experienced the paradox of a prophetic call from God, a reversal of his life's direction, by means of the revelation of God's Son ''in me'' (1:16). The gospel is the exclusive norm for the preacher who proclaims it. For Paul preaching is a servant role, the offering of one's self to the Christ who ''gave himself'' for us (1:4).

Finally, the authority of the gospel is such that it imposes a serious and solemn obligation on the preacher. This is quite clear from the curse formula of 1:8. Since the preaching of the gospel is the presentation of Christ and the execution of his saving lordship, the nature and content of preaching is *singular*. Christ is at its heart and center. And any preaching which departs from that center invites disaster.

CHAPTER FOUR

CROSS, RESURRECTION, AND MINISTRY: THEOLOGY OF PREACHING IN THE CORINTHIAN CORRESPONDENCE

Paul's correspondence with the congregation at Corinth constitutes the largest single collection of material which we have from the apostle. This alone makes 1 and 2 Corinthians important for any investigation of his theology, since it provides access to a greater depth and range of Paul's thought. To this advantage we can also add another, the fact that Paul speaks to specific issues and concerns that have arisen in the congregation's practice of the Christian faith subsequent to his departure from the city. This allows us to observe the manner in which Paul's theology functions in actual experience. For it is clear to even the least observant that Paul's answers to the congregation's questions and his responses to reports of their conduct are not merely practical advice but flow from his theological convictions. The apostle is engaged in what has been aptly called "applied theology."[1]

Our investigation of Paul's theology of preaching, therefore, finds itself in a fortuitous position when we come to examine the Corinthian correspondence. For our greatest number of references to preaching appear in this collection. In addition, Paul's references to preaching occur in contexts in which

---

[1]Hans Conzelmann, *First Corinthians* (Philadelphia: Fortress, 1975), 9.

he treats some of the most crucial themes of his theology. In 1 Cor. 1:17–2:5 Paul speaks of preaching in direct relation to the cross of Christ, a theme reinforced in 1 Cor. 9:14-18. In 1 Cor. 15:1-12 preaching is treated within the context of his important discussion of the resurrection. And in 2 Cor. 4:1-6 the apostle argues that the ministry of preaching the gospel implies the lordship of Christ with the preacher as servant. From these texts, together with several other related passages, important dimensions of Paul's theology of preaching emerge, particularly as regards the function and nature of preaching.

THE HISTORICAL SITUATION OF FIRST CORINTHIANS

The congregation at Corinth was established by the apostle Paul during his so-called second missionary journey (Acts 18). The city was historically an important commercial port and was made the center of the Roman province of Achaia. Paul apparently worked there a considerable period of time, and when he departed for Ephesus, he left behind a thriving church, made up principally of gentiles.[2]

After Paul was gone from Corinth, certain problems arose within the congregation. The apostle dealt with them by means of the letter we know as 1 Corinthians. That the apostle Paul is the author of the letter is not seriously challenged today. Scholars are generally content that he wrote 1 Corinthians from Ephesus, probably in the spring of 54 or 55 A.D.[3] The stimulus for his taking pen in hand was two-fold, first a personal report from "Chloe's people" (1:11) about strife in the congregation and then a letter from Corinth seeking the apostle's advice on certain questions of conduct (7:1, 8:1, 12:1).

Two other aspects regarding the nature of the document are not quite so easily settled. The first is the question of whether 1 Corinthians constitutes a unity. It has long been noted, for example, that the well known hymn of Christian love in 1 Cor. 13 intrudes awkwardly into the discussion about spiritual gifts, which continues from chapter 12 through chapter 14. And chapter 9, a defense of Paul's practice of not accepting financial support from the congregation for his ministry, interrupts the train of thought in chapters 8 to 10, which deal with the subject of eating.[4] In addition, certain statements are

---

[2]For a useful, comprehensive description of Paul's dealings with the Corinthian church see Bornkamm, *Paul,* 68-77. For a social description and analysis of the congregation see also Gerd Theissen, *The Social Setting of Pauline Christianity* (Philadelphia: Fortress, 1982), 69-120.

[3]Kümmel, *Introduction,* 275, 279; Marxsen, *Introduction,* 71ff.; Perrin, *Introduction,* 101ff.

[4]Conzelmann provides a list of the breaks and dislocations (*1 Corinthians,* 3).

made which appear to be contradictory, as when in chapter 4 Paul speaks of his imminent arrival in Corinth and then in chapter 16 speaks of his being delayed.[5] As a result, some scholars, such as Weiss and Hering, have concluded that 1 Corinthians is really a compilation of two or more letters and have set about reconstructing what they believe to have been their original forms.[6] Their attempts have not been widely accepted. As Conzelmann observes, in order to be convincing those who argue that 1 Corinthians is a compilation must show that "different situations are presupposed for different parts of the epistle."[7]

This brings us to the other unresolved aspect, the question of the historical circumstances and the nature of the problem with which Paul tries to deal. In this respect the most thorough-going attempt to relate a theory of compilation with a reconstruction of the historical setting is that of Schmithals. By means of literary-critical analysis he divides 1 and 2 Corinthians into six letters. He theorizes that the letters were the product of a conflict between Paul and a group of Jewish gnostic missionaries, whom Paul came to know and understand only gradually over an eight-month period.[8] However, even this brilliant attempt cannot be regarded as successful, although it has had some influence.[9]

There is no denying that 1 Corinthians exhibits a loose construction. This, however, can be understood as traceable to the variety of specific problems that occupy Paul's attention, to the fact that he has two sources of information (a report and a letter), and to the apostle's use of the literary device of the

---

[5]Jean Hering, *The Epistle of St. Paul to the Corinthians* (London: Epworth, 1962), xiii., can be consulted for a complete list. Cf. the analysis of C. K. Barrett, *A Commentary on the First Epistle to the Corinthians* (New York: Harper, 1968), 12-17. In addition, 1:2b and 14:33b-35 are suspected of being later interpolations; for a discussion see Kümmel, *Introduction,* 275f.

[6]Barrett offers a thorough description and analysis of the views of Weiss and Hering (*First Epistle*, 12-17).

[7]Conzelmann, *1 Corinthians,* 3f. He is therefore unconvinced and regards 1 Corinthians as a unity, since he finds no conclusive proof for different situations in the letter.

[8]Walter Schmithals, *Gnosticism in Corinth* (Nashville: Abingdon, 1971), 87-116.

[9]Scholarly reservations are due in large part to the fact that there is a lack of evidence for Schmithals' premise that there was in existence a pre-Christian gnosticism with a redeemed redeemer myth (a tenet of the Bultmann tradition). See Conzelmann for a discussion and review of the gnostic argument and of Schmithals' reconstruction (*1 Corinthians,* 3f. and 14f.). Conzelmann contends that there are no traces of the gnostic myth in Corinth and that such a myth is not required to explain the Corinthian libertinism. However Kümmel and Marxsen have both been influenced by Schmithals' views, even though neither accepts his compilation theory of 1 Corinthians. Kümmel refers to Paul's opposition as an "enthusiastic-Gnostic front" (*Introduction,* 275), while Marxsen identifies the opposition as "representatives of a syncretism in which Christian, Jewish and Gnostic elements are combined" (*Introduction,* 88).

excursus.[10] We can, therefore, with some confidence regard 1 Corinthians as an essential unity. And even if it cannot be shown that it is a complete literary unit, its various discussions fall close enough together in time and basic subject matter to provide a unified framework from which we can carry on our exegetical research.

What, then, is the problem Paul confronts? From an examination of the text of 1 Corinthians we learn that there are divisions and strife within the congregation (1:10ff., 11:17ff.), there is a case of open incest (5:1-13), there are disputes over legal transactions in the courts (6:1-11) and eating of meat offered to idols (8:1ff., 10:23ff.), there is disorder in worship and misunderstanding of spiritual gifts (11:2-14:40), and there are those who deny any resurrection of the dead (15:12ff.). We would be misled, though, if we identified the problems as merely a break-down of moral and religious order. Rather, as Conzelmann sees, what has occurred is an outbreak of "religious enthusiasm."[11] The Christians in Corinth have evidently misunderstood the nature and application of their newfound faith. Conzelmann explains that "their conduct is grounded on a freedom principle (6:12; 10:23); this in turn rests upon 'knowledge' (8:1), and the latter derives from experience of the Spirit (12:4ff.)."[12] All this is grounded, finally, on what Conzelmann terms an "exaltation Christology," meaning that the Corinthians appear to believe that in their baptism they have been united to the risen and exalted Christ in a "movement of spiritual ascent."[13] These ecstatics believe themselves to have left behind all human, earthly constraints. The result, therefore, is an elitist mentality which threatens to fragment the congregation. The enthusiasts, as Bornkamm describes them, "have disavowed responsible obligation toward the rest and thus sought to transcend the limits of time and history imposed on the Christian life."[14]

Against this perversion of the Christian faith Paul argues that the exaltation Christology of the Corinthian ecstatics has no basis because the resurrection is not their present possession, but a future promise (15:20ff.). Instead, it is the cross that is the central controlling symbol of salvation in the present (1:17ff.). This means, in turn, that the true test of spirituality is concern for the fellow Christian and a love that builds up, rather than tears up, the fellowship of the community (8:12-13, 9:19-23, 10:23, 13:1ff.).

---

[10]Kümmel, *Introduction,* 278. He lists as such excursuses 2:6-16, 6:1-11, 9:1-27, 10:1-13, and 13:1-13. See also Conzelmann, *1 Corinthians,* 4, and Barrett, *First Epistle,* 14-17.

[11]Conzelmann, *1 Corinthians,* 14.

[12]Ibid.

[13]Ibid., 15, and Ulrich Wilckens, *Weisheit und Torheit* (Tübingen: Mohr-Siebeck, 1959), 20f. See also Robinson and Koester, *Trajectories,* 32ff. on the relationship of the problem of baptism to the situation in Corinth.

[14]Bornkamm, *Paul,* 73.

FIRST CORINTHIANS 1:17–2:5

A. The Literary Context

The initial text we intend to examine falls within the first major section of the epistle, 1:10-4:21. There Paul deals with the factions in the Corinthian congregation on the basis of the report which he has received from "Chloe's people" (1:11).

He begins with an appeal to the Corinthians to cease their dissension (1:10). He recounts the specific nature of the problem about which he has been informed in the report, namely, that the Corinthian church members appear to have divided themselves into competing factions on the basis of who baptized them (1:12-13). Paul denies that he has had anything to do with baptisms among them (1:14-16). He insists that his call is to preach the gospel, a gospel which is not the same as "eloquent wisdom" but is founded on the cross of Christ (1:17). This key-note is followed by his important argument that the preaching of the cross is the wisdom and power of God, with the consequence that all human boasting is excluded (1:18-31). The apostle points to the actual experience of the Corinthians (1:26-31) as well as his own preaching and experience as evidence of that fact (2:1-5). He assures the Corinthians that there is indeed a wisdom for those mature enough to receive it, a wisdom from God (2:6-16). He has, however, not been able to impart this to the Corinthians since they are yet "babes in Christ" (3:1-2). Paul returns to his theme of divisions. He asks who Apollos and Paul really are and answers that they are to be regarded as servants whose purpose is to build up the congregation on the foundation of Jesus Christ (3:3-17). On this basis he warns the Corinthians not to be deceived into mistaking where their true wisdom lies (3:18-23). In 4:1-5 Paul relates that he and the other apostles should be thought of as "servants of Christ" and therefore as "stewards of the mysteries of God." Paul upbraids the Corinthians for their arrogance and points to his own experience in weakness as an example of the way the gospel is intended to be exercised (4:6-16). Finally he concludes by informing the congregation that he has sent Timothy to them and will soon be coming to them himself (4:17-21).

Paul's discussion of preaching, then, is intended to deal with the problems of dissension, arrogance, and the spiritual elitism of some of the Corinthians. His theology of preaching, as the preaching of the cross, is the foundation of his demand that life in the Corinthian congregation be reordered.

B. Exegesis

> For Christ did not send me to baptize but to preach the gospel, (and) not with eloquent speech, lest the cross of Christ be emptied (v. 17).

From his discussion of the divisions within the Corinthian congregation, which are based, as they seem to have been, in a faulty understanding of baptism, Paul turns abruptly to a new theme in v. 17. In 1:10-16 the apostle severely criticized the presuppositions of the theology and practice which held sway among some of the Corinthians. He measured their divisions according to the essential unity of Christ and found them wanting. Paul emphasizes the fact that he, as their founding apostle, did not personally baptize any of them, with just a few exceptions. The implication is clear. Paul regards their thinking as misguided. He finds no justification for their divisions. So now in v. 17, having demolished their preconceptions about baptism as the center of their faith and practice, Paul offers the first hints as to what he holds to be the authentic center Christian theology and practice. He does so by referring back to his own commission as apostle. The implication here, as will be shown repeatedly in the rest of 1:18–4:21, is that the center of his own calling determines the nature of his mission and consequently the character of both his apostleship and the practice of the churches he has "fathered" (cf. 4:15). And that center is, in Paul's own shorthand, the "cross of Christ" *(ho stauros tou Christou)* which he preaches.

Verse 17, therefore, is a striking transitional verse, even though its abrupt turn of thought and compact terminology make it rather awkward and somewhat difficult to understand.[15] Paul shifts the discussion by means of two antitheses. The first is his insistence that he has been "sent" *(apesteilen)* by Christ to "gospelize" *(euaggelizesthai),* as opposed to baptizing.[16] Paul intends to lead the Corinthians to rethink their theology, and so he returns to the point of origin, his own apostolic commission. The sharp contrast between baptizing, as important as it may be, and the nature of his authentic call, to preach the gospel, makes clear where the point of departure lies for all of Paul's theology and its applications.[17] As we have already seen (1 Thess.

---

[15]As Conzelmann says, it "becomes understandable in the light of the later statements in which Paul shows that the form of preaching cannot be separated from its content (the word of the cross)" (*1 Corinthians,* 37).

[16]Although "sent" is the literal translation, in this context the translation "apostled" could be justified in order to bring out the emphasis on his apostolic commission.

[17]Conzelmann warns us that we should not make the mistake of concluding that Paul devalues baptism. Rather, Paul is simply placing the emphasis on the heart of his commission. As Conzelmann puts it, "Baptism can be administered by anyone. *He* has to preach the gospel to the Gentiles (Gal. 1:16)" (*1 Corinthians,* 36). In addition, we might also point out that for Paul baptism does not stand on its own but is dependent on the nature of the gospel, which for Paul means the cross.

1:5), for Paul the gospel denotes simultaneously the content of the Christian message, the manner of its administration, and the sphere of Christian existence. Thus Paul takes the gospel as axiomatic for his theologizing.

But this shift in thought would not yet have addressed the heart of the problem in Corinth. For the Corinthians do not see any contradiction between baptism and the gospel. In their thinking their baptism connects them with the risen Christ, who is the subject of the gospel, and that in turn means being connected with his resurrection and exaltation. Paul's task, therefore, is to drive a wedge between baptism and exaltation. To do that he introduces the second antithesis, that between a "wisdom of word" *(sophiai logou)* and the "cross of Christ" *(ho stauros tou Christou)*. The apostle understands the Corinthian misconception as marked by a baptism connected with existence in an exalted Lord, which they believe to be expressed in and confirmed by a "wisdom of word." His own position is expressed by the "cross of Christ." These two catchwords, "wisdom" and the "cross," will dominate Paul's following discussion and serve to establish what is the genuine criterion for Christian theology. But how are we to understand these two expressions?

It may very well be that Paul is taking up a formulary expression of the Corinthians when he uses the phrase *en sophiai logou* ("in a wisdom of word").[18] The word *sophia* ("wisdom") introduces an important concept, but one which was understood quite differently in various circles of the ancient world. For the Greeks *sophia* denoted a quality, "a materially complete and hence unusual knowledge and ability."[19] But the term has an altogether different meaning in biblical usage. *Sophia* was used in the Septuagint to translate the Hebrew conception of wisdom. In Old Testament thought wisdom was not theoretical but practical, the "prudent, considered, experienced and competent action to subjugate the world and to master the various problems of life and life itself."[20] In later Jewish thought wisdom became personified and so was understood as a prophetic voice summoning a person (cf. especially Prov. 1-9).[21] Then in gnostic thought *sophia* was again personified, but with a soteriological function. *Sophia* was conceived of as having a supernatural origin and divine nature, the revealer of redemption to the gnostic.[22] Which of these, then, provides the clue for Paul's usage in v. 17ff.? Conzelmann believes Paul's usage originates in Jewish Wisdom speculation, while Schmithals and Wilckens are convinced the word has gnostic overtones.[23] The emphasis in these cases falls on the content of wisdom as a means

[18]Wilckens, *Weisheit*, 19.
[19]U. Wilckens, *TDNT*, 7 (Grand Rapids: Eerdmanns, 1971), 467.
[20]Ibid., 476.
[21]Ibid., 490f.
[22]Ibid. 509.
[23]Conzelmann, *1 Corinthians*, 8f. Schmithals, *Gnosticism in Corinth*, 141f. Wilckens, *TDNT*, 7:519f.

of salvation. But, as Horsley argues, in Paul's discussion the emphasis falls just as much on *sophia* as *speech* (cf. 1:17; 2:1; 2:13; 4:19-20) as it does upon the fact that it is a means of salvation. Horsley believes this double-sided conception of wisdom, understood simultaneously as both eloquence and means of salvation, finds its true home in Hellenistic-Jewish tradition, particularly Philo, Wisdom of Solomon, and Sirach.[24] He notices that, according to Paul, some in Corinth appear to regard eloquence as an "element in their spiritual achievement."[25] Thus Horsley explains that for the Corinthians *sophia* is a means and content of salvation, a means of immortality and perfection, according to the Philonic model. In that case, eloquent speech is an important evidence of that perfection, since "intimacy with *sophia* endowed them with eloquent expression of her revelations (2:4)."[26] This explanation of the Corinthian position fits the context well. We are therefore advised to regard *sophia* as gathering up for the Corinthians the various aspects of redeemed existence which Paul locates only in the sphere of the gospel. *Sophia* has for the Corinthian opponents displaced the gospel as the key descriptive term for the content of the saving message, the manner of its administration, and sphere of existence.[27] *Sophia* has become the competitor of the gospel. Thus Barrett's translation of *ouk en sophiai logou* as "without rhetorical skill" is too weak, while Schmithals comes closer with "not in wise discourse."[28] It is no accident that Paul introduces this key term in a negative sense precisely after his mention of preaching the gospel.

In contrast to a "wisdom of word" Paul emphasizes his own alternative, which corresponds to his preaching of the gospel. It is the "cross of Christ." At this point Paul does not offer an exposition of what he means by this expression. Instead he presupposes knowledge of it.[29] Its significance is to be unfolded in what follows. At this point Paul only wants to do two things. He wants it known where the center of his gospel activity lies. And he wants to indicate the consequences when the criterion for Christian practice becomes a "baptism/wisdom of word" theology. The latter Paul accomplishes by means of a negative purpose clause, *hina mē kenōthē ho stauros tou Christou* ("lest the cross of Christ be emptied").

---

[24]Richard Horsley, "Wisdom of Word and Words of Wisdom in Corinth," *CBQ* 39 (1977): 224f. Cf. Johannes Munck, *Paul and the Salvation of Mankind* (Atlanta: John Knox, 1977), 153, who stays entirely with the emphasis on Greek rhetoric in his interpretation of wisdom in Corinth.

[25]Horsley, "Wisdom of Word," 231.

[26]Ibid., Horsley believes this is traceable possibly to Apollos, even though Paul tries to close ranks with him. He thinks "Paul insists too much" that there is no conflict between the two of them.

[27]Whether *en* (*"in"*) should be instrumental or local here is thus not really significant.

[28]Barrett, *First Epistle*, 49f. Schmithals, *Gnosticism in Corinth*, 142.

[29]Schmithals, *Gnosticism in Corinth*, 136.

The consequence of a theology of wisdom is that the cross is "emptied" *(kenōthē)*. As Paul will argue in v. 18ff., that is disastrous, for the cross of Christ is the very saving power of God (1:18, 21, 14; cf. Rom. 1:15-16). For the cross to be emptied means that it is "emptied of its significance" with respect to salvation.[30] The cross is thus "denuded," made "theologically unimportant."[31] In this way Paul makes it abundantly clear that he is driving a wedge between the gospel of the cross and the Corinthian "gospel" of baptism and wise discourse, which is condensed in the code-word *sophia*. To accept the gospel as preached by Paul means accepting the cross of Christ as paradigm. The Corinthian alternative must be rejected.[32]

> For the word of the cross is folly to those who are on their way to destruction, but to us who are being saved it is the power of God. For it is written, "I will destroy the wisdom of the wise, and the intelligence of the intelligent I will confound. (vv. 18-19).

The terms of reference introduced in v. 17, with the essential antagonism between wisdom and the cross, now in v. 18 become rephrased by Paul into a thesis which he will defend and expound in vv. 19ff. It is important to observe that at this point Paul leaves behind the specific situation in Corinth, which occupied his attention in vv. 10-17, in order to argue his case more broadly, laying down a central principle in the economy of God's salvation (vv. 18-25). This principle, once established, the apostle will then focus once again on the circumstances in Corinth, beginning from v. 26.

Paul's thesis is laid down in v. 18 in the form of a double antithetical parallelism. Those on the way to destruction are set opposite those who are being saved, and folly is set over against the power of God. The subject which determines these fundamental contrasts Paul describes as the "word of the cross," which picks up from the mention of the cross in v. 17. Paul's use of *logos* ("word") at this point most certainly refers to the content of the message, as is indicated by his discussion in 2:1ff. as well as the fact that Paul repeats the use of the article for emphasis: *ho logos ho tou staurou* (which literally could be rendered, "the word, the one which is of the cross").[33] The "word of the cross" becomes Paul's code-word for the gospel, especially when he wants to speak of the gospel polemically in terms of some other interpretation of the Christian message.[34] The expres-

---

[30]Barrett, *First Epistle,* 49.

[31]Wilckens, *Weisheit,* 20.

[32]Schmithals, *Gnosticism in Corinth,* 136.

[33]Cf. Hering (*First Epistle,* 8) who wants to translate *logos* as "instruction." But that is too weak.

[34]This is brought out forcefully by Ernst Käsemann, "The Saving Significance of the Death of Jesus in Paul," in *Perspectives on Paul* (Philadelphia: Fortress, 1971), 35.

sion is an abbreviation, a figure of speech which, in compressed form, elevates the crucial content of the gospel.[35] It is shorthand for "preaching of Christ as the crucified" (cf. 1:23; 2:2).[36]

The effect of the "word of the cross" is stated in terms of a contrast between the "lost" (apollumenois) and the "saved" (sōizomenos). Curiously, though the terminology is eschatological and therefore future (destruction and salvation which are to be consummated at the last day), both terms are participial constructions in the present tense. The implication is that the process is not complete. Why does Paul apply eschatological terms to the present? As Wilckens explains, "The saved and lost judge the preaching of the cross oppositely, and by this contrary judgment they distinguish themselves in the eschatological sense as the saved and the lost."[37] This is no doubt true, but that does not really answer the question. We must not lose sight of the fact that Paul frames his argument with a view to the situation in Corinth. If we are correct in supposing that some of the Corinthians believe that the eschaton has already arrived, it is vital for Paul to describe Christian existence in such a way that the eschaton as a future event remains intact. The use of the present passive participle does exactly that. On the other hand, the use of the same construction for those "on the way to destruction" is a way of leaving the door open. This is important for the Corinthians also, because some of them in their enthusiasm have come to regard the cross as folly, and thus stand perilously close to the lost.

A second aspect of Paul's description of the lost and saved is that both constructions (apollumenois and sōizomenois respectively) are in the dative case. The "word of the cross" is arranged so that it comes "to" those who are being saved and lost. Wilckens argues that there are two co-extensive nuances intended by the apostle. On the surface level each term is understood as being a judgment made by human beings; the lost and saved regard the word of the cross as, respectively, folly or power of God. But the terms also are an expression of the fact that not only is the word of the cross in question, but people are placed in question by that preaching of the cross. Thus the "word of the cross" actually extends folly to the one and the power of God to the other.[38] And this brings us to recognize an important fact, namely that the "word of the cross" has an "eschatological-'critical' power;" it creates an eschatological division among the hearers.[39]

---

[35]Conzelmann, 1 Corinthians, 41.
[36]Wilckens, Weisheit, 24. See also Gal. 3:1.
[37]Ibid., 23.
[38]Ibid., 21f.
[39]Ibid., 23. See also Schütz, Anatomy, 192.

The other two terms of the parallelism are "folly" *(mōria)* and the "power of God" *(dunamis theou)*. This is striking in view of the fact that for the parallelism to remain strictly intact, the opposite of *mōria* should have been *sophia* ("wisdom"). The switch in terms is clearly intentional, as indicated by the addition of *theou* ("of God") which even further breaks the harmony of the parallel members. What does Paul understand by *mōria*, and why does he avoid the use of *sophia* until v. 24? And what is signified by the "power of God" *(dunamis theou)*?

First, the term *mōria* in the New Testament comes to have a theological significance which it had neither in classical Greek, where it referred merely to a physical or intellectual deficiency, nor in the Septuagint, where it appears infrequently. *Mōria* means folly not only in the sense that something is apprehended as stupid or senseless, but also in the fact that it is a violation of taste. For cultured people in the Graeco-Roman world to mention the "cross," an instrument of execution reserved for slaves, was a breach of etiquette.[40] The cross was offensive, almost an obscenity, the symbol of disgrace and utter humiliation to all who belonged to polite circles.[41] Paul cannot help but be conscious of this. His use of the term is both deliberate and understandable. Mention of the cross of Christ strikes hearers as an embarrassment, and to suggest that this is the heart of human salvation is much like a morbid joke. And no amount of argument, no higher *sophia* ("wisdom"), can make the cross appear otherwise. It is not a case of being converted to a Christian "wisdom" by which suddenly the cross makes sense and loses its embarrassing connotations. So Paul certainly does not want to suggest that there may be any such wisdom. In fact, because the problems in Corinth are linked precisely to their desire for wisdom, for Paul to introduce the term at this point would undermine the very point he wishes to make.[42] Thus *sophia* does not appear again until v. 24, after he has redefined the terms of the discussion. Rather, the cross is held up by Paul not as a new wisdom, but as the "power of God," a power which saves those who believe through the instrumentality of shame and weakness, the cross (v. 21; cf. Rom. 1:16).

Paul's thesis of v. 18 is profound, but it is also controversial, as he himself recognizes. It requires the lengthy argument which follows to convince the Corinthians that it is true. The apostle's first line of proof, therefore, is the Scripture, and the quotation of Is. 29:14 (LXX) is intended to

---

[40]G. Bertram, *TDNT,* 4 (Grand Rapids: Eerdmanns, 1967), 845f.

[41]Notice how it is parallel to weakness in v. 25.

[42]Conzelmann thinks that Paul's choice of *dunamis theou* instead of *sophia* "points to the fact that faith is not a habitus which—on a higher plane—again makes possible the independent operation of a wisdom of our 'own' " (*1 Corinthians,* 41 n. 15). See also Wilckens, *Weisheit,* 24.

prove his statement in v. 18, as is indicated by the appearance of the *gar* ("for") at the introduction of the citation. Furthermore, it also demonstrates that wisdom's overthrow is foreordained by God.[43] The point Paul makes is that the overthrow of *sophia/sunesis* ("wisdom/intelligence") is an established principle of the God's operation with people.[44]

But there is still more to Paul's use of the quotation. He has changed the last word from *krupsō* ("I will hide"), which appears in the original version, to *athetēsō* ("I will bring to nothing"), which is probably imported into the text from Ps. 32:10 (LXX; Ps. 33:10 in RSV).[45] This strengthens the thrust of the quotation. It is God's design not merely to conceal the true wisdom but to destroy it! And that is done where the cross of Christ is preached *ouk en sophiai logou* ("not in wisdom of word").[46]

> Where is the wise man? Where is the scribe? Where is the disputant of this age? Did not God make foolish the wisdom of the world? For since in the wisdom of God the world did not acknowledge God through wisdom, God resolved to save those who believe through the folly of what is preached. (vv. 20-21).

Having stated his thesis in v. 18 that the cross of Christ is, paradoxically, the power of God, and having proven from the Old Testament that it is God's intention to destroy the wisdom of the wise (vv. 18-19), Paul now draws out the implications for his readers. The fundamental significance is that the wisdom of the world is in a state of total collapse. Paul makes this point emphatically through the rhetorical questions of v. 20.

The first three questions are descriptive of persons and represent a change from the abstract nature of the argument up to this point. Is this because, as Conzelmann suggests, the apostle is alluding to Scriptural formulations in Isaiah?[47] Or is it because Paul wants to throw the light of biblical truth on the Corinthians who fancy that they have become "wise" (1 Cor. 4:8-10)? For the answer to the question, "Where is the wise, the scribe, the disputant of this age?" is obviously expected to be: such a person does not exist!

The questions are arranged anaphorically, with the triple repetition of *pou* ("where"). The climax is in the third member, as is apparent from its

---

[43]Barrett, *First Epistle*, 52 Conzelmann, *1 Corinthians, 42.*

[44]Hering (*First Epistle*, 8) notes that *sophia* and *sunesis* are almost synonymous here, due to the parallelism of Hebrew poetry. He does not think they are meant pejoratively in the quotation. However, cf. Conzelmann (*1 Corinthians*, 42) who argues that both words stand for an attitude of *hubris* ("pride, arrogance").

[45]Conzelmann, *1 Corinthians*, 42 n. 21.

[46]Wilckens, *Weisheit*, 25f. Robin Barbour, "Wisdom and the Cross in 1 Corinthians 1 and 2," in *Theologia Crucis—Signum Crucis* (Tübingen: Mohr-Siebeck, 1979), 63, also notes that through the use of the quotation Paul broadens the impact with a universal note. Schütz makes a similar observation (*Anatomy*, 193).

[47]Conzelmann, *1 Corinthians*, 42f. See Is. 19:11f. and 33:18f. Wilckens raises this question too but does not answer it (*Weisheit*, 26 n. 1).

length.[48] Who, then, is meant by each of the three terms, *sophos* (*"wise"*), *grammateus* (*"scribe"*), *suzētētēs* (*"disputant"*)? Wilckens contends that *sophos* is the more comprehensive term, which is then made more specific by the use of *grammateus*, a reference to the scribe who represents Jewish theology, while *suzētētēs* is descriptive of Greek philosophy. Each of these is the *sophos* in their respective cultures. In this way Paul unfolds the meaning of the *sophos* in such a way as to characterize wisdom as the wisdom of the world (v. 20b.).[49]

Paul intends to strike a universal note. This can be seen in the closing words of the third question, *tou aiōnos toutou* (*"of this age"*). The phrase should be understood as also implied in the other two questions.[50] "This age" is a term from Jewish apocalyptic, where it is used to differentiate the present evil age from that of the coming messianic era. The expression had a qualitative as well as temporal significance, since it was used to represent life in the present as lived under enslavement to powers that are hostile to God. Thus it is almost synonymous with the expressions "this world" or "the world," the latter of which appears in v. 20b.[51] The thrust of the rhetorical questions, therefore, is not only that, in view of God's destruction of wisdom (v. 19), the "wise" do not exist, but every attempt at resurrecting such a wisdom is a sign of one's enslavement to powers which are enemies of God.

Of course, Paul knows full well that there still are in the world people recognized as "wise" according to the usual human standards. By their criteria the cross is "folly." Does Paul mean, then, that theirs is a pseudo-wisdom? Not very likely, answers Wilckens, in view of the fact that in v. 18 the contrary term to "folly" was not "wisdom" but the "power of God." Rather, Wilckens goes on, "Does it not follow that if God makes nothing the wisdom of the wise, then it becomes nothing as such?"[52] That this is an accurate understanding of the text is evident from v. 21b, where Paul, again in the form of a final rhetorical question, asserts that God "made foolish the wisdom of the world." His statement must be taken literally in order to obtain its full force. Paul is not saying that God shows up the world's wisdom as foolish, but God actually "makes its wisdom

---

[48]Conzelmann, *1 Corinthians*, 43.

[49]Wilckens, *Weisheit*, 28. See also Barbour, "Wisdom and the Cross," 63f. But cf. Hering, who thinks *sophos* refers to the Greek, *grammateus* to the Jew, and *sudzētētēs* to the sophist, either Greek or Jew (*First Epistle*, 9).

[50]Conzelmann, *1 Corinthians*, 43.

[51]Schütz, *Anatomy*, 193. Barrett, *First Epistle*, 53. Conzelmann, *1 Corinthians*, 43. Conzelmann points out, though, that in apocalyptic thought the counterpart to "this age" was "the coming age," an expression which is absent in Paul. This suggests that Paul's eschatology is not based on a strictly apocalyptic outlook.

[52]Wilckens, *Weisheit*, 26.

foolish.''[53] That is to say, all human attempts at wisdom God reduces to folly, in both senses in which *mōria* (''folly'') was explained above; that is, wisdom is reduced not only to intellectual chaos, but to disgrace! And that in turn is comprehensible in view of the fact that ''wisdom'' *(sophia)*, as we have seen, is an attitude which tries to make a claim on God according to one's own criteria (cf. Rom. 1:22ff.).[54]

The fact that ''wisdom'' is characterized by such an attitude explains why wisdom is now described at the end of v. 20 as ''the wisdom of the world'' *(tēn sophian tou kosmou)*. The *kosmos* (''world'') represents the comprehensive, ''temporal-historical'' dimension of the ''wise'' *(sophos)*, and thus of ''wisdom'' *(sophia)*.[55]*Kosmos* thereby makes Paul's reference to ''wisdom'' more precise. At the same time the term suggests two important nuances, as can be seen from Paul's usage elsewhere; namely, the *kosmos* is sphere of the lordship of sin and death, and for that reason it has only a provisional status in view of its end on the last day.[56] Therefore, as Wilckens sees, it is understandable how and why Paul adds *tou aiōnos toutou* (''of this age'') in v. 20a. The additional reference not only takes into its embrace the Greeks, but all the ''wise,'' both Jews as well as Greeks. Wilckens summarizes, ''In this way Paul simultaneously places *sophia tou kosmou* in theologically implicit proximity to sin.''[57]

Verse 21 explains the attitude and action of God which Paul has described in vv. 19-20. Whereas the previous two verses dealt with God's having made foolish the wisdom of the world in an absolute sense, now Paul turns to supply the proof of that fact in historical terms. That is clear from the opening words of the verse, *epeidē gar* (''for since''), which introduces the causal clause.[58]

The construction of the sentence itself provides an important clue to the direction of Paul's argument. It is, first of all, composed of a double antithesis. The *sophia* (''wisdom'') of God appears in opposition to that of the world, a *sophia* which is ranged in opposition to the *mōria* (''foolishness'') of the proclamation which saves.[59] But then there is also the important fact that a change in subject occurs halfway through the verse, *kosmos* (''world'') being the subject of the causal clause and *ho theos* (''God'') being the new subject in the second clause.[60] To this fact must

---

[53]Conzelmann, *1 Corinthians*, 43.

[54]Ibid., 44 n. 45.

[55]Wilckens, *Weisheit*, 28.

[56]Ibid. See 1 Cor. 11:32 and 7:29, for example.

[57]Ibid., 29.

[58]*Epeidē* is causal in the New Testament. See Wilckens, *Weisheit*, 29, and Conzelmann, *1 Corinthians*, 44 n. 51.

[59]Conzelmann, *1 Corinthians*, 45.

[60]Wilckens, *Weisheit*, 29.

be added another, related, feature of the sentence. The conclusion does not flow logically from the causal clause. Since the world "did not know God through wisdom," one expects to be told of God's punitive action. Instead we are informed of God's decision to save.[61] Finally, the verse is constructed of verbs in the aorist tense, which implies past activity, even though Paul's chief interest is in the present (cf. the prominence of the present tense in vv. 18 and 22-25). This would seem to be due to Paul's focus on the turning-point in God's dealings with the world, a matter which occurred in the past but which has importance in interpreting the present.[62] The verse is constructed, therefore, in such a way that although a historical opposition between the world and God is set forth, we are not to imagine this implies a stand-off. From Paul's perspective God and the world are not equal partners in the conflict (v. 25!). It is God's action that Paul is especially concerned with. The change of subject, the concluding assertion, and the past/punctiliar force of the aorist all point to the decisiveness of God's saving activity through the "folly of the proclamation" of Christ crucified (v. 23). Paul's absolute assertions of vv. 19-20 are now located historically in such a way as to provide the theme which he will carry out in vv. 22ff., a theme which embraces the congregation at Corinth.[63] The movement of Paul's thought is downward, from macrocosmic broad truth in the economy of God to the cosmic reality in human history and finally to the microcosmic interpretation of Christian experience in Corinth (vv. 26-31) and in Paul's own apostolic activity (2:1-5).

The causal clause of v. 21a addresses an essential opposition between God and the world. In fact, it is a basic contradiction. On the one hand, even though human wisdom has been destroyed (v. 19), there still is a certain wisdom available in the world. But the world failed to capitalize on it. That wisdom is referred to by the expression *en tēi sophiai tou theou* ("in the wisdom of God"). But what exactly is God's wisdom, and what force does the *en* ("in") have? When those two closely-related questions are answered, we can begin to see why it was necessary for God to act as he is said to have done in the concluding clause.

Although it is a matter of dispute among scholars, the reference to the "wisdom of God" is very likely to be understood in terms of the created order, as can be seen by the close parallel in Rom. 1:18-23.[64] This interpretation

---

[61]Schütz, *Anatomy*, 195.

[62]Wilckens, *Weisheit*, 30. Schütz, *Anatomy*, 194.

[63]Schütz, *Anatomy*, 194.

[64]Wilckens, *Weisheit*, 32-34. Hering, *First Epistle*, 10. Conzelmann doubts this, although he admits this is the simplest explanation. Instead, he believes Paul is borrowing from Jewish wisdom speculation of a particular type: "vanished" wisdom. The myth runs as follows: " . . . (wisdom) appeared in the world, was rejected, withdrew to heaven, appeared again from there,

is strengthened if, as Wilckens argues, the *en* ("in") is taken in its "local basic meaning," instead of being construed in a temporal or instrumental sense.[65] This explanation, like the former, is simplest and fits well with the context. *En* would thus reflect a spatial understanding. It would be the area of the world's existence and therefore also a means to knowledge of God.[66] What then is Paul trying to say? Wilckens answers, "The world was 'In the midst of wisdom,' i.e. surrounded by it, so that it has been the world's area of existence. But just the same, the world did not recognize God in it, i.e. it turned away from God."[67] Why so? Because the world insisted on knowing God by means of its own wisdom, *dia tēs sophias* ("through wisdom").[68] The world of both Jews and Greeks (vv. 20, 22), demands "that the kerygma conform to their own norms and criteria."[69]

In view of the heavily charged atmosphere of v. 21a it should come as no surprise that the expression *ouk egnō* ("did not know") has a pregnant sense. From the Old Testament Paul works with the idea that knowledge of God is a relationship term. Knowing God means to know him in his saving action (particularly the Exodus) and acknowledging him in obedience.[70] Therefore, as Wilckens explains, the fact that the world "did not know God" means "not so much something like ignorance, but non-recognition, i.e. rejection of

---

but now only to the small circle of the chosen, i.e., the wise." Thus for Paul wisdom of God would be a sphere of existence and of knowledge, simultaneously (*1 Corinthians*, 45f.) Conzelmann may be correct with regard to his latter point, but the fact that Paul does not speak of wisdom withdrawing, as Conzelmann is forced to admit, raises serious questions about Jewish wisdom speculation being the background. Cf. Archibald Robertson and Alfred Plummer, *A Critical and Exegetical Commentary on the First Epistle of St. Paul to the Corinthians* (Edinburgh: Clark, 1914), 21; they believe the reference is to God's acts in the history of religions.

[65]Conzelmann points out that *en* in the temporal sense would be unusual for Paul, since nowhere does he speak of an epoch without sin (*1 Corinthians*, 45). He also notes that the instrumental use of *en* is made doubtful because of the appearance of *dia* in the instrumental sense at the end of the causal clause ("through wisdom"); while such a change for rhetorical reasons conforms to Paul's style, here it would leave *tou theou* ("of God") isolated and difficult to understand in the context (Ibid., 45 n. 56).

[66]Ibid., 45.

[67]Wilckens, *Weisheit*, 34.

[68]Notice the use here of *sophia* ("wisdom") conspicuously without the addition of *tou theou* ("of God"). See again Rom. 1:18-23. Clearly implied is that "wisdom" refers to human wisdom, as in vv. 17, 19-20. See also Barrett (*First Epistle*, 54), whose reflections on this point are worth quoting: "God is as truly manifest in his creation as any artist is manifest in his workmanship, but God is not apprehended in his creation because there is no manifestation of God that man's essentially self-regarding wisdom does not twist until it has made God in its own image."

[69]Wilckens, *Weisheit*, 34.

[70]Ibid., 30. In hellenistic Judaism *ouk egnō* ("did not know") became a key term in their mission to the heathen. The heathen do not know God, so they worship idols. Acknowledging God was the first step to faith (Ibid., 30f.).

God.''[71] Not to be overlooked is the fact that this reproach of ''not knowing God,'' which was often hurled at the world by Jewish theology, is here turned against the Jews themselves, since they are a part of the world which in its entirety has rejected God.[72]

It is this failure on the part of the world which explains why God has acted, why God suddenly becomes the subject in the second part of the verse. For all its own vaunted wisdom, the world stands impotent before the one thing in all the world worth knowing, God himself. As we noted before, the surprising aspect is that God has not acted in judgment. This would be completely expected in view of the world's refusal to acknowledge God. Yet Paul sets forth that God has ''decided to save those who believe.'' That this salvation belongs entirely on the side of God is obvious from the choice of the verb *eudokēsen* (''he was pleased/he decided;'' cf. Gal. 1:15!). The verb implies a free, sovereign choice on God's part. But that choice does not imply some new knowledge of God. Instead it is an ''act of salvation intended for the world'' (cf. 2 Cor. 5:19).[73]

If it is surprising that God has decided to save rather than destroy, it is utterly astonishing that he has elected to do so ''through the folly of what is proclaimed'' (*dia tēs mōrias tou kērugmatos*). It is important to observe, especially for Paul's theology of preaching, that the sovereign decision of God embraces *both* his purpose (salvation) and his instrument (the folly of the proclamation).[74]

What is the ''folly of the proclamation'' of which Paul speaks? The clear implication is that foolishness and preaching are inseparable, as Conzelmann observes in saying, ''Preaching is not merely *considered* to be foolish; it *is* foolish, by God's resolve.''[75] There is an essential offensiveness which characterizes preaching. And preaching must be understood here as meaning both in its content and its very activity. This interpretation is supported by the choice of words Paul has made. *Kērugma* as the description of preaching, like its verbal form *kērussein* which appears in v. 23, addresses the matter from the aspect of the preaching *activity,* rather than from the point of view of its content (cf. 2:4).[76] ''Proclamation'' was in the ancient world the work of the ''herald'' (*kērux*), who made a public declaration of an event (laws and ordinances, terms of peace, the public notification of games) on the authority

---

[71]Ibid., 31. Conzelmann describes it as an ''active refusal of recognition'' (*1 Corinthians,* 45).

[72]Wilckens, *Weisheit,* 31.

[73]Conzelmann, *1 Corinthians,* 46. See also Schütz, *Anatomy,* 195.

[74]See Conzelmann, *1 Corinthians,* 46.

[75]Ibid. See also Wilckens, *Weisheit,* 36-37.

[76]G. Friedrich, *TDNT,* 3 (Grand Rapids: Eerdmanns, 1965), 703-704. This article is the source for the description which follows (Ibid., 703-717).

of a king or god, an event which became enacted in its very announcement. The content is important to the *kērugma,* of course, because that is what is actualized in the proclamation. In this case, Paul will go on to specify the content of the Christian message as "Christ crucified" (v. 23). But at this point the crucial significance for the use of the term *kērugma* is the issue of *authority.* Without the herald's being commissioned by someone in power, someone whose high authority is recognized, the herald's word is foundationless, "empty" (cf. v. 17! and Rom. 10:15). And that is exactly why the activity of preaching, no less than its content, is offensive. For the knowledge of the power and authority of God are precisely the question, as v. 21a shows. Since the world refuses to acknowledge God, it does not recognize his authority, and thus for any herald to offer a public declaration in his behalf constitutes an absurdity and unbecoming conduct. The *kērugma* as a form of Christian address, then, precisely because from the perspective of this world it represents utter weakness (cf. v. 25), is a scandal and a folly (v. 23). Proclamation does not seek to convince the world on the basis of the world's criteria. God does not offer a "new" *sophia,* he does not meet the world on its terms, but he overturns its wisdom.[77] And on the basis of the world's failure, God simply "declares" his salvation as located in the cross of Christ.[78] And the fact that God intends for his salvation to be universal, for the entire world, comes to light in Paul's concluding words, "for those who believe" (*tous pisteuontas*).

> While Jews demand signs and Greeks seek wisdom, we preach Christ crucified, to Jews a scandal and to the gentiles folly, but to the ones who are called, both Jews and Greeks, Christ is the power of God and the wisdom of God; because the foolishness of God is wiser than men, and the weakness of God is stronger than men (vv. 22-25).

The repetition of *epeidē* ("since, because"), which introduced the decisive statement of v. 21, signifies that what follows is a sharper restatement of the thought.[79] In the context of vv. 19-20 the Jews and Greeks represent the civilized, cultured world, but here the concern is even more the division of the world into the two groups representing psychological attitudes.[80] The Jews "demand" (*aitousin*) miracles. The Greeks "seek" (*zētousin*) wisdom. Common to both is "the demand for a *proof* of the divine truth," thus to be in a position to pass judgment on God.[81] It is this attitude which accounts for the world's refusal to acknowledge God (v. 21a).

---

[77]Schütz, *Anatomy,* 194.

[78]Ibid., 195.

[79]Barrett, *First Epistle,* 54.

[80]Conzelmann, *1 Corinthians,* 46.

[81]Ibid., 47. On the reputed characteristic of the Jews to demand signs being a demonstration of their wickedness Conzelmann points to Mark 8:11, Matthew 12:38f., Luke 11:16, and John 6:30. He notes that *zētein* ("ask") is a term referring to philosophical investigation, but

As v. 22 restates v. 21a, so also vv. 23-24 restate the theme-note of salvation in v. 21b. Since God does not capitulate to human demands, he puts his salvation into motion through his "foolish" proclamation. As a result, Paul can say as herald and apostle of God, "we proclaim Christ crucified" (*kērussomen Christon estaurōmenon*).

There are two essential thrusts to the apostle's description of this task. One is the fact that Christ is proclaimed as having been crucified. Notice that Paul uses the perfect tense in the word *estaurōmenon* ("who has been crucified"), because the Greek perfect denotes an action in the past which has continuing significance in the present. This means that the emphasis lies not on the manner of his dying, but on the continuing status of his death, so that, as Robinson restates it, "Though Christ did not remain dead, but is alive, he remains—as the risen Christ—the crucified one."[82] His ignominious death cannot be quickly brushed aside as having been simply dismissed by the resurrection, as the Corinthians very likely think. The fact that Christ has been crucified remains in force, its offensiveness unremitting.

The other, and even more important, thrust is the emphasis on *kērussomen* ("we proclaim"), as can be seen by the attention given to the act of preaching in vv. 21, 23, 2:2, and 2:4.[83] This interpretation is confirmed on the one hand by Horsley's investigation, which shows that *sophia* ("wisdom") in this context is important as a form of speech, and on the other by Conzelmann's observation that Paul's use of the first person plural makes the style of the statement that of a confession.[84] Thus Paul does not regard the essence of his ministry of God's gospel as engaging the attention of humanity by means of demonstration of wonders or by wisdom speculation. Rather it is a case of heralding the message that the one whom God raised from the dead is exactly the same one who bears the marks of degradation in his having been crucified. Or, as Schütz says, "The proclamation of the cross is the

---

suggests it means here only "desire" (Ibid., 46 n. 75). However, if the significance, as Conzelmann says, is that both Jews and Greeks insist on proof of God's claims, then to translate *zētein* as "desire" is much too weak. See also Robertson-Plummer, *Critical and Exegetical Commentary*, 22. Robinson observes that *sēmeia* ("sign"), *sophian* ("wisdom"), and *kērugma* ("proclamation") occur together in vv. 21-22, but elsewhere only at Matthew 12:38-42 and parallel in Luke 11:29-32, which is from the Q source. This suggests, he says, that the Corinthians may have found the sayings of Q "congenial to their positions" (*Trajectories*, 42f.).

[82]William Childs Robinson, Jr., "Word and Power (1 Corinthians 1:17–2:5)," in *Soli Deo Gloria*, edited by J. McDowell Richards (Richmond: John Knox, 1968), 71.

[83]Ibid., 73. Thus Robinson insists, against Schmithals and Wilckens, that the emphasis is not on the Corinthian rejection of the soteriological understanding of Jesus' death, but on the fact of its being central to the proclamation.

[84]Horsley, "Wisdom of Word," 224-231. Conzelmann, *1 Corinthians*, 47.

bridge from the deed itself to those who are called, for whom Christ is the power and wisdom of God.''[85]

In view of the fact that the Christ who is proclaimed by Paul as the center of God's salvation remains the crucified and that this is delivered to people by public proclamation, it is no surprise that the world, both Jews and Greeks, find this proclamation a "scandal" (*skandalon*) and "folly" (*mōrian*). Since we have already examined the significance of folly, it only remains for us here to say what is meant by "scandal." *Skandalon* means an "offence," some thing which arouses revulsion and opposition.[86] Munck is probably quite correct in regarding the term as being close to "blasphemy."[87] The accent on revulsion, then, parallels the intense feeling of repugnance which accompanies "folly" (*mōria*). Paul insists that the proclaiming of Christ crucified is destined to meet with utter revulsion on the part of the world. This is not only because certain expectations and sensibilities have been transgressed. It is also because if such a proclamation is true, then every human boast, all "sinful self-reliance before God" is collapsed.[88] Few have said it better than Käsemann:

> The cross always remains scandal and foolishness for Jew and Gentile, inasmuch as it exposes man's illusion that he can transcend himself and effect his own salvation, that he can all by himself maintain his own strength, his own wisdom, his own piety and his own self-praise even towards God. In the light of the cross God shows all this, and ourselves as well, to be foolish, vain and godless. For everyone is foolish, vain, and godless who wants to do, without God and contrary to God, what only God himself can do. Whether it is the devout man who makes the attempt or whether it is the criminal is in the last resort unimportant. Only the creator can be the creature's salvation, not his own works.[89]

What Paul accomplishes with his accent on the proclamation of the crucified Christ is the establishment of a "new and controlling paradigm of God's mode of action."[90]

Having revealed and substantiated that the character of the gospel of Christ is a double offense, in that the Christ is the crucified and in that salvation is enacted by merely heralding the crucified Christ, Paul now turns to describe its surprising results for those who accept it. It is interesting that after referring to the recipients of salvation as *sōizomenois* ("the saved") in v. 18 and

---

[85]Schütz, *Anatomy*, 196.

[86]*BAG*, 760.

[87]Munck, *Paul and the Salvation*, 149. Hering is doubtless correct in describing the cross as *skandalon* ("stumbling block") to the Jews in the sense that it is an "insult to their messianic hopes, which were essentially political. A suffering Messiah was completely unknown at that period" (*First Epistle*, 10f.). However, for Paul the issue is not messianism, but the larger issue of human expectations and criteria.

[88]Robinson, Jr., "Word and Power," 75.

[89]Käsemann, "The Saving Significance," 40-41.

[90]Meeks, *First Urban Christians*, 180.

as *pisteuontas* ("believers") in v. 21, Paul now changes the designation to *klētois* ("called").[91] This descriptive term for Christians reemphasizes that one does not achieve salvation, but receives it as a gift of God.[92] One comes to God only by invitation. Here the term appears in the third person plural, which gives an objectifying sense to the term and leaves the invitation of God open to all, as is apparent from the inclusion of "both Jews and Greeks."[93] The word *klētois* ("called") is strengthened by the pronoun *autois* (literally "themselves" or "the very ones," a turn of phrase difficult to translate into English) which stands in the emphatic position at the beginning of the verse.[94] The "called" are those who are the focus of the proclamation of Christ and by this means are granted the "power of God and the wisdom of God" in Christ.[95] Of course Paul means this in a paradoxical sense.[96] By the world's standards it is a form of disgraceful nonsense. That is why it must be a power and wisdom located only in God, as is shown by the fact that Paul repeats *theou* ("of God").[97] And only now, after he has described the demise of the world's wisdom by God's act and located God's salvation in the foolish proclamation of the crucified Christ, does Paul use the term which we expected already in v. 18, *sophia* ("wisdom"). Paul can use the term only after investing it with new content, lest it be misunderstood as a new worldly wisdom.[98] As Schütz points out, "There can be no Christ the *sophia theou* ["wisdom of God"] without there being first Christ the *mōria* ["folly"] by this world's standards, and the *mōria kērugmatos* ["folly of preaching"] based on that."[99]

Verse 25 serves as a concise, broadly formulated conclusion. It also makes a transition to the following passage.[100] The saying is set off by its parallelism and chiastic relation to v. 24—*to mōron* ("the foolish") relates to *sophian* ("wisdom") and *to asthenes* ("the weak") to *dunamis* ("power")—so that it stands on its own as a maxim which "becomes a definition of the historical

---

[91]Conzelmann, *1 Corinthians*, 47 n. 81.

[92]*BAG*, 437. See also Conzelmann, *1 Corinthians*, 27f.

[93]Conzelmann, *1 Corinthians*, 47.

[94]Robertson-Plummer point out that *autois* ("themselves") corresponds to *humin* ("you") in v. 18 and is an appeal to personal experience (*Critical and Exegetical Commentary*, 23).

[95]Although the participle "crucified" is not repeated, it is obviously understood as implied. See Robertson-Plummer, *Critical and Exegetical Commentary*, 23. Also, the conjunction of *dunamis* ("power") and *sophia* ("wisdom") here shows, as Conzelmann says, that *sophia* is not understood as a hypostasis (*1 Corinthians*, 48).

[96]Barrett, *First Epistle*, 56.

[97]Wilckens, *Weisheit*, 39f. Wilckens calls attention to the repeated mention of "God" (*theos*) in this whole section (Ibid., 215ff.).

[98]Ibid., 38. See also Schütz, *Anatomy*, 195.

[99]Schütz, *Anatomy*, 195.

[100]Hering, *First Epistle*, 11.

relationship which God establishes through the cross.''[101] Because God is the sovereign of the world, he dictates the terms of strength and weakness, wisdom and foolishness. We must note that Paul has changed the expression from the abstract noun *mōria* (''folly''), which he has used continuously through his argument (vv. 18, 21, 23), to the neuter adjective *mōron* (''foolish''), thus orienting the word to a ''particular act of 'foolishness.' ''[102] The same would be true of the neuter adjective *asthenes* (''weak''). There is no doubt that Paul, though broadening the statement to be generally descriptive of God's relationship to the world, still has the cross in mind. Barrett provides a useful summary and concluding point: ''What God has done in Christ crucified is a direct contradiction of human ideas of wisdom and power, yet it achieved what human wisdom and power fail to achieve. It does convey the truth about God (and man), and it does deliver man from his bondage.''[103]

> For look at your calling, brothers; namely, that not many (of you) are wise according to the flesh, not many powerful, not many of noble birth. But God chose the foolish things of the world in order to disgrace the wise, and God chose the weak things of the world in order to disgrace the strong, and the ignoble and contemptible things of the world, things that do not exist, God chose in order to reduce to nothing the things that are, so that no flesh might boast in the presence of God. You are, then, by it [i.e., God's election] in Christ Jesus, who by God was made wisdom for us, (our) righteousness and sanctification and redemption, in order that, as it is written, ''Let him who boasts boast in the Lord'' (vv. 26-31).

As further proof of his argument in vv. 18-25 Paul directs the attention of the Corinthians to their own experience. The connection with the preceding is indicated by the appearance of *gar* (''for'') at the beginning of the sentence.[104] The style of the passage is striking for its obvious rhetorical features. Its diatribe style introduces a dialogical element which engages the reader.[105] The forcefulness of the argument is also enhanced by the repetition of key phrases.[106] Both features testify to the importance the apostle attaches to his address at this point.

Paul calls the Corinthians to ''look at'' (*blepete*) their own ''calling'' (*klēsin*). The latter connects with his reference to the ''called'' (*klētoi*) in

---

[101]Conzelmann, *1 Corinthians*, 48.

[102]Barrett, *First Epistle*, 56. But cf. Robertson-Plummer (*Critical and Exegetical Commentary*, 23), who caution that the expression should not be pressed. Hering's interpretation (*First Epistle*, 11) that what is meant is the ''so-called foolishness of God'' is far too weak.

[103]Barrett, *First Epistle*, 56.

[104]Schütz, *Anatomy*, 97. See also Conzelmann (*1 Corinthians*, 49 n. 1), who calls attention to the fact that *gar* (''for'') with the imperative corresponds to the inferential sense described in *BAG* (section 3). Cf. *BAG*, 151.

[105]Conzelmann, *1 Corinthians*, 49.

[106]This, says Hering, is according to the anaphoristic style of the Greek orators (*First Epistle*, 12). Note the repetition of the phrases ''not many'' (*ou polloi*), ''of the world'' (*tou kosmou*), and ''God chose'' (*exelexato ho theos*).

v. 24.[107] Here the emphasis falls on the act of calling rather than on the state of their being called.[108] This is borne out by the explanation that follows in which the stress falls on *exelexato ho theos* ("God chose").[109] The fact of the matter, Paul points out, is that the very composition of the Corinthian congregation is evidence of the character of God's manner of working. For God called "not many" (*ou polloi*) who were "wise" (*sophoi*), "powerful" (*dunatoi*), or "of noble birth" (*eugeneis*). And to make more precise what he means the apostle adds the significant phrase *kata sarka* ("according to the flesh") to the word *sophoi* ("wise").[110] This qualifer is doubtless also to be understood as applying to the other two words, "powerful" and "of noble birth."[111] The phrase *kata sarka* means "by human standards."[112] The three adjectives, therefore, are sociologically descriptive terms. *Sophos* ("wise") refers to the educated people, *dunatoi* ("powerful") to the politically influential, and *eugeneis* ("nobly born") to those of distinguished family.[113]

Paul's reference to the sociological composition of the congregation introduces an important aspect into the interpretation of the text. If it is true that not many were educated, influential or well-born, then there are some few who were. On the basis of this observation Theissen has performed pioneering work in his attempt to describe the social differences and stratification of the Corinthian congregation, based on sociological clues found in the Corinthian letters and literature from the Greco-Roman world.[114] The results of his investigation indicate that the church encompassed various social strata, but with the power and leadership focused in

---

[107]Wilckens, *Weisheit*, 41.

[108]Ibid., 42. Conzelmann, *1 Corinthians*, 49. Schütz, *Anatomy*, 197. Cf. Barrett, who thinks it refers to the circumstances in which they were called (*First Epistle*, 57).

[109]Wilckens, *Weisheit*, 42.

[110]Conzelmann, *1 Corinthians*, 50.

[111]However, Conzelmann thinks *kata sarka* ("according to the flesh") is added to *sophoi* ("wise") because the term is equivocal in the context, while *dunatoi* ("powerful") and *eugeneis* ("of noble birth") are not (*1 Corinthians*, 49).

[112]Barrett, *First Epistle*, 57. Schütz understands *kata sarka* ("according to the flesh") as refering to *sophia tou kosmou* ("wisdom of the world") in v. 21 (*Anatomy*, 197). Hering says it is synonymous with *kosmos* ("world") (*First Epistle*, 12). Conzelmann points out that *kata sarka* combines with the adjective *sophos* ("wise"), while *tou kosmou* ("of the world") combines with the substantive *sophia* ("wisdom") (*1 Corinthians*, 49f.)

[113]Conzelmann, *1 Corinthians*, 50. Wilckens, *Weisheit*, 41. Theissen especially notes that this is supported by the fact that *eugeneis* ("nobly born") is set opposite *mē onta* ("things that are not"), both of which, for the Greeks, are sociological terms (*Social Setting*, 70-73). But cf. Horsley ("Wisdom of Word," 233), who argues that the terms come from the Philonic description of those who are in perfection of religious status. Cf. also Munck, *Paul and the Salvation*, 162.

[114]Theissen, *Social Setting*, 69-119.

the "not many" who were members of higher social status.[115] Theissen believes that the new multi-level social group meant a profound altering of social relationships so that a new pattern of social integration occurred which he calls "love patriarchalism."[116] In this arrangement the majority of poorer, low-status members looked to the few higher-status members to supply their needs, while the higher-status members expected a trusting submission on the part of the low-status members, all within a context of mutual care and respect.[117] According to Theissen this new pattern of "love patriarchalism" did not function without problems, however, and there were conflicts in terms of relationships both within and outside the community.[118] Within the church these conflicts had to do with the distribution of power and authority, and this is probably reflected in the squabbling among people who attached themselves to the "powerful" figures referred to in 1:10-16.[119]

This new, somewhat problematical arrangement may also have been complicated by one other factor. Meeks has suggested there is evidence in Corinth of what he calls "high status inconsistency."[120] This means that for members of the community "their achieved status is higher than their attributed status."[121] Or, to put it differently, in a mercantile city such as Corinth, begun as a Roman colony of freedmen, where a certain upward mobility was possible in terms of the accumulation of wealth, one could achieve a higher station in life, as measured by material prosperity, but yet not be accorded the recognition expected from a higher socio-economic position, since social status has more than one dimension.[122] Such persons, for instance, may be deficient in the social criteria of education, political influence, or family background. Meeks hypothesizes that Christianity may very well have been attractive to exactly such persons whose social status was ambiguous, because the "emotionally effective symbols" of the proclamation of the exaltation of the crucified Messiah may have lent a strong sense of personal power and prominence to them.[123]

---

[115]Ibid., 96, 106. On the basis of New Testament material the socio-economic levels that appear most frequently, those of the "typical Christian," are the free artisan and the tradesman, according to Wayne Meeks, "The Social Context of Pauline Theology," *Int* 37 (July, 1982): 270.

[116]Ibid., 109. Meeks refers to the arrangement as patronage (*First Urban Christians*, 98, 119).

[117]Theissen, *Social Setting*, 108-110.

[118]Theissen finds these conflicts reflected in the questions of eating meat offered to idols and of the arrangements for the Lord's Supper (*Social Setting*, 121-174).

[119]Meeks, *First Urban Christians*, 117ff. See also Schütz, *Anatomy*, 187-203.

[120]Meeks, "Social Context," 271.

[121]Ibid.

[122]Ibid., 267ff. Meeks gives as a modern example the case of the university professor whose "occupation lends him a prestige he cannot afford to live up to" (Ibid., 268).

[123]Ibid., 271ff.

If the social description of Theissen and Meeks is accurate, it is completely intelligible why *sophia* (''wisdom'') could become a vital concern for those in Corinth who aspired to a higher status, whether they be from among the wealthy patrons or even among the artisans and poorer people. For *sophia* connoted, as we have seen, a certain recognizable sophistication. Denied the status accorded by virtue of belonging to the educated classes (*sophoi*), the message of Christ could easily be construed as a new substitute, a Christian *sophia* which accorded recognition and status, at least among the members of their own group. It is a seductive idea, and it is this Paul hastens to demolish with his argument of 1:18ff. Paul turns their attention back to the origins of their faith. They were called in the preaching of the crucified, a socially weak message and medium, which means any power and status is derived from God alone. Their status consists in the fact that God chose them, not in their worldly status, for few in the congregation came with any socially recognized credentials. The implication is, as Paul makes plain in what follows, that if their origin is characterized by God's choice, his call, then the model of their present conduct cannot be any *sophia* of the world, but rather his continued free choice.

That the congregation exists by God's free choice provides a positive alternative to worldly status; the Corinthians enjoy the place accorded those who are the ''called'' (*klētoi*) of God, v. 24. The other side of that new status, which Paul now elaborates in vv. 28-29, is God's ''negative act of creation,'' as Wilckens refers to it.[124] That is, God has made those of no status his choice precisely that he might ''disgrace'' (*kataischunēi*) and ''reduce to nothing'' (*katargēsēi*) all that which is accorded exalted status by the ''world'' (*tou kosmou*). This election testifies to God's sovereign power as creator.[125] He not only creates the world, but as its only sovereign he creates the criteria of its status, its exaltation, its ''boast'' (cf. v. 29). This God does first of all negatively, by overturning the world's standards. Instead of the symbols of fleshly power—education, political influence, and birth—God elects the ''foolish'' (*ta mōra*), the ''weak'' (*ta asthenē*), and the ''ignoble'' (*ta agenē*).[126] The purpose of this choice is to ''shame'' the wise and powerful.[127] It is to ''reduce to nothing'' the

---

[124]Wilckens, *Weisheit*, 43.

[125]Conzelmann, *1 Corinthians*, 50. The allusion to creation is plain from the *ex nihilo* reference in v. 28. See Schütz, *Anatomy*, 198, and Wilckens, *Weisheit*, 42f. But cf. Theissen, who informs us that the term *mē on* is a Greek sociological designation for those who are ''nothing'' (*Social Setting*, 72). Most likely the expression is doubly nuanced, a play on words which serves to orient social status in terms of the creation of God.

[126]The use of the neuter adjective emphasizes the attributes and generalizes the references, according to Conzelmann (*1 Corinthians*, 50 n. 15) and Barrett, *First Epistle*, 58).

[127]*Kataischunein* does not mean a ''mental condition of shame,'' Conzelmann says, but a ''situation of ignominy'' (*1 Corinthians*, 50 n. 20).

things which count for so much in the world.[128] In their place God creates, from all that is nothing, a "new creation," a new order of existence (cf. 2 Cor. 5:17!; Gal. 6:15). This corresponds precisely to the preaching of the cross. The existence of the Corinthian congregation is the very proclamation of the gospel as it can be seen in its effects, tearing down the old order and creating the new.

The motive in God's manner of working is revealed in the purpose clause of v. 29, "so that" *(hopōs)* no one "might boast before God."[129] "Boast" *(kauchēsis, kauchasthai)* in vv. 29 and 31 refers to a human attitude over against God, a matter of self-glorification which one "pursues by means of sophia ("wisdom")."[130] God's inversion of the standards of exaltation leave human beings without any possibility of a self-manufactured exaltation.[131]

Paul's argument from the Corinthian experience now circles back in his concluding statements of vv. 30-31. The apostle's reference to their call in v. 26 was described in terms of God's elective act, followed in vv. 27-29 by the negative implications, namely, his destruction of the world's standards. Now the call of the Corinthians is taken up again in vv. 30f., but this time the positive implications are elaborated. The world has been debased, but for the called there is a new existence. The *humeis* ("you") is emphatic here.[132] The Corinthians enjoy a new status "in Christ Jesus" *(en Christōi Iēsou),* which they have "by it" *(ex autou),* meaning God's act of election.[133]

In their new existence "in Christ" the Corinthians have received indeed a *sophia* ("wisdom"). But it is very carefully described by Paul in v. 30. It does not reside within the Corinthians, but resides in Christ. It is a wisdom that comes "from God" *(apo theou).* It is a wisdom that is "for us" *(hēmin,* note the dative), but not belonging to us.[134] And it is a wisdom that is immediately qualified in terms that are both soteriological and relational: Christ is their "righteousness" *(dikaiosunē),* "sanctification" *(hagiasmos),* and

---

[128]Barrett emphasizes that *katargēsein* is an eschatological term, meaning "do away with." He calls our attention to 2 Cor. 3:11 *(First Epistle,* 58).

[129]Hering is impressed by the "flagrant Hebraism" of the expression in v. 29, which, literally translated, is "that all flesh may not boast" *(First Epistle,* 13). Conzelmann regards it as a means of emphasis *(1 Corinthians,* 51).

[130]Conzelmann, *1 Corinthians,* 51.

[131]Ibid.

[132]Barrett, *First Epistle,* 59.

[133]Conzelmann, *1 Corinthians,* 51. He refers to 3:23 as evidence. Schütz observes that the believer lives *en Christōi* ("in Christ") versus existence *en sophiai* ("in wisdom"), v. 21 *(Anatomy,* 199).

[134]Schütz, *Anatomy,* 197.

"redemption" *(apolutrōsis)*.[135] This means that "wisdom," as reinterpreted by Paul, is a dimension of salvation and therefore has God alone as its origin. The "direction" of salvation is "from God, 'in Christ,' to us."[136] If there is to be any "boast" in the presence of God, therefore, the only legitimate boast is *en kuriōi* ("in the Lord"), as Paul emphasizes by his allusion to Jer. 9:22f. in v. 31.[137]

> And I, when I came to you, brothers, did not come proclaiming to you the mystery of God with a preeminence of word or wisdom. For I resolved not to know anything among you except Jesus Christ and him crucified (2:1-2).

Having supplied evidence for his argument in 1:18-25 on the basis of the experience of the Corinthians in 1:26-31, Paul now refers to himself as a further example of his claim that God has nullified the wisdom of the world in the proclamation of a crucified Christ.[138] In both cases, that of the experience of the Corinthians and of himself, the apostle refers back to the origin of the community, as is shown by the reference to his "coming" *(elthōn)*.[139] Paul describes the manner of his own initial proclamation among them in these verses, first in negative and then in positive terms.

At the outset it is important to observe that Paul describes the foundational work among the Corinthians in terms of preaching. The essential nature of his apostolic task is "proclaiming to you the mystery of God" *(kataggellōn humin to mustērion tou theou)*. Paul employs the verb *kataggelein* here, which has the dictionary meaning "to proclaim solemnly."[140] But though the word is different, Paul has the same preaching activity in mind as he did in 1:18-25, where he used *kērussein* ("to proclaim"). This is borne out by the reference to "Christ crucified" in v. 2, as well as the appearance of *kērugma* ("proclamation"). Of more importance is the fact that the word appears in the present tense, because it describes "the way in which the visit was occupied."[141] And the content of that activity is characterized as preaching the "mystery of God" *(to mustērion tou theou)*. This expression, however, is problematical. First there is a textual problem in that many manuscripts have *marturion* ("witness") instead of *mustērion*. Secondly, it is hard to decide whether the genitive *tou theou* ("of God") should be construed as objective or subjective. As to the first, *mustērion* ("mystery") would appear to

---

[135]Barrett especially emphasizes these terms as indicative of how the human being is related to God *(First Epistle*, 59).

[136]Conzelmann, *1 Corinthians*, 52.

[137]Ibid. Hering, *First Epistle*, 13.

[138]Conzelmann points out that *kagō* ("and I") is transitional, corresponding to *blepete* ("look") in 1:26, *(1 Corinthians*, 54).

[139]Ibid. Wilckens, *Weisheit*, 44. Cf. 1 Thess. 1:4ff., 2:1ff.

[140]*BAG*, 410. Hering's translation, "announce," is too feeble *(First Epistle*, 14).

[141]Robertson-Plummer, *Critical and Exegetical Commentary*, 30.

enjoy slightly better arguments, in that the word prepares for Paul's further discussion in 2:7ff. and also because the two verses here are parallel in thought structure, the expression "mystery of God" becoming connected with "Jesus Christ and him crucified" (2:2). In the context of Paul's whole argument this understanding fits best, since the cross is represented as a "mystery of divine providence."[142] This helps to answer the second question, about the correct understanding of the genitive construction. In the context, for Paul to speak of proclaiming the mystery *about* God (objective genitive) introduces an alien and essentially countervailing element into his argument, because then the expression would imply that Paul brought a special insight, a new *sophia* ("wisdom"), about God. And this is precisely what he has been arguing against. Instead, it is surely the mystery *from* God (subjective genitive), for this implies the revelatory activity of God and the demise of all human wisdom as a means to God, as Paul argued in 1:21.[143]

If Paul's foundational work was essentially occupied with preaching, then the way in which the "mystery of God" was borne to them is now described by the apostle, first negatively and then positively. Negatively, Paul did not arrive in Corinth preaching "with a preeminence of word or wisdom" *(kath huperochēn logou ē sophias)*. The word *huperochēn* carries with it connotations of superiority, prominence, and superfluity.[144] Paul means that he did not overwhelm them with an abundance "of word or wisdom" *(logou ē sophias)*. The conjunction of these two terms reminds us of their appearance together at the very start of Paul's argument in 1:17. There we noted that wisdom and speech were probably intertwined in the minds of the Corinthians. As a result Paul probably does not refer here to rhetorical skill, since, as Schütz explains, 1:17 "set the stage for a discussion not of dialectical skill but of the basic opposition between the cross and wisdom *as a principle* [emphasis mine]."[145] Rather, the discussion is about the criterion for his apostolic ministry, and by implication the pattern for congregational life (2:5).[146]

---

[142]Hering, *First Epistle*, 14f. The reading *mustērion* ("mystery") is also supported by Schütz (*Anatomy*, 199) and by the textual critic Metzger (*Textual Commentary*, 545). But *marturion* ("witness") is adopted by Barrett (*First Epistle*, 62f.) and Robertson-Plummer, who follow Lightfoot (*Critical and Exegetical Commentary*, 30). Conzelmann is hard pressed to decide between them (*1 Corinthians*, 53 n. 6).

[143]Those who opt for the objective genitive are, therefore, those who also adopt the reading *marturion* ("witness"). See Robertson-Plummer, *Critical and Exegetical Commentary*, 30, and Barrett, *First Epistle*, 63.

[144]*BAG*, 849, which notes in addition that *kata* "denotes kind and manner." Cf. Barrett, who turns *huperochēn* into an adjective, "preeminent" (*First Epistle*, 63), and Hering, who translates "a prominent point, eminence" (*First Epistle*, 14).

[145]Schütz, *Anatomy*, 199. Cf. the rhetorical interpretations of Barrett (*First Epistle*, 63) and Hering (*First Epistle*, 14).

[146]See Schütz's discussion, which focuses more on the content than on the manner of Paul and lifts up the importance of the criterion (*Anatomy*, 199f.).

Paul rejects any suggestion that the "mystery of God" be proclaimed in such a way as to be recognized by the criteria of "word or wisdom."

What, then, is Paul's criterion as represented in his *modus operandi?* The apostle answers that by his positive description in v. 2. Paul "resolved" *(ekrina)* not to "know anything" *(ti eidenai)* among the Corinthians except "Jesus Christ and him crucified" *(Iēsoun Christon kai touton estaurōmenon).* Paul's choice of the word *ekrina* ("resolved/decided") must not mislead us into thinking this represented a departure from his usual practice. The contrast is not between what he did in Corinth as opposed to his custom elsewhere, but between what he does everywhere as over against what others wish to do in Corinth.[147] And when the apostle refers to "not knowing anything" *(ti eidenai),* he does not mean general knowledge, but theological knowledge, which implies that the nature of his administration of the gospel is grounded in the cross.[148] It is also possible that the expression is intended in much the same sense as Paul used the term in 1:21. In that case Paul is saying he refuses to "acknowledge" or "recognize" any other standard than the cross. This interpretation is reinforced by Wilckens' observation that *eidenai* ("to know") corresponds content-wise (and, we might add, also in terms of the parallelism of structure) to *huperochēn logou ē sophias* ("preeminence of word or wisdom") in v. 1.[149]

The thrust of Paul's argument reaches its climax with the expression "Jesus Christ and him crucified." As Conzelmann proposes, this "shows that the corresponding statements in 1:17, 23 were intended to be exhaustive."[150] The heart of his proclamation, the "mystery" of God, is the cross, and that fact determines not only the content but the corresponding activity of preaching. Preaching is cruciform.

> And I was among you in weakness and in fear and in much trembling, and my message and my proclamation was not in persuasive words of wisdom, but in a demonstration of the Spirit and power, in order that your faith might not be in a wisdom of men but in the power of God (2:3-5).

The repetition of the initial word *kagō* ("and I") from 2:1 shows that vv. 3-5 constitute an extension of the same thought progression. The difference is that "vv. 1 and 2 show the unity between the form and content of preaching, vv. 3-5 the unity between the preaching and the existence of the preacher."[151] Paul's existence as preacher is represented in v. 3 by a

---

[147]Barrett, *First Epistle,* 64. He follows Moffatt. See also Munck, *Paul and the Salvation,* 147. The idea that Paul changed tactics because of the disastrous results of his attempted preaching in Athens (Acts 17:16-34), a view supported by Hering (*First Epistle,* 7f.), lacks any evidence, as Barrett points out (*First Epistle,* 63).

[148]Conzelmann, *1 Corinthians,* 54.

[149]Wilckens, *Weisheit,* 46.

[150]Conzelmann, *1 Corinthians,* 54.

[151]Ibid., 53f.

threefold characterization, "in weakness and fear and much trembling" *(en astheneiai kai en phobōi kai en tromōi pollōi).* But what precisely does he mean? It is possible that *astheneiai* ("weakness") refers to Paul's un-impressive speaking ability, or to illness.[152] And "fear and great trembling" *(en phobōi kai tromōi pollōi)* could mean his consciousness of bearing a great responsibility in preaching the gospel.[153] But more persuasive is the position adopted by Conzelmann and Wilckens, that the whole expression is to be understood in a "strictly theological sense."[154] Much more than a mere external appearance of weakness, Wilckens argues, Paul's "weakness" consists in the fact that "one misses in his appearance/demeanor *pneumatic dunamis,* which likely means 'signs of an apostle.' "[155] In addition, Wilckens informs us, the expression "fear and great trembling" marks the introduction of an Old Testament formula, also frequent in apocalyptic texts, which is descriptive of the experience of an epiphany, especially of an eschatological judgment.[156] This threefold characterization, Wilckens maintains, "corresponds exactly to the situation of the preacher of the proclamation of the cross."[157] He explains:

> As his preaching does not have *logos* ["word"] or *sophia* ["wisdom"] as its content, but Christ as crucified, thus he is marked in view of his own person not through strength, but rather through his own weakness, which consists in this, that he has at his disposal nothing of his own except the content of his proclamation. This situation as *the crisis of everything of one's own* Paul describes with the traditional formula "fear and trembling."[158]

Paul's weakness, then, is to be understood as based on the Christology which is oriented to the cross.[159] The cross is the symbol of weakness, and therefore the preacher's conduct in its proclamation must conform to it.

As Paul explained the nature of his missionary activity among the Corinthians both negatively and positively in vv. 1-2, so also in v. 4 he explains the weakness of his existence as preacher first negatively and then positively. His speaking of "message and proclamation" *(logos kai kērugma)* represents a "rhetorical duplication," as Conzelmann refers to it, and we should see no

---

[152]The former is the interpretation of Barrett (*First Epistle,* 64) and Robertson-Plummer (*Critical and Exegetical Commentary,* 32), while Conzelmann raises the latter possibility (*1 Corinthians,* 54).

[153]Barrett, *First Epistle,* 65. See also Robertson-Plummer, who call attention to the fact that *phobos kai tromos* ("fear and trembling") appear together in Eph. 6:5 to describe the slave's duty toward the master; the words are also combined at 2 Cor. 7:15 and Phil. 2:12 (*Critical and Exegetical Commentary,* 32).

[154]Conzelmann, *1 Corinthians,* 54. Wilckens, *Weisheit,* 46ff.

[155]Wilckens, *Weisheit,* 46f. He refers to the context and to 2 Cor. 10:1, 10 for support.

[156]Ibid., 47.

[157]Ibid., 48.

[158]Ibid.

[159]Ibid.

essential difference between the two words.[160] The double expression simply continues Paul's focus on the proclamatory nature of his mission activity in Corinth. The important aspect is the negative expression that his proclamation was not "in persuasive words of wisdom" *(en peithois sophias logois)*. This expression is troublesome textually, since there are eleven different variant readings, most of which revolve around the fact that *peithois* ("persuasive") does not occur anywhere else in all Greek literature.[161] The reading we have adopted, along with Conzelmann, is probably to be preferred.[162] In any event, it is apparent Paul does not want the proof or validity of his proclamation to be made subject to *sophia* ("wisdom"). Instead, the authenticity of the proclamation of Christ crucified consists in the "demonstration of the Spirit and power" *(apodeixei pneumatos kai dunameōs)*.[163] The appearance of "Spirit and power" are reminiscent of 1 Thess. 1:4-6, where Paul uses these terms to refer to the reception of the gospel by the Thessalonians. In that case the apostle is underscoring the fact that the very existence of the congregation is a sign that the proclamation of the cross, regarded as utter "weakness" by the world's standards, is in fact the operation of the power of God (1:18). The purpose clause which follows in v. 5 makes this interpretation all the more likely.

The purpose clause of v. 5, like v. 4, is also constructed antithetically. Only now the focus shifts (notice the change of the subject) to "faith" *(pistis)*, more specifically the faith of the Corinthians. Paul has not only proclaimed what he proclaimed, Christ crucified, but he has proclaimed *as* he did with God's ultimate purpose in mind. The purpose is, negatively, that the faith of his converts might not be "in human wisdom" *(en sophiai anthrōpōn)*.[164] Rather, the aim is that their faith should be, positively, in the "power of God" *(en dunamei theou)*. The fact that faith resides in the power of God,

---

[160]Conzelmann, *1 Corinthians*, 54. Barrett, however, thinks *logos* means "argument" here (*First Epistle*, 65).

[161]Metzger, *Textual Commentary*, 546. He also points out that *logois* ("words") is missing in several important manuscripts. Barrett suggests *peithois* ("persuasive") may have been coined by Paul (*First Epistle*, 65).

[162]Conzelmann, *1 Corinthians*, 55. See also Metzger, *Textual Commentary*, 546. But cf. Hering (*First Epistle*, 15), who thinks this reading is "inadmissible."

[163]Both Barrett (*First Epistle*, 65) and Wilckens (*Weisheit*, 51) support the idea that *apodeixei* refers here to "proof." Whether *pneumatos kai dunameōs* ("of the Spirit and power") is objective or subjective genitive is difficult to decide. Barrett may be quite right that Paul has both in mind (*First Epistle*, 65). On the other hand, for these words to be an objective genitive would mean Paul is taking a posture similar to the Corinthians, and since he is trying to collapse that position, we may be better advised to regard it as subjective. See Conzelmann, *1 Corinthians*, 55.

[164]Conzelmann thinks the introduction of *anthrōpōn* ("of men") in v. 5 may contain a "barb directed against the 'human' party slogans" and points to 3:3f. as evidence (*1 Corinthians,* 55).

not in human wisdom, has two vital facets. The first is that, if faith relies exclusively on the power of God, then it is "impossible for the believer to demonstrate his faith by displaying his power."[165] And the second is related to it. As Schütz observes, "If the Corinthians must be reminded *that* God 'chose what is foolish,' etc., then they must be reminded also of *how* he did so. He did so through the preaching of Paul, which is itself the very demonstration of God's power."[166] The accent in this concluding phrase, therefore, brings the argument full circle (see 1:18) and shows that Paul intends for his argument to address the specific problems in Corinth. If the power of God is the basis for the gospel and their existence as a congregation, then there is no basis for spiritual elitism (see 4:8ff.) nor for dissensions over relations to powerful figures (1:11ff.; cf. 3:5ff.). Instead, the exercise of their faith must conform to faith's basis, living out of the weakness of the gospel on the foundation of the power of God. Or, as Schütz puts it, "the apostolic paradigm is not merely an embodiment of the gospel ('the word of the cross') but a model for the church."[167]

C. Preliminary Observations

Various aspects of Paul's theology of preaching have come to light in 1 Cor. 1:18–2:5. Perhaps the most important is the disclosure of the basic model for preaching, which turns out to be the herald. Therefore, functionally speaking, the preaching of the gospel involves the public declaration, the heralding, of the terms and conditions of existence on the basis of God's authority. But because God's authority is not obvious, as measured by human standards, the preacher as herald stands in a vulnerable position. Preaching is thus a weak medium, both in content and form. It is conformed to the gospel, which has as its center the crucified Christ. Nonetheless, it is a powerful proclamation, for it establishes God's new creation, which is his church.

EXCURSUS ON FIRST CORINTHIANS 9:14-18

Paul's argument in 1 Cor. 2:1-5 appears again in the letter of 1 Corinthians. A parallel is to be found in 1 Cor. 9:14-18, where Paul demonstrates that his apostolic existence is keyed to the gospel and then turns his practice into a paradigm for the Corinthians. The passage is of particular interest to our

---

[165]Ibid.
[166]Schütz, *Anatomy*, 201f.
[167]Ibid., 203.

study of Paul's theology of preaching since there is a special concentration on his obligation to preach.

Paul's discussion in these verses deals with a problem that he himself has evidently created, albeit unintentionally, in supporting himself by working with his hands. The general context (unless, as some scholars suggest, chap. 9 is an interpolation) is chapters 8-10, where Paul takes up the issue of eating meat which has been offered to idols (see 8:1-13 and 10:14ff.).[168] The apostle's argument is that while the Christian knows that idols have no real existence and therefore the Christian is free to eat meat which has been sacrificed to them, at the same time if it does harm to the conscience of the brother, then the proper course of action is to renounce one's own rights and privileges in the other person's interests (see 8:9-13 and 10:31ff.). This principle is illustrated in chapter 9 by reference to his own apostolic practice of renouncing his legitimate right to receive financial support from the congregation to whom he is ministering. Paul says he has adopted this practice so as not to put an encumbrance in the way of their engagement with the gospel of Christ (9:21b).

The key issue of the chapter is set forth immediately in the rhetorical questions of 9:1-2. That issue is his apostolic freedom.[169] It seems that in Corinth his practice of working with his hands, as opposed to direct financial support by the congregation, has generated confusion or doubt about his claim to be an apostle. If Paul does not conform to the customary apostolic practice, then it is not difficult to imagine some members in Corinth harboring serious reservations as to whether Paul is in fact fully an apostle. Paul answers with a series of arguments marshalled to prove that he has every legitimate claim to financial support, but that he operates as he does because of the nature of his calling.[170] A "necessity" (anagkē) is laid upon him (9:16). He therefore works under a divine "constraint."[171] This means Paul is conscious of a destiny, a "compulsion exercised on (him) from the outside."[172] It is not, therefore, a matter of an inner personal feeling nor a sense of obligation. Instead, "His commission, and the compulsion arising out of it originate with his Lord."[173] And that commission is not only to preach the gospel, but to preach it "free of charge" (adapanon).

---

[168]Regarding the possibility that 1 Cor. 9 is an interpolation, see the Conzelmann's discussion (1 Corinthians, 3f.).

[169]Conzelmann, 1 Corinthians, 151.

[170]Barrett emphasizes that the array of arguments—from reason, common experience, the Old Testament, universal religious practice, and a saying of Jesus—indicates how important is the case Paul is making (First Epistle, 208).

[171]Conzelmann, 1 Corinthians, 157.

[172]Käsemann, "The Saving Significance," 229. He especially makes anagkē ("necessity") the focus of his interpretation of 9:14-18, which he believes is traceable to prophetic precedent, particularly Jeremiah.

[173]Ibid., 229. He criticizes vehemently and at length all those whose interpretations of this text try to psychologize Paul's motives.

From what basis does Paul's argument proceed? The clue to that question is the slavery motif which emerges in the critical section of 9:14-18. Two aspects of the text make this plain. Both emerge in the surprising conclusion of 9:17. First, the parallelism of the structure in v. 17 leads us to expect the apodosis of the second conditional clause to read, "I do not have a reward," but the apostle changes the wording to read, "I am entrusted with a commission" (*oikonomian pepisteumai*).[174] As Käsemann points out, the rationale of the change "can only be to exclude the motif of reward altogether," thereby bringing out "the will of the Gospel as the sole motivation in the apostle's work."[175] This means that Paul has no claim on the gospel he preaches, but only that the gospel has claimed him as its slave.[176] This interpretation is confirmed by the second aspect of the verse, namely, the word *oikonomian* (literally "stewardship"). This word usually signified an office laid upon a slave or freedman.[177] When we consider the emphasis of this verse together with Paul's climactic statement of v. 19 that "I have made myself a slave to all" (*pasin emauton edoulōsa*) and his renunciation of any "boast" (*kauchēma*) in v. 16, it is unmistakable that Paul's argument proceeds from the fact that he is a slave to Christ, a slave to the gospel, and therefore a slave to all for the gospel's sake (see 2 Cor. 4:5). The commission he has from the Lord is to preach the gospel free of charge. He has no choice, as is made clear by his exclamation, "Woe to me if I do not preach the gospel" (v. 16). His whole orientation, even to the financial terms under which he operates, is determined by this divine "necessity" (*anagkē*).

The nature of his argument is evident from the thoroughly paradoxical way in which his thought is laid out. Paul's "boast" (*kauchēma*) is that he has none at all.[178] His "reward" (*misthos*) is that he receives no pay for carrying out his stewardship as a preacher of the gospel except to work without any.[179] His "destiny" (*anagkē*) is not blind fate, as that word was commonly understood among the Greek and Roman thinkers, but requires obedience, a free decision.[180] And his "freedom" (*eleutheros*) consists precisely in his becom-

---

[174]Ibid., 231.

[175]Ibid.

[176]Holmberg, *Paul and Power*, 93.

[177]Barrett, *First Epistle*, 210.

[178]Conzelmann, *1 Corinthians*, 157. Thus there is no contradiction here between this and his chief argument that no one has a boast before the Lord, i.e. his theology of the cross.

[179]Barrett, *First Epistle*, 210. Conzelmann, *1 Corinthians*, 158. Conzelmann regards the *hina* ("so that") clause as defining the reward "exhaustively" and criticizes Käsemann for himself psychologizing Paul (Ibid., 158 n. 30). Cf. Käsemann, "Saving Significance," 232.

[180]Käsemann, "The Saving Significance," 230. Conzelmann, *1 Corinthians*, 157f.

ing a slave.[181] Every source of personal claim, every presumption, is thereby excluded by the apostle. The gospel of Christ has taken him captive (see Phil. 3:12).

Paul's argument is made all the more comprehensible by recent sociological studies. Hock, whose investigation is focused on the social context of Paul's tentmaking ministry, has discovered that among Greco-Roman philosophers there were four recognized alternatives for financial support, the relative merits of which were vigorously debated. They included charging fees, entering the household of a wealthy person as as resident intellectual, begging, or working.[182] Of these, the least desirable, from the point of view of both philosophers and society, was working as a laborer.[183] In fact, "to those of wealth and power, the appearance *(schēma)* of the artisan was that befitting a slave *(douloprepes)*."[184] As a result, when Paul chose to work with his hands to support himself and his work in Corinth, he had placed himself in a socially undesirable position. For not only was labor regarded as the least desirable option of philosopher-teachers, but generally working with one's hands was stigmatized by the Greco-Roman world as demeaning.[185]

Since laborers were accorded no social status, therefore, the Corinthians could mistake Paul's renunciation of support as simply indicative of his lack of full apostolic status. Instead of appearing with signs of authenticity and power emanating from his obvious personal freedom, so highly prized in the Greek speaking world, Paul appeared in the guise of a slave. This was part of his "weakness" *(astheneia)*, Hock believes, not merely that he appeared ill or emotionally shaken or with a speech impediment, as is often supposed, but that his whole comportment as an apostle left a great deal to be desired.[186] Paul did not fit the generally accepted pattern. This also means, we might add, that Paul's *astheneia* ("weakness") mentioned in 1 Cor. 2:3 should not be understood in as strictly a theological sense as Conzelmann and Wilckens have argued, even though they are quite correct in saying that Paul has interpreted his weakness in theological terms.[187] It is a question of Paul's whole apostolic bearing, an important part of which is the socially debilitating status

---

[181]Hock, *Social Context,* 60f. He reminds us that personal freedom was a central concern of Greek philosophy and a primary issue related to the question of the philosopher's means of support. The question was, how could one support oneself without compromising one's philosophy, one's liberty?

[182]Ibid., 52-59.

[183]Ibid., 59.

[184]Ibid., 60.

[185]Ibid., 35f. Trades were, for example, despised as slavish (most workshops employing almost entirely slaves), as leaving little time for development of the soul, as unnecessary, and as only catering to luxury.

[186]Ibid., 59f.

[187]See the discussion above on 1 Cor. 2:3, p. 115f.

he brings with him as a tradesman. Hock finds this line of interpretation verified by Paul's reference to his weakness in 1 Cor. 4:9-13, where he describes himself as serving the Corinthians in weariness of toil and in want.[188]

This passage (9:14-18) underscores the sharpness of Paul's argument in 1 Cor. 1:17–2:5, especially 2:1-5. The cross is for Paul the symbol of weakness, not only in the political or philosophical sense, but also in the sense that it testifies to total and utter humiliation. Jesus died in disgrace, completely dominated by the political-cultural forces which held the field in his day. Yet he has become the source of salvation because God has made the proclamation of the crucified Christ the means of access to his own divine power. God raised up and exalted an utterly humiliated Jesus (see Phil. 2:5-11!). All human possibilities have therefore been thrown over. It becomes crucial, then, that the gospel and the bearer of the gospel conform to the center of the gospel, the crucified Jesus Christ. For them to be otherwise would be to displace the absolute power of God with some form of human potency. For Paul, who knows himself to be called as apostle and even chosen from his mother's womb (Gal. 1:15f.), as preacher of the gospel his whole bearing must share in the weakness of the cross. And that weakness is physical, cultural, political, and social. Only in that way will the faith of the hearers rest solely on the absolute power of God. Once again Paul's theology of preaching is stamped as thoroughly cruciform.

FIRST CORINTHIANS 15:1-14

A. The Literary Context

The next important discussion of Paul's preaching in 1 Corinthians takes us to the end of the letter. Chapter 15 takes up an integral theme, the resurrection of the dead, and may very well represent the climax of the letter and the keystone which holds it together, as Barth contended.[189] In connection with 1 Cor. 4:8ff., as we have seen in the introductory discussion, the resurrection theme provides important evidence for the situation of Paul and the Corinthian community at the time of the writing. At the same time, the opening verses of chapter 15 begin afresh with no clear reference to what precedes

---

[188]Hock, *Social Context*, 60.

[189]Karl Barth, *The Resurrection of the Dead* (New York: Fleming H. Revell, 1933), 13-124. Beker (*Paul the Apostle,* 164) thinks Barth's arguments for the unity of 1 Corinthians are confirmed in 1 Cor. 1:4-9. Beker notices how the language of vv. 5-7 relates especially to chapters 1-15, setting the stage: "speech" corresponds to the discussion in chapters 1-4; "knowledge" surfaces in chapters 8-10; "spiritual gifts" in chapters 12-14; and the "revealing of our Lord Jesus Christ" in chapter 15.

it, and the reasons for addressing the subject do not appear until v. 12.[190] As Conzelmann describes it, the chapter represents a "self-contained treatise on the resurrection of the dead."[191]

The heart of the argument in chapter 15 is located in vv. 12-28, where Paul insists that the resurrection of the dead is the indispensable core of the gospel, of faith, and of salvation. His argument is two-sided. Negatively Paul contends that to dismiss the resurrection of the dead results in a faith without basis (vv. 13-19). Positively he describes the resurrection of Christ as the "first fruits of those who have fallen asleep" (v. 20), and then, using apocalyptic language, emphasizes the future resurrection of all believers.[192] Thus for Paul Christ's resurrection is the inauguration event of the coming Parousia.[193] In the remainder of the chapter the apostle tries to convince the Corinthians of the correctness of his position, partly by calling attention to their own conduct (v. 29ff.) and partly by answering the expected questions and objections (vv. 35ff.). Paul climaxes the discussion with a revelatory description of the resurrection of the dead at the Parousia, the fulfillment of Scripture (vv. 51ff.), and concludes on a parenetic note in which the Corinthians are urged to remain "steadfast, immovable, always abounding in the work of the Lord" (v. 58).

If this is Paul's position, then what were his opponents in Corinth saying? Obviously they believe in the resurrection, since they are said to have accepted the tradition that "he was raised on the third day" (v. 4). The resurrection chapter is not, therefore, as has often been supposed, an attempt to prove the historicity of the raising of Jesus. Instead, it is plain that Paul and some in Corinth have a basic disagreement on what the resurrection means and how it applies to Christian experience. There have been various attempts to reconstruct the opposing position in Corinth. Bultmann and his pupil Schmithals believe Paul's opponents hold a gnostic position which denies the realistic nature of the resurrection, as understood in Jewish and primitive Christian tradition, and spiritualizes any resurrection expectations.[194] Beker believes the problems are located in the fact that the Corinthians share a "non-apocalyptic hellenistic world view" by which the resurrection is interpreted as a present reality that is theirs by virtue of their sacramental unity with Christ.[195] Similar to Beker's conception is that of Bartsch. He also believes Paul's framework is apocalyptic, while that of his opponents is not, and that

---

[190]Barrett, *First Epistle*, 335.

[191]Conzelmann, *1 Corinthians*, 249.

[192]Schütz, *Anatomy*, 85.

[193]Hans-Werner Bartsch, "Die Argumentation des Paulus in 1 Cor. 15:3-11," *ZNW* 55 (1964): 267ff.

[194]Bultmann, *Theology*, 169. Schmithals, *Gnosticism in Corinth*, 156.

[195]Beker, *Paul the Apostle*, 163ff.

the problem has come about because the opponents have identified the resurrection of Christ with the new life and the Parousia. Thus the opponents would have believed "that with the appearances of the resurrected Lord the new being *[Dasein]* took on a bodily concrete reality."[196] More impressive and more finely nuanced, however, is the reconstruction offered by Schütz. He has noted that the discussion in chapter 15 is not only about the resurrection, but also about death (vv. 6b, 27!). Schütz concludes, therefore, that the Corinthian position has "two foci: proleptically it assumes the fullness of the eschaton which has not yet arrived; it denies the reality and power of death."[197]

Common to all the above reconstructions is the supposition that the Corinthians have misconstrued the resurrection of Christ, disregarding its meaning for the future and seizing upon it as a present reality. Against this Paul insists on the "resurrection of the dead" (v. 12). For him death is a continuing reality, and Christ's resurrection has ushered in the promise of the future expectation.

The verses we are to examine appear at the very beginning of chapter 15. Verses 1-11 are preparatory. They lay the foundation for what Paul will say in the rest of the chapter.[198] Verses 12-14 are the start of his actual argument. These opening verses, while oriented around the theme of the resurrection of the dead, initiate the discussion in the context of the gospel (vv. 1-2), Christian tradition (vv. 3-5), apostolic authority (vv. 6-11), and preaching (vv. 12-14). This text, then, is alive with potential for our examination of Paul's theology of preaching. We need to see how these all fit together and why, surprisingly, in v. 12 Paul bases his entire argument on the fact that Christ is "preached" *(kērussetai!)* as "raised from the dead."

B. Exegesis

> I make known to you, brothers, the gospel which I preached to you, which you received, in which you also have taken (your) stand, through which you also are being saved, if you hold fast with what word I preached (it) to you, unless you believed to no purpose (vv. 1-2).

These opening words, although quite difficult to translate into acceptable English, are Paul's attempt to establish a comprehensive framework for all that is to follow. It is the "gospel" *(euaggelion)* which is the basis of the discussion, introduced in a solemn declaration "I make known to you" *(gnōrizō).*[199] Paul's starting point is the gospel which he "gospeled"

---

[196]Bartsch, "Die Argumentation," 267-270. The quotation is from page 270.
[197]Schütz, *Anatomy,* 86.
[198]Conzelmann, *1 Corinthians,* 249. Karl Kertelge, "Das Apostelamt des Paulus, sein Urprung und seine Bedeutung," *BZ* 14 (1970): 167.
[199]Conzelmann, 250.

(euēggelisamēn) to the Corinthians. But lest the gospel be understood as an objective quantity, and therefore possibly taken by the Corinthians to mean something at their disposal (as they evidently regarded so much else to be, cf. 4:8ff.), Paul describes the gospel as a comprehensive reality which has them at *its disposal.* They have "received" it *(parelabete)* to be sure, since it comes in the form of a message. But it also constitutes the sphere in which they "have taken (their) stand" *(estēkate),* the realm of their existence. Furthermore, the gospel is the means "through which (they) are being saved" *(di hou kai sō-izesthe).* To this final point, however, Paul adds a condition, "if you hold fast" *(ei katechete).* All this corresponds to the larger argument in the chapter and in 1 Corinthians generally, in which Paul asserts that salvation lies in the future.[200] So at the very outset Paul places his readers clearly within the orbit of the gospel's power and suggests that their salvation, rather than an assured result, is at stake in their holding fast.

But holding fast to what? One wants to answer, to the gospel. But that would mean putting the gospel back into a position of being at the disposal of the Corinthians. Besides that, the Corinthians are already said to have accepted the gospel and to stand within it. Rather, the answer lies in the expression *tini logōi euēggelisamēn humin* ("with what word I gospeled it to you"). As Robertson and Plummer note, paying close attention to the Greek construction, the words *ei katechete* ("if you hold fast") are displaced to the end of the clause, which in turn puts the emphasis on *tini logōi.*[201] This latter phrase is best translated "with what word."[202] Paul is recalling to the minds of the Corinthians not merely the gospel as message, as historical report, but the gospel as a "pregnant entity," to borrow Schütz's description.[203] The gospel as a totality includes the *terms* in which it is preached.[204] What this all means is that, despite the mention of the tradition in vv. 3-5, as Schütz says, "the gospel is not identical with the paradosis but represents its effective interpretation."[205] Or, as he also explains it, "For Paul the authority [of the gospel] rests in the *implications* of the historical report, and only the report so interpreted is genuinely 'the gospel.'"[206]

---

[200] The future aspect is clear from the use of the present tense *sōizesthe* ("you are being saved"), as Barrett observes (*First Epistle,* 336). See also 1 Cor. 1:18.

[201] Robertson-Plummer, *Critical and Exegetical Commentary,* 332.

[202] Ibid. This translation has the effect of covering both the form and the substance of the preaching of the gospel. Cf. Barrett (*First Epistle,* 336) who translates, "in what form of words," and Hering (*First Epistle,* 157) who translates, "in what way."

[203] Schütz, *Anatomy,* 109.

[204] This point is reflected in the RSV translation, "in what terms I preached to you the gospel."

[205] Schütz, *Anatomy,* 110.

[206] Ibid., 109.

These first two verses have disclosed an important dimension of Paul's theology of preaching. Paul understands preaching as exercising an authoritative *interpretive* function. That is why, in v. 12, Paul will set down the fundamental basis of his argument not by appealing to the tradition (vv. 3-5), nor even to the resurrection witnesses (vv. 6-8), but rather to the fact of preaching! Both the Corinthians and Paul agree that Christ was raised. Both can appeal to the tradition for their respective positions (vv. 3-5). But the key question is, "in what terms" is this to be understood and applied? What is needed is an interpretive medium, and Paul locates that within the context of the preaching of the gospel. Interpretation is not outside the gospel's sphere, external to preaching, but an extension of it.

Paul's argument is not conclusive at this point, however. For the Corinthians can still ask, even if they concede that preaching the gospel implies also its interpretation, what constitutes Paul's authority for *his* interpretation. The apostle deals with that issue in vv. 3-11, in which Christian tradition, resurrection witness, and his own apostolic authority are all linked together.

> For I delivered to you, among the first and most important matters, that which I also received, namely that Christ died for our sins according to the Scriptures, and that he was buried, and that he was raised on the third day according to the Scriptures, and that he appeared to Cephas, then to the twelve. After that he appeared to more than five hundred brothers at once, the majority of whom remain till now, but some have fallen asleep. After that he appeared to James, then to all the apostle. Last of all, then, as it were to an abortion, he appeared also to me (vv. 3-8)

Paul began with the gospel as the foundation for his intepretation in what is to follow, and more specifically the terms in which he proclaimed the gospel. Now Paul attempts to demonstrate that his interpretation stands within the recognized authoritative sphere in the early church. He therefore appeals to Christian tradition, both in the form of a confessional formula (vv. 3-5) and in the form of a list of witnesses to the resurrection of Christ (vv. 6-7). At the end he includes himself within that tradition (vv. 8-11).

Paul starts with the fact that in preaching the gospel he has delivered to the Corinthians the same tradition, the same creed, which he received.[207] The credal elements were the starting point, as his expression *en prōtois* (literally "among the first things") indicates.[208] And that creed embraced two vital

---

[207]It is quite true, as Stuhlmacher admits, that since vv. 1-2 are from Paul, it is not absolutely certain that *euaggelion* ("gospel") should be connected with the tradition in vv. 3ff. But on the basis of his tradition-historical inquiry in Acts 10:34ff., where *euaggelion* ("gospel") and *logon* ("word") appear together, the connection seems confirmed (*Das Evangelium*, 267).

[208]The phrase is ambiguous. It could have a temporal meaning, or it could indicate importance, or both. Conzelmann prefers the former (*1 Corinthians*, 251), while Hering takes up both in the translation we have followed, "among the first and most important elements taught" (*First Epistle*, 158). But Barrett wants to retain the ambiguity in translating simply, "in the first place" (*First Epistle*, 337).

points, that "Christ died for our sins" *(Christos apethanon huper tōn ha-martiōn hēmōn)* and that he "was raised on the third day" *(egēgertai tēi hēm-erai tēi tritēi),* both having taken place "according to the Scriptures" *(kata tas graphas).* Each of these two elements is then further elaborated. His death is underscored by *etaphē* ("he was buried") and his having been raised by *ōphthē Kēphai, eita tois dōdeka* ("he appeared to Cephas, then to the twelve").[209] How much more of what follows should be regarded as also be-longing to the credal tradition is a matter of question. Generally scholars tend to regard the citation as concluding with v. 5, since the grammatical structure changes with v. 6.[210] It is also supposed that Paul received the tradition from either Damascus or Antioch.[211] But more important for our purposes than either of these factors is the observation, made by Bartsch, that Paul begins with *paredōka gar humin* ("For I delivered to you") and concludes with *houtōs kērussomen kai houtōs episteusate* ("thus we preach and thus you believed") in v. 11.[212] The significance of vv. 3ff., then, lies in its totality, wherever its origin and whatever the various traditional elements included. The credal for-mulation of vv. 3-5 is understood by Paul in the context of the further state-ments of vv. 6-8, which serve to add interpretive support to his further argument.

Whether Paul knew and incorporated the traditions about the resurrec-tion appearances in vv. 6-7 as a group or compiled them from independent sources, it is quite clear that they do represent traditional material. The language of the report about the appearance to the "five hundred brothers" in v. 6a is not characteristically pauline, as is apparent from the use of *epanō* ("more than") and *ephapax* ("at once").[213] Nor does v. 7 seem likely to have come from Paul, since its concluding expression *apostolois pasin* ("to all the apostles") would seem to leave Paul outside the circle of the apostolate, when his intention is precisely to include himself within it (v. 9ff.). Also it is parallel in structure to v. 5, which indicates that it is meant probably to be understood as a unit.[214] On the other hand, Paul's own hand is evident in v. 6b and in v. 8. These verses doubtless are in-

[209]Conzelmann, *1 Corinthians,* 251.

[210]The string of *hoti* ("that") clauses stops at v. 5. Conzelmann, *1 Corinthians,* 252. Schütz, *Anatomy,* 94f. Bartsch, "Die Argumentation," 271. But cf. Hering, who thinks the citation concludes with v. 4 (*First Epistle,* 158).

[211]Beker says Antioch (*Paul the Apostle,* 173). Hering thinks Damascus (*First Epistle,* 158). But Stuhlmacher advises, on the basis of his tradition-historical investigation, that it could have been mediated from Jerusalem (*Das Evangelium,* 272).

[212]Bartsch, "Die Argumentation," 263.

[213]Stuhlmacher, *Das Evangelium,* 268. See also Bartsch, "Die Argumentation," 263f.

[214]Stuhlmacher, *Das Evangelium,* 268. See also Schütz, *Anatomy,* 95. Bartsch believes that v. 5 and v. 7 represent competing traditions, since there are different names for those who received the first appearance ("Die Argumentation," 264).

tended to indicate what Paul wants the Corinthians to see in his additional list of resurrection witnesses.[215]

What does Paul mean by his own additions? The apostle's first addition in v. 6b, "most of whom remain till now, but some fell asleep" *(ex hōn pleiones menousin heōs arti, tines de ekoimēthēsan),* is peculiar. If his purpose was to pile up an impressive number of witnesses as proof of the resurrection, it would have been enough to mention that many are still alive, which would suggest his list could be documented. But since that is really not the case, as we have seen, the point of the statement lies in the second clause. The important thing is that "some died."[216] If, as we have supposed, the Corinthians take the position that the resurrection is already an existing reality in their present life and imparts to them a power which rules out death, then it is altogether intelligible why Paul should refer to the death of some of the resurrection witnesses. He is emphasizing that even fellow Christians who have themselves received appearances of the risen Lord have not been rendered immune to death. They died! This means the very presupposition of the Corinthian position collapses.[217] Furthermore, by reference to the fact that Christ died, which is emphasized in v. 4a by his being "buried" *(etaphē),* and that the witnesses of the resurrected Lord have died, Paul introduces his thesis that the resurrection of Christ must be understood as a resurrection "from the dead" *(ek nekrōn)* (vv. 12ff.).[218]

The second series of words Paul attaches to the tradition (v. 8) begins with the fact that the risen Lord "appeared even to me" *(ōphthē kamoi).* This statement, coming immediately on the heels of the tradition that the risen Lord appeared to "all the apostles" *(apostolois pasin),* explains why Paul links together this chain of resurrection witnesses. He intends to include himself within the circle of authoritative leadership, the apostolate, of the church.[219] Simultaneously, if Bartsch is correct that Paul may be assembling competing traditions in vv. 6-7, then Paul is presenting the interpretive authority of the church as a united front.[220] From Paul's point of view all the traditions concur about the way in which the resurrection is to be correctly understood, as he will make clear in v. 11 and v. 12.

While on the one hand Paul includes himself within the authoritative apostolic tradition and emphasizes its essential unity with respect to the

---

[215]Schütz, *Anatomy,* 95. Bartsch, "Die Argumentation," 272f. Stuhlmacher, *Das Evangelium,* 269.

[216]Conzelmann, *1 Corinthians,* 258. Schütz, *Anatomy,* 85. Bartsch, "Die Argumentation," 272f.

[217]Conzelmann, *1 Corinthians,* 258. Schütz, *Anatomy,* 85. Bartsch, "Die Argumentation," 272f.

[218]Bartsch, "Die Argumentation," 272.

[219]Schütz, *Anatomy,* 96. Stuhlmacher, *Das Evangelium,* 268.

[220]Bartsch, "Die Argumentation," 264.

resurrection of Christ, on the other hand in v. 8 he also distinguishes himself in two ways. First, he declares that he is the "last" *(eschaton)* of the line of those who have received an appearance of the risen Lord.[221] Does Paul mean last historically or last in importance? In view of the sequential nature of the list, most likely he means "last" chronologically.[222] If that is the case, then Paul means to close off the resurrection appearances with Christ's appearance to himself, thereby making it impossible for the Corinthians to claim any direct access to the risen Lord.[223] In that way the apostle shuts off their access to the foundation for their argument. Whatever powerful experiences the Corinthians have had—and Paul admits they are rich in every spiritual way (1:4-7)—these experiences are not appearances of the risen Lord and therefore, as a basis for their position, are not on the same level with the apostolic tradition. Paul is part of the authoritative tradition of the "*one* gospel of the *one* church," while the Corinthians are not.[224] As an apostle (vv. 9-10), he therefore has the authority to interpret the Christian faith as subsumed within the preaching of the gospel.

The second factor that distinguishes Paul from the other apostles is the concession that his calling to the apostolate is irregular.[225] Whatever else the puzzling term *ektrōma* ("abortion") in v. 8 means, in view of the context that much is certain. It is entirely likely that Paul is taking up an insulting term hurled at him by his opponents.[226] This supposition becomes all the more attractive with the observation that *ektrōma,* as an premature birth, does not fit easily with the emphasis that he is the "last."[227] It is only within the context, however, that we really understand what Paul means by the term, as Conzelmann emphasizes.[228] And there are two aspects which emerge from the

---

[221]Paul's full expression is "last of all" *(eschaton pantōn). Pantōn* ("all") can be neuter or masculine, but as Robertson-Plummer suggest, in the context the latter is surely intended (*Critical and Exegetical Commentary*, 339).

[222]Barrett, *First Epistle*, 344. See also Conzelmann, *1 Corinthians*, 259, and Erhard Güttgemanns, *Der leidende Apostel und sein Herr* (Göttingen: Vandenhoeck & Ruprecht, 1966), 88 n. 89. But cf. Schütz (*Anatomy*, 105), who believes it is to be taken in the context of apostleship (vv. 9-10), by which through being "least" he becomes the best example of apostolic life.

[223]Conzelmann, *1 Corinthians*, 259. He argues that the point of the list is to put temporal distance between the present and the resurrection of Christ. This may be overstating the case, since, as Kertelge argues against Conzelmann, the intention clearly seems to be to extend the list of appearances to the present, to Paul ("Das Apostelamt," 168f.).

[224]The phrase is Kertelge's ("Das Apostelamt," 171).

[225]Ibid., 166.

[226]Barrett, *First Epistle*, 344. Hering, *First Epistle*, 162. Robertson-Plummer, *Critical and Exegetical Commentary*, 340. Güttgemanns, *Der leidende Apostel*, 89. But cf. Schütz (*Anatomy*, 104), who says it is not necessarily abusive and may in fact be Paul's own term.

[227]Güttgemanns, *Der leidende Apostel*, 89.

[228]Conzelmann, *1 Corinthians*, 259.

context. The first is the accent on the fact that he is an apostle strictly by God's "grace" *(charis)*, v. 10. That means that Paul understands *ektrōma* ("abortion") to focus not on the process of birth but on the result, a result that is incapable of sustaining life on its own.[229] Secondly, and more important, is the accent on the fact that Paul, as an apostle, appears to the Corinthians as an "outsider," particularly if they regard his understanding of the resurrection as being at odds with that of the other apostles.[230] That would explain why in vv. 9f. Paul insists on his apostolic status, despite all appearances and despite all prior history. Even though he does not seem to the Corinthians to manifest the apostolic credentials they might have expected, either historically or in his interpretation of the kerygma, he is in fact an apostle, and his authority is equal to all the other apostles.[231] As a result, when Paul interprets the tradition, in vv. 12ff., so that the resurrection of Jesus "from the dead" is incorporated within the structure and sphere of the preaching of the gospel, he does so on the basis of his divinely ordained apostleship.

Our interpretation of v. 8 is made all the more probable by the sociological investigation of Holmberg relative to Paul's apostolic position. He believes there is evidence for two different apostolates in the early church: the "Jerusalem Easter apostolate" and the "wandering missionary apostolate," the difference between them being that only the former group was regarded as "sent by the Risen Lord Himself," while the latter was authorized by a human sender in the form of a local congregation.[232] This of course meant that the Jerusalem apostles were the more important, the first line of authority in the church, to which even Paul was obligated.[233] To which of these does Paul belong? Holmberg answers by noting that Paul, at first glance, belongs logically to the missionary apostolate, since he is sent out by the church in Antioch. On the other hand, Paul argues vigorously that he is an apostle by virtue of the appearance of the risen Lord and that his apostolic status was fully recognized by Jerusalem (Gal. 1:16, 2:2b, 2:7-9). The recognition by Jerusalem, though, appears to have been "private" (Gal. 2:2b), thus putting Paul in the position of being "materially" recognized, but suffering from the "formal deficiency" that his apostolic status was not recognized publicly.[234]

[229]Schütz, *Anatomy,* 104f. See also Barrett, *First Epistle,* 344.

[230]Güttgemanns, *Der leidende Apostel,* 89f. He thinks Paul's understanding of resurrection is best described as emphasizing the "Christological distance" between the risen Christ and believers, while his opponents want to see an identity between them.

[231]Both Güttgemanns (*Der leidende Apostel,* 88-92) and Kertelge ("Das Apostelamt," 170f.) emphasize that Paul's apostleship is at issue here.

[232]Holmberg, *Paul and Power,* 52f.

[233]Ibid, 54.

[234]Ibid., 55. Holmberg believes (with Dix) that it was private so as not be a provocation to the Jews.

The upshot of all this is that Paul was probably "somewhere half-way between the two categories of apostles."[235]

If this analysis is accurate, it is not hard to imagine why Paul is continually arguing his apostolic position in his letters, and particularly in the Corinthian correspondence where there are such sharp differences between the congregation and himself. As Schütz has seen, Paul wants to exercise authority in Corinth, he "wants to control a tradition he regards as illegitimately exploited."[236] His apostolic authority is vitally important if he is to position his interpretation within the framework of the preaching of the gospel (vv. 11, 12). And he absolutely must do that, for Paul's specific commission is limited to preaching the gospel to the gentiles (Gal. 1:15f.). If his interpretive authority does not lie within the preaching of the gospel, then he cannot exercise interpretive authority in Corinth.

> For I am the least of the apostles, unfit to be called an apostle, because I persecuted the church of God. But by the grace of God I am what I am, and his grace which is in me did not prove to be fruitless, but I labored more abundantly than all of them, yet not I but the grace of God which was with me. Therefore, whether it was I or they, thus we preach and thus you believed (vv. 9-11).

In vv. 9-10 Paul elaborates what he means by referring to himself in v. 8 as an "abortion" (ektrōma). He is the "least" (elachistos) of the apostles, because his past history was one of persecuting the church of God. That makes him the least likely candidate for the apostolic office, at least by normal human expectations. He is not "fit" (hikanos) to be called an apostle.[237] On the other hand, we must not imagine that Paul is employing the word here in an entirely self-debasing manner. There is a certain irony in that for Paul the fact that he is the "least" of the apostles, understood on his own terms, means "he is the best example of what is quintessential in apostleship."[238] For in his own experience Paul sees the best illustration of the creative, redemptive power of the grace of God. Precisely where there was nothing to be expected, humanly speaking, there, by God's grace, Paul has been called to new life, to apostleship (cf. Gal. 1:11-16).

The fact that Paul's apostleship as an expression of the "grace of God" (hē charis tou theou) is especially emphasized in v. 10. Three times the word charis ("grace") appears. Despite the fact that he was the least of all, Paul

---

[235]Ibid.

[236]Schütz, *Anatomy*, 102.

[237]The translation, "fit," follows the RSV and Conzelmann, *1 Corinthians*, 248. *Hikanos* actually means "sufficient" and is an important term in 2 Corinthians. As Conzelmann suggests, we rather expect *axiōs* ("worthy"), so it may mean Paul is using a catchword of his opponents (Ibid., 260f.). But cf. Barrett, who thinks the word is oriented toward Paul's standpoint before Christ, not the opponents (*First Epistle*, 345).

[238]Schütz, *Anatomy*, 103.

is nonetheless an apostle by the grace of God. Grace means not only that his calling is a matter of God's gift to him, but also that it is an absolutely free act of God.[239] In order to document the power of God's grace in his apostolic calling Paul points to his own ministry. God's grace has not proved "fruitless" *(kenē)*, because Paul "labored more abundantly than all of them" *(perissoteron autōn pantōn ekopiasa)*.

By speaking of his abundant labor Paul is not merely referring to the extraordinary efforts he exerted in his missionary activity. He also includes the results, the congregations he has established (cf. 2 Cor. 10:13ff. and 11:21ff.).[240] For these results, as Schütz is doubtless correct in arguing, are in the final analysis all that the apostle can appeal to for the certification of the gospel.[241] Schütz goes on, "For Paul a description of apostolic activity is itself a statement of apostolic authority," and in that way it is therefore also "an expression of the authority of the gospel itself."[242] Kertelge is probably correct, then, when he claims that while Paul intends to include himself within the list of resurrection witnesses and therefore within the authoritative tradition of the early church, at the same time by emphasizing his apostolic work he "simultaneously also distances himself from the tradition."[243] In that way Paul is able to claim apostolic authority to interpret the tradition independently. However, lest that be taken to indicate he is boasting in himself or is somehow not accountable, he adds the disclaimer that his work was not actually his own but the grace of God which is "with me" *(sun emoi)*.

With v. 11 Paul returns to the basic line of his argumentation, begun in v. 1, as can be seen from the inferential particle *oun* ("therefore").[244] Three essential points surface in the statement. The first is "whether I or they" *(eite oun egō eite ekeinoi)*. Güttgemanns is surely right that this is meant polemically by Paul.[245] The apostle will not allow the Corinthians to isolate him and his preaching of the resurrection from the rest of the Christian apostles, from authoritative tradition. With respect to the preaching of the resurrection Paul and the rest of the authorities are one.

The second feature of v. 11 is the *houtōs* ("thus"), which is stressed by its being repeated. The word does not take us back to the creed (vv. 3-5), as Conzelmann believes, nor to the content of the kerygma, as Hering thinks.[246]

---

[239]Bultmann, *Theology*, 284. See also Conzelmann, *1 Corinthians*, 260, and Kertelge, "Das Apostelamt," 165.

[240]Conzelmann, *1 Corinthians*, 260. Holmberg, *Paul and Power*, 199.

[241]Schütz, *Anatomy*, 112.

[242]Ibid.

[243]Kertelge, "Das Apostelamt," 166.

[244]Conzelmann, *1 Corinthians*, 260. Hering, *First Epistle*, 162. Robertson-Plummer, *Critical and Exegetical Commentary*, 342.

[245]Güttgemanns, *Der leidende Apostel*, 91.

[246]Conzelmann, *1 Corinthians*, 260. Hering, *First Epistle*, 162.

Instead, it connects us with the crucial phrase *tini logōi* ("by what word") in v. 2.[247] Paul insists that the Corinthians are called to accept not only the gospel, expressed in the creed and tradition, but the terms in which that gospel of the resurrection was delivered to them. That means the resurrection must be understood as the resurrection "from the dead" (v. 12ff).

The third and final point is the appearance of the two verbs, "we preach" *(kērussomen)* and "you believed" *(episteusate)*. These two verbs disclose the relationship between the Corinthians and the authoritative apostolic interpretation. Paul stands with church authority, as is evident from the fact that "we" preach. The Corinthians stand under interpretive authority and are expected to accept it. Paul began with the terms of his personal preaching (v. 2), but his conclusion in v. 11 represents a remarkable shift. Schütz describes it by saying, "The net effect of the movement in vv. 1-11 is to broaden the spectrum of what constitutes authoritative preaching and still show that this expansion neither adds to nor subtracts from the tradition which the Corinthians first accepted and believed."[248]

> Now if Christ is proclaimed as having been raised from the dead, how can some among you say that there is no resurrection of the dead? But if there is no resurrection of the dead, neither has Christ been raised; if Christ has not been raised, then our kerygma is empty and your faith is equally empty. (vv. 12-14).

These verses are the heart of Paul's argument in 1 Cor. 15. His theme is made clear by the addition of the words *ek nekrōn* ("from the dead") to the statement that Christ has been raised. And since his designation for the risen Lord is here again *Christos* without the article, as in v. 3, shows that Paul understands the creed to mean that the resurrection of the person Jesus on the third day is, in fact, a resurrection "from the dead."[249]

But what does Paul mean by *ek nekrōn* ("from the dead")? That question can only be answered in the context of the rest of the chapter and in what is implied by "resurrection" *(anastasis)*. Paul's understanding of the resurrection is shared by the early church and is rooted in apocalyptic thinking. The resurrection of the dead was expected as the inaugural act of the new, messianic age ordained by God. The resurrection of Jesus, therefore, is not understood as an isolated wonder, but as the prelude to the general resurrection of all the dead at the Parousia, at which time the godless are to be judged and the faithful vindicated. The new life in God's perfect righteousness and peace would then be experienced by all God's people. Thus the resurrection

---

[247]Robertson-Plummer, *Critical and Exegetical Commentary,* 342. See also Schütz, *Anatomy,* 102.

[248]Schütz, *Anatomy,* 102.

[249]Conzelmann, *1 Corinthians,* 265.

of Jesus is for Christians the basis for the future expectation.[250] That is why in vv. 21-28 Paul describes Christ as the "first fruits" *(aparchē)* of the dead, as the origin of the new age of life (as opposed to the age of death begun by Adam, v. 22), and as the appointed agent of God who will defeat all God's enemies so that the kingdom of God is the sole undisputed realm of human existence. When this perspective on the resurrection is understood in the context of God as the creator *ex nihilo* (1 Cor. 1:24ff., 2 Cor. 5:17ff.), it is comprehensible why Paul insists on the resurrection "of the dead" *(ek nekron)*. For death signifies the ultimate limit of human life and human potential. Flesh and blood "cannot inherit the kingdom of God" (v. 50)! Therefore, the kingdom must mean a totally new creation, and God creates "from nothing." At death, where all human potential ceases, at that very point God brings about the new creation.

If it is true that the Corinthians have individualized the resurrection hope and tried to make it their own possession within their lifetime, it is plain why Paul must insist on the resurrection of the dead. Otherwise, the resurrection of Christ will mean little more than a "souped up" version of life as we know it, which is no real salvation at all (v. 29!). As Barth clearly saw, it is not merely a doctrine that is at stake, but the entire structure of Christian faith.[251] That is why Paul goes to such great lengths to explain his position in what follows, noting that the resurrection of the dead is the foundation for everything.

Paul's logic in these verses is an argument *ad absurdum*. Strikingly, Paul begins from the foundation of preaching! If Christ is "preached" *(kērussetai)* as raised from the dead, how can some say "there is no resurrection of the dead?"[252] The resurrection of the dead is "identical with the proclamation of Christ," the proclaiming of the gospel.[253] For the gospel is what gives preaching its authority (Gal. 1:6ff.). As a result, the resurrection of the dead is not only essential to the gospel as message, but it is the foundation for the activity of preaching as the authoritative interpretation of the gospel! It is from the basis of preaching that Paul can recall the Corinthians to a correct understanding of the gospel.

Since the authoritative voice of proclamation has interpreted Christ's resurrection as the resurrection of the dead, Paul asks the Corinthians how they

---

[250]A. Oepke, *TDNT,* 1 (Grand Rapids: Eerdmanns, 1964), 368-371. See also A. Oepke, *TDNT,* 2 (Grand Rapids: Eerdmanns, 1964), 334-337.

[251]Barth, *Resurrection,* 112f.

[252]Schmithals believes these words are a quotation of the triumphant message of Paul's gnostic opponents (*Gnosticism in Corinth,* 158). Along the same lines, Güttgemanns argues that Paul emphasizes *Christos* (without the article), thus an individual, as over against the gnostic conception of the "mythical Anthropos" (*Der leidende Apostel,* 74f.).

[253]Conzelmann, *1 Corinthians,* 265. See also Barrett, *First Epistle,* 347.

can deny it? The obvious implication is that they cannot. Paul proceeds to show how its denial undermines everything. His logic moves from the general to the single occurrence: "If the dead are not raised, then neither has Christ been raised."[254] Paul can say this because his emphasis in vv. 3ff. was that Christ died and was "buried" *(etaphē)*.[255] Since Christ himself actually died, if there is to be any resurrection at all, it must be a resurrection from the dead! If not, then there is no resurrection at all, with the inevitable result, as the inferential particle *ara* ("in that case") shows, that there is no basis for "proclamation" *(kērugma)* or "faith" *(pistis),* v. 14.[256] It is not only the Christian proclamation that is groundless, but faith is also "devoid of reality" *(kenē)*.[257] Presupposed is that the Corinthians have had the experience of salvation through the gospel, and therefore they know for a fact that it is not empty (see 1:4ff.). Thus Paul's conclusion is that "to dispute one's own resurrection is to abrogate the presupposition of one's own existence, the kerygma and therewith also faith."[258]

C. Preliminary Observations

By way of summation we could say that Paul proceeds from the authority of God, which is located in the act of creation. God has brought about the "new creation" by raising Jesus from the dead (see 2 Cor. 5:17ff.). Now those who believe are incorporated within the new created order by means of the gospel, and that happens when his authorized apostle preaches the gospel which is based on the resurrection of Jesus Christ from the dead (see 1 Cor. 1:25–2:5). Since preaching is always the preaching of the gospel, grounded in the resurrection from the dead, preaching is simultaneously empowered to interpret the gospel for the church.

Two things are implied in this summary. The first is that preaching is not only foundational for the Christian congregation, but it also has an ongoing function in the church's life. Preaching functions as authoritative interpretation. If a parallel is sought in the Old Testament, it might very well be the fact that God is revealed not only as the creator but also the preserver of his creation. Preaching the gospel carries on God's preservation in his "new creation."

Secondly, Paul stresses that the congregation at Corinth does not exist independently. Once having been "gospeled," they do not then "fly solo."

---

[254]Schütz, *Anatomy,* 88f. Hering calls attention to the fact that presupposed here is Christ's humanity (*First Epistle,* 163).

[255]Güttgemanns, *Der leidende Apostel,* 75.

[256]Robertson-Plummer, *Critical and Exegetical Commentary,* 348.

[257]Ibid. They note how *kenos* and *kenē* ("empty") are emphatic by position.

[258]Conzelmann, *1 Corinthians,* 265.

Instead, they are incorporated within the gospel's terms of reference and are obligated to it. Thus Paul understands the Corinthian congregation to be bound to apostolic preaching, just as he is bound to the gospel by his apostolic calling!

THE HISTORICAL SITUATION OF SECOND CORINTHIANS

The final passage for our investigation of Paul's theology of preaching within the Corinthian letters is 2 Cor. 4:1-6. But before we can deal with that passage, it is necessary to describe the circumstances in which the text was written. For between the first and second epistles there has been an important change in the situation at Corinth. The apostle's problems in dealing with the congregation have intensified to the point where a fracture of their relationship is immanent. The words of this final text, and the theology of preaching resident within them, are therefore part of a decisive argument the apostle advances in meeting this crisis.

The question of the situation in Corinth, however, does not exist in isolation. It is bound up with the issue of the integrity of the document we call Second Corinthians. While few scholars today doubt that the epistle comes from Paul about 54 or 56 A.D., it has long been recognized that there are serious dislocations in the document.[259] The most obvious one is the sharp difference in content, style and tone between chapters 1-9 and 10-13. But chapters 1-9 do not seem to constitute a unity either. The letter begun at 1:1 apparently leaves off at 2:13 and resumes at 7:5. This isolates 2:14–7:4 as a separate piece of literature, within which 6:14–7:1 is widely regarded as a non-pauline interpolation.[260] In addition, chapters 8 and 9 impress the reader as having initially existed as independent units, since neither of them appears to connect directly with what preceeds. The conclusion seems inescapable, then, that 2 Corinthians is in fact a "collection of fragments," as Perrin refers to it.[261] How can they be reconstructed so

---

[259]Dieter Georgi, "Corinthians, Second," *IDB*, Supplement (Nashville: Abingdon, 1976), 184. Perrin, *Introduction*, 104. Kümmel, *Introduction*, 293. Marxsen provides a useful survey of the literary dislocations (*Introduction*, 77-79). We follow him in our description.

[260]Marxsen, *Introduction*, 78f. Georgi, "Corinthians, Second," 184f. Perrin, *Introduction*, 105. But cf. C. K. Barrett, *The Second Epistle to the Corinthians* (New York: Harper & Row, 1973), 192f.; he makes a case for the authenticity of 6:14–7:1. And Kümmel, after reviewing all the difficulties, still is not convinced that the passage is inauthentic (*Introduction*, 287f.).

[261]Perrin, *Introduction*, 104. Marxsen, *Introduction*, 79. Cf. Barrett, who argues for the unity and order of the canonical text (*Second Epistle*, 19-21). However, in order to support his case Barrett is forced to postulate two groups of opponents and a doubtful role of Titus. Most damaging is his own concession that it is simplest and most natural to take chapters 10-13 as prior to chapters 1-9 (Ibid., 11f.). See also Munck, *Paul and the Salvation*, 168ff. Kümmel also admits the difficulties, but he is inclined to accept the unity of the letter; he thinks the problems are explained by interruptions and the complicated situation (*Introduction*, 290-293).

as to provide not only a plausible continuity, but also a framework in which the crisis between Paul and the Corinthians comes to light?

A careful, convincing reconstruction of the letter and events has been worked out by Bornkamm, and it has been subsequently supported and amplified by Georgi's study of Paul's opponents.[262] Bornkamm argues that, following the events and letter we refer to as First Corinthians, certain "itinerant preachers," who were outsiders, appeared on the scene in Corinth. They insinuated themselves into the congregation in part by presenting letters of recommendation from previous congregations they had visited. These letters established, in their own minds at least, their claim to be called "apostles" and "servants of Christ" (11:5, 23; 12:11)[263] Evidently they meant to supplant Paul and take over the congregation at Corinth as their base of operations.[264] News of this situation reached Paul by means of Titus, whom he had dispatched to Corinth to complete the collection for Jerusalem.[265]

When Paul learned of this ominous turn of events, he first responded by writing an apologetic letter, which Georgi characterizes as similar to a "political speech," composed of 2:14–7:4 (except for 6:14–7:1).[266] Unfortunately this failed to dislodge the intruders, so Paul paid a personal visit to Corinth, a visit which apparently turned out disastrously (2:1ff., 7:5ff., 12:14, 13:1).[267] Then, with his apostolic authority hanging in the balance, the apostle wrote a second letter, chapters 10-13, a vehement polemic modeled after the philosophical apology.[268] Along with many scholars we believe this letter to be the "letter of tears" referred to in 2:4.[269] This "tearful letter" appears to have worked, and the congregation came back around to support Paul. With the crisis resolved, the apostle wrote a letter of reconciliation (1:1–2:13 and

---

[262]Bornkamm, *Paul*, 68-77, 244-246. Georgi, "Corinthians, Second," 183-186. Cf. Kümmel, however, who thinks Bornkamm's explanation of how the text came to be as we have it today is not adequate (*Introduction*, 292).

[263]Bornkamm, *Paul*, 74.

[264]Georgi, "Corinthians, Second," 184.

[265]Ibid. For evidence he points to 1 Cor. 16:3-9; 2 Cor. 8:6, 10; 9:2; and 12:18.

[266]Ibid.

[267]Ibid.

[268]Ibid. Most notable in this section is the "fool's speech" of 11:1–12:18, whose origin is in hellenistic mime (Ibid.). On the style see especially Hans Dieter Betz, *Paul's Apology in II Corinthians 10-13 and the Socratic Tradition* (Berkeley: Center for Hermeneutical Studies, 1975), 15.

[269]Bornkamm (*Paul*, 77, 245) and Perrin (*Introduction*, 104) identify chapters 10-13 as the "tearful letter." Marxsen (*Introduction*, 79f.) agrees, but he allows for the possibility that chapters 10-13 may not represent the "tearful letter" in its complete form. Cf. Jean Hering, *The Second Epistle of St. Paul to the Corinthians* (London: Epworth, 1967), xii.; he is doubtful. And Barrett (*Second Epistle*, 8) believes the "tearful letter" is lost, which is not surprising since his case for the canonical order of 2 Corinthians cannot allow otherwise.

7:5-16) and followed it up with two later letters concerning the successful completion of the collection for Jerusalem (chapters 8 and 9).[270]

Who were the intruders, the opponents of Paul, in Corinth? Barrett has attempted to classify Paul's opponents as Palestinian "Judaizers."[271] Schmithals argues that they are Jewish Christian "Gnostics," in line with his theory of the single-front opposition faced by Paul.[272] But neither of these arguments is as persuasive as that of Georgi, who has demonstrated that Paul's opposition is comprised of Hellenistic Jews, wandering preachers, influenced by the Hellenistic-Jewish apologetic.[273] That they are Christian missionaries is indicated by their titles: *diakonoi Christou* ("servants of Christ") in 11:23, *apostoloi Christou* ("apostles of Christ") at 11:13, and *ergatai* ("workers") at 11:13.[274] Georgi thinks their model was the *theios anēr* ("divine man") of Hellenistic Judaism and that Moses was their chief exhibit.[275] More importantly, for Paul and the congregation at Corinth, the opponents see *Jesus* as a *theios anēr* through whose earthly life the Spirit had been preeminently revealed and to which they themselves now have access.[276] As proof of their spiritual superiority they offered "letters of recommendation" (3:1), which documented their miraculous achievements and ecstatic experiences.[277] What these Jewish Christian missionaries were really after was the inheritance of the Jewish mission, by which they intended to gain prestige and extend their own work. Their program consisted of the attempt, "by means of retrospect to the past, demonstration of power in the present, and ecstatic experiences which broke through into the future, to transcend present existence."[278] This they seem to have made available to the Corinthians through their pneumatic interpretation of Scripture (probably allegorical). In view of the Corinthian interest in powerful, pneumatic experiences, it is altogether understandable that the opponents' position was very attractive to them.

The opponents disparaged Paul's authority by leveling a series of accusations against him. They contend there is a discrepancy between Paul's hu-

---

[270]Georgi, "Corinthians, Second," 184. Perrin, *Introduction,* 105. Bornkamm, *Paul,* 77, 245.

[271]Barrett, *Second Epistle,* 28-30. See his fuller argument in "Paul's Opponents in II Corinthians," *NTS* 17 (3, 1971): 233-254. Cf. Kümmel (*Introduction,* 286), who tries to combine all the elements by saying that Paul's opponents are "Gnostic-Palestinian-Jewish-Christian" and "antipauline."

[272]Schmithals, *Gnosticism in Corinth,* 87-116.

[273]Dieter Georgi, *Die Gegner des Paulus im zweite Korintherbrief* (Neukirchen-Vluyn: Verlag des Erziehungsverein, 1964), 31-218, 301.

[274]Ibid., 31-50. See also a summary of his argument in Roy Bowen Ward, "The Opponents of Paul," *Restoration Quarterly* 10 (1967): 190.

[275]Georgi, *Die Gegner,* 220ff.

[276]Ibid., 282ff.

[277]Ibid., 241ff. See also the description in his *IDB,* Supplement, article, "Corinthians, Second," 186.

[278]Georgi, *Die Gegner,* 301.

mility when face to face versus his boldness when at a distance, especially noticeable in the impression his letters make compared with the impression he makes in person (10:1, 10).[279] They question whether he belongs to Christ (10:7). They reproach him for not accepting financial remuneration, suggesting that by crafty methods he takes advantage of the congregation (11:7, 12:16). And they seem to have suggested that Paul lacked the transcendent, ecstatic experiences one expects of an apostle (12:1ff.).

As Paul defends himself against these charges, the central issue that emerges is his apostolic authority. Paul is faced with a "rival apostolate," as Barrett aptly refers to it.[280] The essential question is the *criteria* by which the authentic apostle is to be distinguished from the false apostle (11:13, 12:12).[281] Therefore, as Barrett has so appropriately emphasized, although Paul delivers an ardent polemic against his opponents, it is not to them that he writes, but to the church at Corinth, for the Corinthians are the ones who must decide between him and his opponents.[282] Georgi claims, though, that at an even more profound level the issue is Christology; for Paul apostleship relates directly to Christ and to Spirit and to gospel, all of which are inextricably connected (4:7-12; 11:4).[283] For Paul it is not the mere mention of the name of Jesus that spells salvation, but rather a correct understanding of who Jesus is. As a result, Paul defends his Christology by defending his apostleship, both of which he views in relation to salvation.[284]

SECOND CORINTHIANS 4:1-6

A. The Literary Context

Our text falls in the middle of the letter which constitutes the heart of Paul's argument in 2 Corinthians, the letter of 2:14–7:4. Georgi characterizes it as in its entirety "an apology of the apostolate."[285] Paul tries to drive a wedge between the opponents and the Corinthians who have been attracted to the opponents' conception of the Christian faith. His argument is set forth in a series of antitheses designed to persuade the Corinthians that his own presen-

---

[279]Our list of accusations follows Schütz, *Anatomy*, 166.

[280]Barrett, "Opponents of Paul," 233. See also Rudolf Bultmann, *Der zweite Brief an die Korinther* (Göttingen: Vandenhoeck & Rupprecht, 1976), 21.

[281]Barrett, "Opponents of Paul," 233.

[282]Ibid., 241ff.

[283]Ibid., 284ff.

[284]Schütz contends that Paul must argue in this fashion because for his opponents gospel, Christ and apostle have been collapsed together, while for him they are not. Thus his thought moves along an axis between gospel and apostle (*Anatomy*, 183f.).

[285]Georgi, *Die Gegner*, 284.

tation of the gospel is the authentic one. Because Paul is confident that the gospel he preaches is the authentic revelation of God, he regards his ministry as superior to that of the opponents, and therefore he can argue that if the Corinthians are truly committed to the "transcendental character of revelation, they would stay with (him)."[286]

Paul begins with a doxology praising God for the life-giving knowledge of Christ, whose "fragrance" (*osmēn*) is made available to those who are being saved (2:14). This work of spreading that fragrance is his own, since he is the divinely commissioned representative who speaks in Christ. The opponents, on the other hand, are "peddlers of God's word" (2:15-17). It is his commission that makes him "sufficient" (*hikanos*) for this ministry (2:16). Since this is the case, Paul does not need "letters of recommendation" written by human hand, for his recommendation comes from the Spirit of God who has written it on the hearts of the Corinthians (3:1-3). Paul argues that the Spirit is superior to the "letter" (*gramma*), since the Spirit is able to give life, while the letter kills, and through the Spirit Paul knows himself to have been qualified to be a minister of the "new covenant" (3:4-6). Therefore, he stands before God in complete "confidence" (*pepoithēsin*) (3:4).

The claims Paul has made require some form of proof, and the apostle supplies it in the form of an exegesis of Ex. 34:29-35, which recounts the glory of God in the face of Moses upon his receiving the law. Paul admits that the giving of the law, "letters carved in stone," was glorious, but he contends it has been superceded by the "ministry of the Spirit" (*hē diakonia tou pneumatos*), which he also refers to as the "ministry of righteousness" (*hē diakonia tēs dikaiosunēs*), because it is permanent, while the glory of the law, as reflected on the face of Moses, faded (3:7-11). Since Paul understands himself to stand within the ministry of the Spirit, Paul does not have to imitate Moses in putting on a "veil" (*kalumma*) to separate the glory of God from the people (3:13). In fact, Paul implies that Moses put on the veil so as to hide from the people the fact that his shining countenance was fading. Since Paul represents the new and permanant ministry of the Spirit, he can come to the people with "much boldness" (*pollēi parrēsiai*) (3:12). Then, in a play on words, Paul suggests that the "veil," rather than being a symbol of the glory of God, instead represents an obstacle to the correct understanding of the old covenant. It stands for the people's "hardness of heart," which can only be removed by Christ (3:14-16). Paul reaches the climax of his argument in 3:17-18, where he emphatically claims that the Spirit of the Lord brings freedom and the gift of access to the glory of God for all believers, without the need of any veil.

---

[286]Georgi, "Corinthians, Second," 186.

Clearly Paul means to characterize his own ministry in conscious contrast to that of his opponents in Corinth. In rapid succession he devalues their notion of letter, old covenant, Moses, and the veil, all of which were surely key terms of reference for the opponents and would have been regarded by them as signs of the presence of the Spirit.[287] Paul sets the Spirit in opposition to all of these and lays claim to that Spirit in his own ministry.

The character of his ministry is described by Paul in 4:1-6, which is the text we will consider in detail. The apostle describes his ministry in terms of preaching. Paul preaches "Jesus Christ as Lord," and in that open proclamation of the gospel comes the glory of God.

But Paul wants it known that the "treasure" of the revelation of God in Christ comes in "earthen vessels," meaning that it is resident in the weak humanness of the apostle (4:7). That weakness is spelled out in 4:8-10, where Paul takes as his model the "death of Jesus." The paradox is that in the apostle's death "for Jesus' sake" life comes to those he serves (4:11-15).

The theme of life offered through death in the apostle is amplified and defended by means of an argument from bodily experience (4:16–5:10). The mortal nature of the body does not preclude the presence of the glory of God, since we are daily renewed in our "inner nature" by God who has given his Spirit as the "guarantee" (*arrabōn*). On the other hand, the "eternal weight of glory" (4:17) is being prepared for the believer as a future possession, to be received when each must appear before the judgment seat of Christ (5:10).

With 5:11-15 Paul sums up his argument. The marks of true apostleship are not to be found "in appearances" (*en prosōpōi*), but in an appeal aimed at the hearts of people (5:11-12). The basis for this approach is the death of Christ, in whom "all have died" (5:14). Since Christ died for all, believers no longer live for themselves but for him (5:15).

The outcome of his whole argument is Paul's call to the Corinthians to be reconciled with God and with himself as the apostle of God. This offer is made by Paul in 5:16–6:12. Since there is a "new creation" in Christ, all that is old is gone and superceded, even the earthly Jesus (5:16-17). In his stead there is now the "ministry of reconciliation" carried on by the apostle, the "ambassador of Christ," who appeals to the hearer to be reconciled with God and thus to receive his forgiveness and righteousness (5:18-21). Paul appeals to the Corinthians to accept the offer of God and be reconciled with God and himself, since in his own experience of affliction there is a clear parallel to the model of Jesus' death (6:1-13). The apostle then closes with an expression of confidence in the anticipated happy outcome of their differences (7:2-4).

---

[287]See Georgi's argument which construes the veil as allegorical interpretation (*Die Gegner*, 267-273).

From our survey of Paul's argument it is plain that his chief concern is the question of apostolic criteria. By what signs can the authentic apostle be recognized? His answer is equally plain. The model of genuine apostolic ministry is the death of Jesus, God's act of reconciliation for the world. Apostolic ministry is therefore the ministry of reconciliation. And how is that accomplished? It happens with the appeal to conscience in the act of preaching (4:2)! Preaching emerges once again at the vital center of Paul's apostolic work. We turn now to examine more closely Paul's theology of preaching in the context of reconciliation.

B. Exegesis

> For this reason, since we have this ministry, even as we have been shown mercy, we are not intimidated. But we renounced the hidden things of shame, neither walking in unscrupulousness nor adulterating the word of God. Instead, by the open disclosure of the truth we commend ourselves to every human conscience in the sight of God (vv. 1-2).

Paul drew a vivid contrast between his own ministry and that of his opponents in 2:14-3:18. Now he begins to make more specific the nature and function of the ministry he exercises. "Because of this" (*dia touto*), that is, in view of all the preceding discussion in which he elevated the ministry of the Spirit above the ministry of the letter, Paul intends to characterize his own authentic apostolic work.[288] The key descriptive word which catches up his emphasis is "ministry" (*diakonia*). It is a ministry, Paul says, which is his as a result of his having "been shown mercy" (*kathōs eleēthēmen*), meaning that he has received it as the gift of God through Christ (see 3:4-6).[289] This precludes any claim to the apostolic ministry which he might have made on his own. In this way Paul reinforces again the distinction between himself, who has received his "sufficiency" (*hikanotēs*) from God (3:5-6), and his opponents, who are trying to document their own apostolic status by means of letters of recommendation (3:1-3; 5:12). In addition, precisely because Paul knows himself to have been commissioned with "this" (*tautēn*) ministry (4:1), meaning with the ministry of open "boldness" (*parrēsia*) and open access to the Spirit (3:12-18), Paul is "not intimidated" (*ouk egkakoumen*).[290] Paul ob-

---

[288]We follow Bultmann in taking *dia touto* ("for this reason") as referring to the whole preceding argument (*Der zweite Brief*, 101f.). Barrett says the expression can look forward as well as back, i.e. to the "mercy of God" (*Second Epistle*, 127).

[289]Bultmann, *Der zweite Brief*, 102.

[290]Bultmann notices how *ouk egkakoumen* corresponds to *pollēi parrēsiai* ("much boldness") in 3:12 and therefore adopts the translation, "we are not despondent" (with Lietzmann) or, "we are not cowardly" (*Der zweite Brief*, 102). Cf. Alfred Plummer, *A Critical and Exegetical Commentary on the Second Epistle of St. Paul to the Corinthians* (Edinburgh: T. & T. Clark, 1915), 110. Plummer interprets *egkakoumen* as a "silence to escape criticism" and so translates, as does the RSV, "we do not lose heart." Cf. also Barrett's translation, "we do not neglect our duty" (*Second Epistle*, 127).

viously means to emphasize that he is not cowardly, but this expression is probably also intended to contrast with his opponents, whose work is characterized by a certain secretiveness. For Paul everything is to be out in the open, as he will make clear in v. 2b.

What exactly, then, is Paul's *diakonia* ("ministry")? That can be seen partly by what he says elsewhere in this letter and partly by the amplification the apostle supplies in v. 2. Already in 3:4-18 Paul referred to the authentic Christian ministry as being a ministry "of the new covenant" (*kainēs diathēkes*), a ministry "of the Spirit" (*tou pneumatos*), and a ministry "of righteousness" *(tēs dikaiosunēs).* These descriptive phrases were in contrast to the opponents, who are pictured operating according to the old covenant, to the letter, and to a ministry which brings condemnation. But beyond these phrases Paul has not yet provided a graphic picture of what he means by "ministry." Now, however, in v. 2 the apostle reveals the heart of his ministry. It consists in preaching. That is what is meant by his referring to its exercise by means of the "open disclosure of the truth" (*tēi phanerōsei tēs alētheias).* The "truth" here means the gospel, since it stands in correspondence to the "word of God" (*ton logon tou theou*), v. 2a, and is similarly employed by Paul in 6:7 as well as elsewhere in his letters.[291] And *phanerōsei* ("open disclosure") takes us back to the opening words of this letter, 2:14ff., where Paul praises God for having made him the means for disseminating (*phanerounti*) the word of God and speaks of the commission laid upon him to "speak in Christ" (*en Christoi laloumen*).

Paul portrays his preaching in 2:14ff. as a "revelation-event, and himself as a mediator of revelation," to use Georgi's description.[292] Georgi emphasizes that Paul reproaches his opponents, who make claims for themselves by reference to their own capacities and gifts, for not seeing that "in preaching a comprehensive, effective, and decisive revelation occurs in which the central issue is life and death."[293] Paul accuses the opponents of underestimating and undermining the gospel by treating it as a commodity, like "peddlers" (*kapēleuontes*), who want to profit from it (2:17).[294] That explains why Paul in 4:2 speaks of his preaching ministry not only positively as an "open disclosure" (*phanerōsei*), but also negatively as the renunciation of "hidden

---

[291]R. Bultmann, *TDNT*, 1 (Grand Rapids: Eerdmanns, 1964), 244. He directs us to Gal. 2:5, 14 and Col. 1:15. Plummer notes that the expression is used in all places "as a protest against misrepresentations of the gospel and spurious substitutes for it, especially such as destroyed Christian liberty" (*Critical and Exegetical Commentary*, 112). Barrett, however, believes the term has a frame of reference wider than the gospel and that it means the "true message" (*Second Epistle*, 130).

[292]Georgi, *Die Gegner*, 225.

[293]Ibid.

[294]Ibid., 227. Schütz, *Anatomy*, 172.

things of shame'' (*ta krupta tēs aischunēs*).[295] Paul wants to dissociate preaching from any form of ministry which operates by means that are unscrupulous (*en panourgiai*) and "adulterates" (*dolountes*) the word of God (v. 2a).

For Paul, since the the gospel is the truth, deriving from the God who is true and reliable, it does not need the "help" of human manipulation.[296] Rather, it is aimed at the "human conscience" (*suneidēsin anthrōpōn*) in full view of God (v. 2b). And it is from the conscience, as struck by the preaching of the gospel, that Paul expects his ministry to be recognized as that of a genuine apostle.[297] By what line of reasoning is Paul so convinced? Bultmann explains that the answer is to be found in relation to the term "sincerity" (*eilekrineia*), introduced in 2:17, as a description of apostolic integrity:

> For it is plain why the recitation of the correct teaching can prove the *eilikrineia* ["sincerity"] of the preacher: the *alētheia* ["truth"] is not grasped by considered thought but by *suneidēsis* ["conscience"], meaning that the honest hearer becomes so determined by the character of the *aletheia* that he becomes himself *eilikrines* ["sincere"] and thus can see also that the preacher of such *aletheia* is determined through *eilikrineia*[298]

It is the truth of the gospel, therefore, that is recognizable to the reflective consciousness of the honest person and thus "recommends" (*sunistanontes*) the apostle.

Our picture of Paul's preaching ministry thus far, however, does not exhaust the apostle's understanding of it. In fact, we are given an example of his preaching ministry in actual operation in 5:16ff., where Paul refers to it as a "ministry of reconciliation" (*diakonian tēs katallagēs*). Through Christ, Paul proclaims, God has "reconciled us to himself" by doing away with our sin (5:19, 21). What is more, God has entrusted Paul with the "ministry of reconciliation," which is exercised by means of the "word of reconciliation" (*ton logon tes katallagēs*), 5:18-19. On the basis of God's reconciling act in Christ the ministry of reconciliation is enacted by saying, "We beseech

---

[295]*Ta krupta tēs aischunēs* ("hidden things of shame") is not altogether clear, but its meaning is expressed in the participles which follow, according to Plummer (*Critical and Exegetical Commentary*, 111). Barrett describes the expression as "things one may do, but will do only under cover and with shame if found out" (*Second Epistle*, 128). Cf. Bultmann's translation, which keeps closer to the context, "we reject all cowardly secrets" (*Der zweite Brief*, 103). Hering identifies the genitive as a genitive of quality and so translates, " 'underhand dealings' of which one should be ashamed" (*Second Epistle*, 29).

[296]While *alētheia* ("truth") in the New Testament can have a variety of meanings, the term is related to the Old Testament word *emeth*, which denotes that which is "solid, firm, reliable," according to Quell and Bultmann, *TDNT*, 1:232, 238-241.

[297]Bultmann, *Der zweite Brief*, 105.

[298]Ibid., 104. See also Christian Maurer, *TDNT*, 7 (Grand Rapids: Eerdmanns, 1971), 898-919. He describes the conscience as the "central self-consciousness of the knowing and acting man" (Ibid., 917).

you, on behalf of Christ, be reconciled to God'' (*deometha huper Christou, katallagēte tōi theōi*), 5:20! As Schütz explains, ''Christ is thus extended through his ambassadors. Reconciliation, far from being confined to his death, is accomplished through the ministry by which God makes his appeal,'' which means that ''the gospel is the extension of the Christ-event.''[299] For this reason Paul can dare to designate himself, in his preaching ministry, as the ''co-worker'' (*sunergountes*) of God (6:1)![300] By effecting reconciliation with God in preaching, the apostle actually makes available God's eschatological salvation: ''Behold now is the day of salvation'' (6:2).

It should be evident from all we have just seen that for Paul ''ministry'' (*diakonia*) as a description of his apostolic office, his activity of preaching, is freighted heavily. If, as we believe, Paul has chosen this term in conscious opposition to his opponents, who refer to themselves as ''ministers of Christ'' (*diakonoi Christou*) (11:23), then he has completely reinterpreted it.[301] Paul draws out the implications of service and submission inherent in the root meaning of the term *diakonia,* a submission to God and service to the congregation (4:5b).[302] That service does not lay hold of power-filled demonstrations of the Spirit, but rather works by the plain, unadulterated disclosure of the truth, which is the gospel of God. It is a risky business. It entails suffering and weakness on the part of the apostle, which follows the pattern of the death of Christ (4:8-10). Yet as the apostle's preaching consigns him to death, it results in life for the hearers (2:14ff., 4:11f.), so that the ''transcendent power belongs to God and not to us'' (4:7).

> But if also our gospel is veiled, it is veiled only to those who are perishing; in their case the god of this age blinded the minds of the unbelievers so that they may not see the illumination of the gospel of the glory of Christ, who is the image of God (vv. 3-4).

The polemic Paul has expressed through the antithetical structure of his argument continues in these explanatory verses. The polemical aspect needs to be emphasized in our interpretation because it appears at first glance that Paul is on the defensive, perhaps taking up an accusation made against him

---

[299]Schütz, *Anatomy,* 181. He emphasizes, following Georgi, that Paul's position here comes from the stress on the discontinuity with the past, where *kata sarka* (''according to the flesh'') connects with *Christon* (''Christ'') in v. 16. Thus Paul relegates the earthly Christ to the past, meaning that he cannot serve, as his opponents think, as a *theios anēr* (''divine man'') whose power is available to them. Instead, the eschatological event in Christ is the new creation (v. 17). This is a radical cleavage, so that Christ is now available only in the ministry of reconciliation given to Paul (Ibid., 176ff.). See also Georgi, *Die Gegner,* 256f.

[300]Ibid.

[301]Schütz, *Anatomy,* 178.

[302]Ibid., 179. See also Hermann Beyer, *TDNT,* 2 (Grand Rapids: Eerdmanns, 1964), 81-93.

that his gospel is "veiled" (*kekalummenon*).[303] And yet, a careful analysis of the argument and the grammatical structure of v. 3 suggests the opposite.[304] Paul is engaged in polemic, not apologetic. From the grammatical perspective the verse is striking because of the position of *ei de kai estin* ("but if even") and the position of *hēmōn* ("ours") in v. 3a, both of which are emphatic.[305] In that case *ei de kai* should be linked to *hēmōn* rather than *kekalummenon*, which means, as Georgi says, "Paul does not want to say that his gospel is *also veiled*, but that *also his* gospel is veiled."[306] This also fits with the context. In the argument of chapter 3 Paul takes up the fact that the opponents place a high positive value on the veil of Moses, which they seem to have regarded as a symbol for their own pedagogical device.[307] But Paul turns it into a negative concept (3:12-15).[308] Here Paul does the same again. Just like his opponents, he too can claim that a veil rests over his gospel, but it is a veil in an ironical sense. It is a veil upon those who are "perishing" (*apollumenois*).[309] The connotation is bold and vivid. A "veil" is not a help, but an obstruction to Christian faith and life. In fact, it can separate one from the gospel and thus from the source of salvation.

It should be stressed that the subject of these verses is the gospel. The word "gospel" (*euaggelion*) appears both at the start (v. 3a) and at the end (v. 4b). That is to be expected in view of Paul's emphasis on preaching as the "open disclosure of the truth" (v. 2). The veil that lies over his gospel exists not in the gospel itself, but in the minds of the opponents (v. 4).[310] The gospel is an open disclosure. Only the mind of the hearer closes it off. In fact, the preaching of the gospel is given a profound, sweeping significance when Paul says in v. 4 that it is "the illumination of the gospel of the glory of Christ" (*ton phōtismon tou euaggeliou tēs doxēs tou Christou*). This plerophoristic

---

[303]Barrett (*Second Epistle*, 130) and Plummer (*Critical and Exegetical Commentary*, 113) interpret this as Paul dealing with a charge leveled against him.

[304]Georgi is keenly aware of the polemic. He points to the "strong polemically oriented Christological explanation" in 4:1ff. which, he argues, Paul has "formulated antithetically to the statements about Moses (and tradition) in 3:7ff.," with 4:1-2 forming the connection (*Die Gegner*, 253f.).

[305]Plummer stresses that *ei de kai estin* ("even if it is") is emphatic by position. He also observes that one normally would expect *kai ei* instead of *ei kai* (*Critical and Exegetical Commentary*, 113). However, Plummer fails to see that *hēmōn* ("ours") at the end of v. 3a is equally emphatic. It is Georgi who brings this to our attention (*Die Gegner*, 268).

[306]Georgi, *Die Gegner*, 269. See also Schütz (*Anatomy*, 174f.), who follows Georgi.

[307]Georgi, *Die Gegner*, 267-271. Schütz, *Anatomy*, 174.

[308]Georgi, *Die Gegner*, 269. Schütz, *Anatomy*, 174.

[309]The full expression is *en tois apollumenois* ("in the case of those who are perishing"). The phrase *en tois* could mean "among," or it could be taken as a simple dative, the latter being Barrett's preference (*Second Epistle*, 130). But more probably, as Plummer suggests, it means "in their case" (*Critical and Exegetical Commentary*, 114). For the term *apollumenois* see 1 Cor. 1:18ff. and our discussion of it, page 96f. above.

[310]Plummer, *Critical and Exegetical Commentary*, 113.

string of key terms in the genitive case has the effect of pointing to the succession of divine authority, since it forms a chain ending with "God" (*theou*).[311] The easiest way to understand it is to work it backwards. God is the ultimate source of all illumination (cf. 4:6), but he is not accessible except as he reveals himself. In the Scriptures God's revelation, usually accompanied by the presence of light, is his "glory" (*doxa*).[312] In Christ that glory of God has been made permanently resident, because Christ is the "image" (*eikōn*) of God. That is to say, he is the very reflection of the numinous, not an inferior representation but the actual equivalent.[313] Or, as Plummer succinctly phrases it, "Christ is the one visible representative of the invisible God."[314] Still the glory of Christ, which is of God, is not directly available to believers either, since the dawning of the "new creation" has made the Jesus of history no longer accessible (see 5:16-17). How then is the divine illumination to be received? Certainly not, as the opponents believe, from the glory of Moses or Jesus in pneumatic interpretations of the Mosaic tradition. It is doubtless against just such a position that Paul has carefully selected his terms here.[315] Rather, it is received through the gospel! That is noticeable from the conspicuous way the word *euaggelion* ("gospel") intrudes between *phōtismon* ("illumination") and *doxēs* ("glory").[316]

And yet, as Bultmann observes, that is precisely the problem which Paul has with the Corinthians and his opponents. Because Paul regards the glory of God in Christ to be resident exclusively in the preaching of the gospel, which is nothing more than the open disclosure of the truth, he seems to his detractors "not to give evidence of *doxa* ["glory"], appears not to mediate *Pneuma*

---

[311]Various origins have been suggested for the expression. Barrett thinks it is a "Jewish Greek" language, borrowed from gnosticism (*Second Epistle,* 131). Bultmann also construes it as gnostic, but he believes its roots are related to the "cosmological Son-of-God speculation" in Philo and the hermetic writings, especially the reference to *eikōn* ("image") (*Theology,* 132; see also *Der zweite Brief,* 108f.). Plummer suggests it may come from the Book of Wisdom. He quotes Testament of Napthtali 14:4: *to phōs tou nomou to dothen eis phōtismon pantos anthrōpou* ("the light of the law which was given for the illumination of all men") (*Critical and Exegetical Commentary,* 117).

[312]G. Kittel, *TDNT,* 2 (Grand Rapids: Eerdmanns, 1964), 232-255. See also Barrett, *Second Epistle,* 131f.

[313]G. Kittel, G. Von Rad, and Kleinknecht, *TDNT,* 2 (Grand Rapids: Eerdmanns, 1964), 381-397. See also Bultmann (*Der zweite Brief,* 109), who alerts us to the fact that the relation of *doxa* ("glory") with *eikōn* ("image") appears clear in 1 Cor. 11:7 and is to be understood primarily as *apaugasma* ("radiance, reflection", as in Heb. 1:3).

[314]Plummer, *Critical and Exegetical Commentary,* 117.

[315]Ibid.

[316]That "gospel" (*euaggelion*) stands out in this passage has been demonstrated by Hering's careful literary analysis. He finds the construction so pleonastic as to be "intolerable" and so strikes *to euaggelion* as a gloss (*Second Epistle,* 30). His analysis is persuasive, but his remedy is not. Rather than "gospel" being a gloss, more likely its awkwardness indicates precisely the words Paul has inserted and thus shows us the apostle's own emphasis!

["Spirit"] and *eleutheria* ["freedom"], as they claimed."[317] The preaching of the gospel, says Bultmann, is "ambiguous." By that he means that "it is concealed simultaneously in its openness, concealed for the curious and pretentious inquiry. For understanding does not rest on the peering intelligence but on the subservient decision of those whose consciences are smitten."[318]

Paul is a realist all the same. He accepts the fact that though the gospel proclaimed is the very glory of God, it will be resisted. This resistance comes from the "god of this age" (*theos tou aiōnos*) who "blinds the minds of the unbelievers" (*etuphlōsen ta noēmata tōn apistōn*). In short, it is the devil's work. This "bold expression for the devil," as Barrett speaks of it, which appears only here in Paul's letters, points up the fact that Paul understands Christian existence to be lived out in a world of hostile powers, a conception which is based on "the commonplace apocalyptic presupposition that in the present age the devil has usurped God's authority."[319] The world is not a neutral, harmless sphere, but a positive counterforce against God, a force which is both "seductive and ruinous," to quote Bultmann.[320] In the context, therefore, Paul is not simply offering an explanation for a phenomenon, the resistance to the concealed glory of the gospel, but he is simultaneously issuing a warning that those who refuse his gospel are "not merely in error, but fallen into ruin, fallen to Satan.[321]

> For we do not preach ourselves but Jesus Christ as Lord, with ourselves as your slaves because of Jesus, because it is the God who said, "Let light shine out of darkness," who has shone in our hearts for the purpose of the illumination of the knowledge of the glory of God in the face of Jesus Christ (vv. 5-6).

Verse 5 is explanatory, as the word *gar* ("for") indicates. But what does it explain? In view of everything Paul has said in 4:1-4, he means now to explain why his preaching is oriented as it is. Since the starting point is God, whose glory in Christ is the illumination of people's minds through the ministry of the open declaration of the gospel, the content of preaching cannot be any human being. Instead, the very nature of the gift of salvation requires that the focus be on Jesus Christ. And that is precisely how Paul preaches. With his opponents obviously in mind, he makes his bold statement, first negatively and then positively. "We do not preach ourselves" (*ou heautous kērussomen*), Paul emphasizes.[322] Paul means to say, as Georgi points out, that he and his fellow apostles preach "not our pneumatic selves as do the op-

---

[317]Bultmann, *Der zweite Brief,* 105.
[318]Ibid.
[319]Barrett, *Second Epistle,* 130. See also Bultmann, *Der zweite Brief,* 106.
[320]Bultmann, *Der zweite Brief,* 106.
[321]Ibid. Cf. 2 Cor. 11:13f.
[322]*Ou heautous* ("not ourselves") is emphatic by position, as Plummer points out (*Critical and Exegetical Commentary,* 118).

ponents in their powerful demonstrations."[323] To the contrary, Paul preaches "Jesus Christ as Lord" (*Iēsoun Christon kurion*).[324] The apostle's own role is that of "slave" (*doulos*), and not only a slave of Christ, as we could expect (see 1 Cor. 9:14-18; Rom. 1:1; Phil. 1:1), but a slave of the Corinthians "because of Jesus" (*dia Iēsoun*). To be a slave of Christ is to be a slave of those who belong to Christ, and so for Paul the true apostle is recognized by the bondage of his office.[325] This is surely said in conscious contrast to his opponents, whom Paul believes to be making the Corinthians the slaves of themselves (see 2 Cor. 11:20f.!).

But the nerve center of v. 5, which easily could be thematic for the whole of 2 Corinthians, is that Jesus Christ is preached as "Lord" (*kurios*). With this particular phraseology Paul has made a simple, but profound and multi-faceted, assertion. First, he has laid hold of the early credal formula, the confession "Jesus Christ is Lord."[326] By using this as the summary of his preaching Paul lines himself up with the apostolic tradition. It is no mystery where that leaves his opponents. Secondly, Paul has used an expression that is self-consciously soteriological. By *kurios* ("Lord") Paul means none other than the crucified Messiah who is exalted by God through the resurrection to a position of lordship.[327] This means that he is, in Barrett's words, "merciful ruler of the world and victor over all evil powers."[328] It is the lordship of Jesus Christ which expresses Paul's soteriology, and thus it fits perfectly with the context (v. 4b; cf. 2:14ff.). For Paul the issue of apostolic preaching is life or death! The seriousness of the decision which his Corinthian congregation must make is underscored. Thirdly, the term *kurios* has been chosen by Paul quite likely with a view to his opponents and to the word *doulous* ("slaves") which is about to appear next in his thought. If Jesus Christ is Lord, as he has correctly preached in subservience to the Christian tradition, then as apostle he cannot make himself out as a competing "lord." Yet that is exactly what his opponents have done. In preaching themselves, their own pneumatic achievements, they have displaced the true Lord, Jesus Christ, by their own presumption of lordship.[329]

Paul's argument is sharply polemical. His opponents have reproached him for lacking the spiritually potent signs of an apostle and missionary. He in

---

[323]Georgi, *Die Gegner*, 285. See also Schütz, *Anatomy*, 183ff.

[324]As Barrett notes, *kurion* ("lord") without the article is predicative (*Second Epistle*, 134).

[325]Plummer, *Critical and Exegetical Commentary*, 118f. Barrett, *Second Epistle*, 134. Bultmann, *Der zweite Brief*, 109.

[326]Barrett especially notices this (*Second Epistle*, 134). See Rom. 10:9 and 1 Cor. 12:3 for other appearances of the formula in Paul.

[327]Ibid.

[328]Ibid.

[329]Georgi, *Die Gegner*, 285.

turn reproaches them. As Schütz summarizes, "Paul misses in his opponents both a proper respect for Jesus and a sense of his lordship, stressed by the emphatic location of *kurion* ("lord"). In short, *Iēsous,* their term, is countered with *kurios,* Paul's term."[330] As a result, Paul associates salvation with Jesus Christ as *Lord,* while the Jesus of history, who for the opponents is a source of power as a *theios anēr* ("divine man"), becomes paradigmatic for the apostle as slave. For the phrase *dia Iēsoun* ("because of Jesus"), as the basis for apostolic "slavery" to the congregation, is a reference specifically to the cross (4:10ff.!).

There is one more nuance which, though subtle, dare not be overlooked. In v. 5 Paul has succeeded in splitting apart the conception of Jesus Christ as Lord from that of the historical Jesus. At the same time, in using this as his foundation for apostolicity, Paul also separates gospel and apostle![331] And this is precisely where Paul and his opponents are radically different. Paul's opponents do preach themselves, because for them the apostle and the gospel have been "collapsed," as Schütz says, which means they identify themselves with the gospel, which in turn is to identify themselves with Jesus, which in turn is to claim to have access to his power.[332] Paul, on the other hand, understands his role as preacher of the gospel to be distinct from the gospel itself, as becomes even clearer in v. 6. This does not suggest, however, that Paul denies there is an important relationship between gospel and apostle. In fact, he speaks of himself belonging to the gospel as the "fragrance of Christ" (*euōdia Christou*) in 2:14ff., and for that reason, as Bultmann says, "there is no gospel without an apostle, since the gospel is the addressed word of God."[333] Nevertheless, in Paul's mind they are not the same. Gospel is prior to apostle. Paul's argument in v. 5 is aimed to defeat the "Jesus theology" of his opponents in Corinth.[334] The name *Iēsous* alone, without the appended title *Christos,* appears rarely in Paul, and yet astonishingly it turns up not only in v. 5 but also in 4:10, 11, 14 and 11:4. This fact lends important credence to the claim that Paul contends here with a competitive, subversive conception of the earthly Jesus.[335]

In the causal statement of v. 6 Paul supplies the reason why he preaches Christ, not himself. At the same time his words are a majestic climax for his

---

[330]Schütz, *Anatomy,* 117. See also Georgi, *Die Gegner,* 285f.

[331]Schütz, *Anatomy,* 183f.

[332]Ibid.

[333]Bultmann, *Der zweite Brief,* 110. See also Holmberg, *Paul and Power,* 157.

[334]The phrase is Beker's (*Paul the Apostle,* 296). The argument is Georgi's (*Die Gegner,* 286).

[335]Georgi, *Die Gegner,* 286. This point is at the heart of Georgi's reconstruction of the dispute. He points especially to the phrase "another Jesus" (*allon Iēsoun*) at 11:4 as further documentation.

theology of preaching, which is operative throughout this letter. The foundation of everything lies in God the creator. The point of departure is God's creative word, "Let light shine out of darkness," a reference to God's first creative act (Gen. 1:3). Although the expression presents difficulties, it is not impossible to translate. *Ho theos* ("God") must be predicative here (as it is at 1:21 and 5:5), with *ho eipon* ("who said") being adjectival.[336] The important thing to notice is that God is pictured by Paul as creating light, which is the source of all illumination, and doing it precisely in his act of *speaking*. Thus God's creative word and illumination are correlative. The decisive thing for Paul, however, is that God's creative, illuminating act, which is brought to pass by his word, has been focused in the apostle: "It is the God who said, 'Let light shine out of darkness,' who has shone in our hearts." The plural phrase "in our hearts" should not mislead us. Paul means himself personally, as he often does when he uses the plural.[337] The reference to light shining in him undoubtedly refers to his call to apostleship received on the road to Damascus.[338] As Barrett observes, Paul understands that "his apostolic activity resembles the creation of light."[339]

In his preaching ministry Paul speaks the word which provides spiritual illumination. That is clear from the expression in v. 6b, which, while it is parallel to v. 4b, is subtly recast in order to end on a strongly Christological note. The purpose of God's creative illumination in the word of his apostle is that the world may be illuminated, a theme-note begun in 2:14ff.[340] As in v. 4b, it is a case of illumination by the glory of God. Just as Paul inserted "gospel" (*euaggelion*) between "illumination" and "glory" in v. 4b, so now he inserts "knowledge" (*gnōseōs*).[341] The reason, as Bultmann explains, is that "the *phōtismon* ["illumination"] ensues in the preaching whose result is precisely *gnōsis* ["knowledge"]. The *doxa* ["glory"] is no perceptible phenomenon. That the diffusion of *gnōsis* is demonstrated as *phōtismon* is not based on Gen. 1:3, but Gen. 1:3 is cited because preaching is thought of as *phōtismos*."[342] *Gnōsis* ("knowledge") quite clearly means the gospel.[343] But the word is chosen at this point probably to coincide with the image of

---

[336]Bultmann, *Der zweite Brief*, 110.

[337]Ibid., 111.

[338]Ibid. *Lampsei* ("let shine") and *elampsen* ("shone") are both intransitive in the passage. See Plummer, *Critical and Exegetical Commentary*, 120, and Bultmann, *Der zweite Brief*, 111.

[339]Barrett, *Second Epistle*, 135. He follows Bultmann.

[340]Bultmann, *Der zweite Brief*, 111. He particularly notices the correspondence between v. 6b and 2:14.

[341]Ibid.

[342]Ibid. Bultmann regards this language usage as coming from gnostics.

[343]Barrett, *Second Epistle*, 135. He believes Paul's usage is polemical and that he has appropriated current Corinthian terminology.

God's creation of light, which in Jewish thought was considered to be the source of all knowledge in the world.[344] In other words, the illuminating power of God is in his apostles with a view to their illuminating others by means of their apostolic work, which consists in the preaching of the gospel.[345] And that illumination from God is "in the face of Christ" (*en prosōpōi Christou*), which explains why he is preached as Lord (v. 5). The reference is probably not to an ecstatic vision, but, as Bultmann notes, to "faith in the preached word."[346] God's glory appears in the face of Christ, so whoever sees Christ sees God, and that happens when Christ is preached as Lord.[347]

C. Preliminary Observations

From 2 Corinthians 4:1-6 we have gained a much clearer perspective on the function and nature of preaching, according to Paul. Paul understands himself to have been entrusted with a ministry from God. That ministry consists in preaching, which is nothing more or less than the "open disclosure of the truth," the gospel of God. It brings about reconciliation with God by appealing to the conscience, which is illumined by God's revelation in Christ. It is, therefore, fundamentally a service. Paul conceives his role in preaching to be that of a slave, a slave of Christ and also of his congregation. His preaching ministry is limited to the Lord's commission, and he is duty-bound not to call attention to himself as preacher nor to practice manipulation. Preaching is conformed to the gospel, to proclaiming as Lord the Christ who was crucified. Thus the preacher's paradigm is the "death of Jesus."

CONCLUSIONS

Our investigation of the Corinthian letters has turned up a significant number and variety of aspects relating to Paul's theology of preaching. Particularly prominent are statements of the apostle which clarify the function and nature of the preaching task. Now the question arises, How can these all be brought together into a cohesive unity? Where is the thread that binds the pieces together?

An important clue in answering this question can be found in the term Paul repeatedly uses for preaching. That term is "proclaim/preach" (*kērussein*). It is God's good pleasure "to save those who believe" by the folly of "preaching" (1 Cor. 1:21). If Christ is "proclaimed as raised from the dead,

---

[344]Ibid.
[345]Plummer, *Critical and Exegetical Commentary*, 121. Barrett, *Second Epistle*, 135.
[346]Bultmann, *Der zweite Brief*, 111.
[347]Ibid.

how can it be said that the dead are not raised'' (1 Cor. 15:12)? Paul declares that he ''preaches'' Jesus Christ as Lord (2 Cor. 4:5). In each case the controlling verb is *kērussein*. This term, together with Paul's other favorite word *euaggelizesthai* (''preach the gospel/gospelize''), focuses attention on the power that undergirds the preaching of the gospel and thereby points us in the direction of the image which dominates the apostle's thought. For the term *kērussein*, as we have seen, implies that a recognized authority stands behind the word that is delivered by the herald. *Kērussein* is herald's work. The effectiveness and validity of what the herald proclaims are in direct relationship to the authority of the potentate who backs up the message. Paul knows that to be none other than God. It is God the sovereign creator and ruler of the world who issues the saving proclamation.

If God is the sovereign of creation who authorizes the word to be delivered, then this means that the one who delivers the message and those who hear it stand before him as subjects. Thus Paul describes himself as the slave (*doulos*) of God, of Christ, of the gospel (1 Cor. 9:14-18; 2 Cor. 4:5). The members of the congregation in Corinth are the subjects of God because he has liberated them and called them into his new creation (1 Cor. 1:26-31; 2 Cor. 2:14ff.; 2 Cor. 4:6; 2 Cor. 5:17ff.). And the agent by whom God orders this new, redemptive world is Jesus Christ, the crucified one whom God has raised from the dead and made Lord (*kurios*) of all (1 Cor. 1:18ff.; 1 Cor. 15:3-5, 12ff.; cf. Rom. 1:1ff.). This means a renewal of creation, a reordering of human life and human potential through a realignment of relationships. And all of this is enacted by means of preaching!

What are the implications? At the primary level it means that preaching is in fact much more than mere speech. It is an *act,* as is implied in *kērussein,* which means to enact the sovereign's will by means of a public proclamation. It is not a matter of passing along certain information, though that is assumed to be a part of the proclamation (1 Cor. 15:3ff.). It is rather the case that in the herald's proclamation the sovereign lays down the terms and conditions of existence, whether they be terms of peace (2 Cor. 5:18-21), terms of status (1 Cor. 1:28ff.), or terms of life itself (1 Cor. 1:18-25). In the case of God, Paul would have us know, it has ''pleased him'' (*eudokēsen*) to enact salvation (*sōsai*) by means of an act of proclamation.

The salvation that God enacts by means of proclamation is described in the letters of Paul by means of a multiplicity of images.[348] But the image that appears most frequently, either by direct reference or by allusion, is that of the new creation. Proclaiming the gospel is the ministry of ''rec-

---

[348]For a helpful and careful analysis of Paul's soteriological imagery see Gerd Theissen, ''Soteriologische Symbolik in den paulinischen Schriften,'' *KD* 20 (1974): 282-304.

onciliation'' (*kataggelēs*) which calls the hearer into the power structure of the new creation (2 Cor. 5:17–6:2). At the same time there is a negative dimension to the work of proclamation. In the very declaration of the new order of life the old order is brought to an end. Proclaiming the gospel means the destruction of the old age, the old order of life and the old criteria (1 Cor. 1:19-20, 28-29). The preaching of the gospel is therefore *polemical*. It occurs in the context of a battle, a war between the world and its creator. No wonder Paul calls the Corinthians to be ''reconciled'' (2 Cor. 5:20). The old world dies hard. But it does die. The sovereign's proclamation condemns it to destruction. The surprising aspect is that this happens by the ''open disclosure of the truth'' (2 Cor. 4:2). The power of the truth, the saving will of God revealed in the gospel, exposes the futility, pretention and presumption of the old order, while at the same time it enlightens the life of those who believe.

But the work of the preacher who heralds God's tidings does not end with the announcement of the new order and the establishment of the new power structure. God the creator is also God the preserver and sustainer. It follows, therefore, that if God creates by means of his word, operative through the medium of preaching, then he also preserves and sustains in the same way. The word of preaching has a preserving function, which is carried on by means of continuing interpretation. That is to say, it directs and controls the way in which the gospel is appropriated, as Paul makes clear in dealing with the various crises in Corinth (see especially 1 Cor. 15:3ff.). Preaching is an exercise of *authority*.

Since preaching is the exercise and preservation of the salvation God has accomplished in Jesus Christ, that salvation of God impinges upon the office of the preacher, the preacher himself/herself, and the congregation who hears. As to the office of preaching, Paul recognizes that preaching is no greater, worth no more, than the authority who authorizes the message. The foundation for Christian preaching is God, and God alone. It is his act in raising Jesus ''from the dead'' (1 Cor. 15:12-14) which constitutes the warrant for a new order of human existence. Without that warrant, there is nothing to preach and nothing to believe (1 Cor. 15:14).

As we saw, the resurrection of Christ is validated in Paul's argument neither by reference to the resurrection appearances nor to tradition, but by the fact that Christ is *preached* as raised from the dead (1 Cor. 15:12). To the Corinthians Paul is arguing much as follows: ''Since the risen Christ was preached to you, you have become believers in Christ and have entered into the sphere of the gospel. You and I both know this is true because of the great gifts of the Spirit which you have enjoyed [see 1 Cor. 1:4ff.]. The power of the gospel is therefore a recognizable, valid fact to which we both testify. Now if the risen Christ, whose power you so abundantly experience, is *preached* by me and the other apostolic authorities as risen 'from the dead,' then to deny that resurrection from the dead is to deny the very gospel which is constitutive for your entire Christian existence. And, of course, we both know that would be an absurdity.''

This line of reasoning suggests something else crucially important for Paul's theology of preaching. If salvation is by grace, if apostleship is by grace, if sanctification is by grace, then preaching is also by grace. Not only does this mean it is an undeserved gift, but it is a sovereign, free act of God. Grace means the action is entirely on the side of God! If that is the case, if all is on the side of God, and if God exercises his power in the proclamation of the gospel, then preaching cannot draw attention to itself! Preaching is not a self-conscious, mighty act. If preaching gives way to manipulation or calls attention to the power of the preacher (whether in signs or eloquence), then it discredits the power of God who has authorized it and therewith has sown the seeds of its own destruction (2 Cor. 2:17 and 4:2!). The moment there is a human "boast" (*kauchēsis*), the cross of Christ is emptied of its power (1 Cor. 1:17, 30-31; 2:5). Preaching rests on the foundation of the resurrection of the *crucified* Jesus. Since God raised the crucified, this weak and despised and disgraced figure, from the dead, it means God operates out of human weakness so that there can be no confusion as to where the source of salvation is (1 Cor. 1:25; 2:7). It is in God and God alone.

If the warrant for preaching is the resurrection of Christ from the dead, if the character of preaching is to allow the power of God alone to be recognized, and if the function of preaching is to enact the salvation of God by bringing believers into a new power structure, his new creation, then this has profound significance for those who hear the gospel. For it means, as we have seen in Paul's discussion at 1 Cor. 1:17ff., that the awesome power of God is being enacted through a *weak* medium. Here is a divine paradox. And that paradox is not lost on the hearers of this world, particularly its skeptics. This is because the fundamental presupposition of all proclamation is the power and authority of the sovereign. Whether king, prince or conqueror, the message that is heralded is received as authoritative only if the sovereign's claim is recognized. In the case of the warfare of the world against God, however, God's sovereignty is not unmistakably patent. To the contrary, in the eyes of this world God's claim is precisely the question! The world is not prepared to accept God's authority except on its own terms. Thus preaching appears empty. It is perceived as begging the question.

This, of course, presents a dilemma. For as Paul is keenly aware, if God is truly the divine creator and Lord, he cannot be answerable to the criteria of the wisdom of this world. On the other hand, if God operates strictly outside the structures of the world, how can his power be recognized at all? At this point we are again confronted with the testimony borne by the new creation itself. Those who were nothing have been called into a new existence, the church of God, by the weakness of the proclamation of the crucified and risen Christ, and that fact stands as living testimony to God's creative power operative out of weakness (1 Cor. 1:22-31). The demonstration of the Spirit and power in both the congregation and the apostle is, in fact, the final exhibit which documents the claim that God accomplishes his saving work precisely by means of human weakness (1 Cor. 2:1-5).

The hearer of the gospel, therefore, is brought to a decision. It is not God whose credibility is at stake, but the hearer's. Preaching is a suspect medium. It appears as the opposite of what is called for. That is because the hearer is susceptible to the criteria of the world, its "wisdom." Preaching the gospel, therefore, is always bound to meet with resistance. That resistance is made all the more pronounced by the fact that at the heart of the preaching of the gospel is the Lord who was *crucified*. That God should choose to save the world by means of the senseless, disgraceful, tasteless death of the cross presents the hearer with a scandal. If this is the truth, then all human wisdom and pretension and respectibility and social status is a lie. That is hard to accept. And that explains why the salvation of God in the resurrection of the crucified Christ, offered through the medium of preaching, comes to "those who believe." To others, to "those who are perishing," it is nonsense. The act of preaching is conformed to its center, the cross of Christ (1 Cor. 1:22ff.; 2 Cor. 4:5-12). Both the content of the message and the form of its delivery are equally scandalous. They bear witness that what is called for is a total reordering of human life!

Since the whole point of preaching is salvation, not only does that affect the office of preaching and the hearers, but it also influences the bearer of the message. The preacher and her/his exercise of the office must be conformed to the gospel, and that means under the sign of the cross (2 Cor. 4:7-12). Several dimensions of what this signifies surface in Paul's discussion.

First, the key word for the position of the preacher is "slave" (*doulos*). This means not only that the preacher is accountable to her/his Lord but also that her/his exercise of the preaching office is *limited*. The preacher cannot exceed the content or the means of delivery authorized by the sovereign, God. This is not a position agreeable to the power-hungry or the status conscious. It means offering one's neck to the slave's collar.

Secondly, if the preacher is slave, then his/her work is a service. This is brought out by the fact that Paul in 2 Corinthians, precisely where his apostolic work and authority are at stake, speaks of his office as a "ministry'' (*diakonia*). And while his opponents also used that term, they understood it in terms of the "divine man" model, whereas Paul stresses that ministry implies the humble aspect of slavery. Nowhere is that clearer than in his choice of a model for apostolic preaching. That model is the "death of Jesus" (2 Cor. 4:10). The slave's paradigm is the fate of the master.

Third, the preacher's office is not simply something that one can assume. It is a trust that is given by the master (1 Cor. 9:16; 2 Cor. 5:18ff.; 2 Cor. 2:17). It is a commission. It is therefore also an honor, since the crucified Christ has been exalted by God to be "Lord" (*kurios*). As a result, Paul speaks of himself as having his ministry "by the mercy of God" (2 Cor. 4:1).

Finally, the ministry of heralding the gospel of God is an exercise of faith. It is carried on by means of nothing more than the "open disclosure of the truth" (2 Cor. 4:1). It rejects all attempts at human manipulation (2 Cor. 4:2). The preacher operates with the conviction that in delivering the sovereign's message she/he is the instrument of divine illumination for the world, and in this divine illumination resides the instrument of salvation to those whom God has called (2 Cor. 2:14ff.). Preaching requires a posture of faith, a confidence that the gospel of God, precisely because it is the exercise of the power of God, can do its saving work with no other help from the preacher than to deliver the good news of God.

CHAPTER 5

THE RIGHTEOUSNESS OF GOD, FAITH, AND UNITY: THEOLOGY OF PREACHING IN ROMANS

THE HISTORICAL SITUATION

Paul's letter to the Romans is an anomaly. It is longer than any of the apostle's other letters, is directed to a congregation he has never met, and reads more like a theological treatise than a letter. Still, there is little doubt that it comes from the apostle Paul, very likely written in Corinth towards the end of his ministry in Greece and Asia Minor, about the mid–fifties.[1] In this work Paul gives serious and profound thought to some of the fundamental elements of Christian theology as they have arisen in his missionary activity. It is perhaps fitting, therefore, that our examination of the two final passages which have to do with the apostle's theology of preaching should have as their matrix this important epistle.

---

[1]Kümmel, *Introduction*, 310, 314. Marxsen, *Introduction*, 99f. Bornkamm, *Paul*, 91. We leave aside the question of whether chapter 16 belongs with the original letter. It is not necessary for this chapter to be included in order to provide evidence that Paul knew the Roman situation. The apostle had many other channels of information available to him. It is true that the warning in 16:17-20 does seem odd in relation to the concerns of chapters 12-15, and so it may be that the chapter is a fragment from a letter to Ephesus, as Marxsen believes (*Introduction*, 108). But cf. Kümmel (*Introduction*, 318f.) who is not convinced. And cf. also Sam K. Williams, "The 'Righteousness of God' in Romans," *JBL 99* (1980): 251; he contends the burden of proof falls on those who deny the chapter belongs to the original letter and thinks that it is evidence that Paul had acquaintances in Rome.

Since, on the one hand, Romans is so apparently theological and, on the other, comes late in the apostle's ministry, it has been natural to conclude that this letter constitutes his mature theological reflections, a "testament," as Bornkamm refers to it, or a "manifesto," if one favors Munck's term.[2] In fact, since at least the time of the Reformation this letter has been regarded as a summary statement of Christian systematic theology. Despite this appearance, however, there is good reason to believe that a specific set of circumstances lies behind the composition of the epistle. As a result, the consensus among scholars today is that Romans does not present us with a case of theology in the abstract, dogmatic sense, but that there is a concrete situation to which Paul's letter is directed.[3]

The consensus among New Testament scholars begins and ends with that observation, however. There is considerable debate about how to construe the evidence from the text of Romans and a multiplicity of theories about the occasion of its composition. Still, despite the many conflicting views, there have emerged a number of important observations and insights which, when taken together, allow us to arrive at a description of the Roman situation with enough confidence to provide a reliable framework for our exegetical study.

It seems clear that the letter to the Romans came from the hand of Paul on the basis of more than one motivation. To be sure, the most obvious statement of intent, and the one often used as the starting point by scholars, is Paul's announcement that his work in the east is concluded and that therefore he intends to travel west, specifically to Spain, for which he wants the support of the Romans (15:19-24).[4] In fact, Beker goes so far as to suggest that Paul would never have visited Rome were it not for his plans to carry his missionary work to Spain.[5] The argument goes, then, that Paul, having never been to Rome, uses the epistle as a way of introducing himself and demonstrating that his presentation of the gospel is worthy of support by the Roman Christians.[6] There may be some credence to this line of reasoning. But, as Klein points out, this argument hardly does justice to the wealth of theological content in Romans and in some respects threatens to trivialize Paul's thought if the epistle is "nothing but grist for his apostolic calling card."[7]

Spain, however, is not the only destination for the apostle. He also is at the point of a trip to Jerusalem to deliver the collection which he has taken

---

[2]Bornkamm, *Paul*, 96. Munck, *Paul and the Salvation*, 199.

[3]See Karl Donfried, *The Romans Debate* (Minneapolis: Augsburg, 1977), ix.-xvii. He provides a brief history of the treatment given to the situation of Romans.

[4]Kümmel, *Introduction*, 311. Perrin, *Introduction*, 106. Bornkamm, *Paul*, 90. Williams, " 'Righteousness of God', " 246.

[5]Beker, *Paul the Apostle*, 72.

[6]Kümmel, *Introduction*, 312f. Bornkamm, *Paul*, 93.

[7]Günter Klein, "Paul's Purpose in Writing the Epistle to the Romans," in *The Romans Debate*, ed. Karl Donfried (Minneapolis: Augsburg, 1977), 37f.

up among the gentile congregations, and this has some influence in his relationship with Rome and in the timing of his visit. In 1 Cor. 16:3-4 Paul had reported his intention to send the collection by means of others and indicated that he himself would go to Jerusalem only if necessary. Now, however, for reasons not disclosed, Paul plans to go personally to Jerusalem. He expresses his uncertainty about the prospects, asking the Romans to pray for the outcome and his deliverance from hostile elements there (15:25-33). This matter suggests two facts of importance. First, it is obvious that something has occurred during the time since his letters to Corinth which warrants his personal appearance in Jerusalem. Although it may be going too far to conclude from this fact that Romans is really a "hidden letter to Jerusalem," as Beker does, it cannot be denied that the Jerusalem situation is in the back of Paul's mind, so that Kümmel's description of Romans as having a "double biographical-historical situation" is not a bad way of saying it.[8] Second, it is equally clear that something of decisive importance is also going on in Rome, since Paul feels constrained to write a letter of such depth and length to serve as a substitute for his presence until he actually arrives there. It seems probable that if we can successfully clarify each of these situations and then put them together, we might arrive at the historical framework for Paul's letter.

What are the circumstances among the Christians in Rome, then, as suggested by clues in the text of Romans? We begin with this question first, partly because it is to Rome that Paul actually writes and partly because the situation in Rome may very well have triggered a crisis in Jerusalem. In the first place, the Roman congregation appears to have been composed of both Jewish and gentile Christians, as can be seen from the fact that Paul addresses both groups directly in the letter and the fact that the largest portion of the letter is devoted to the relationship between Jews and gentiles under the gospel of Christ.[9] In addition, all does not appear to be well between the two groups. For Paul deals directly with a conflict between the "strong" and the "weak," gentile and Jewish Christians respectively, in 12:1–15:13, a dispute over the laws about food, drink, and holy days.[10] How has such a conflict arisen in Rome? And

---

[8]Beker, *Paul the Apostle*, 71. Kümmel, *Introduction*, 314. See also Ulrich Wilckens, *Der Brief an die Römer* (Zürich, Einsiedeln, Köln: Benziger/Neukirchener Verlag, 1978), vol. 1, 46. He refers to Romans as Paul's "preparation for his defense speech in Jerusalem."

[9]Beker especially makes this clear, arguing that Jews are addressed in 1:16–4:25; 6:1-15; 7:1, 4-6 and chapters 9-11, while the gentiles are directly confronted in 1:5-6, 13, 14; 11:13, 20-21, 25; 14:15; 15:1, 16 (*Paul the Apostle*, 75). See also Wilckens, *Römer*, 1:35, and *Kümmel, Introduction*, 310. Kümmel thinks, however, that most were gentiles. Cf. Marxsen, *Introduction*, 97f. On the other hand, Munck (*Paul and the Salvation*, 201) and Bornkamm (*Paul*, 89) regard the church at Rome as being made up primarily if not exclusively of gentiles.

[10]Marxsen has made a particularly strong case for identifying the "strong" as gentiles and the "weak" as Jewish Christians (*Introduction*, 96ff.) See also Beker, *Paul the Apostle*, 73f.; Wilckens, *Römer*, 1:35; and Hans-Werner Bartsch, "The Historical Situation of Romans,"

how is it that the conflict has reached such proportions that the apostle must devote almost eleven full chapters of serious theological discussion about God's dealings with Jews and gentiles before his stated intention in 1:14-17, to preach the gospel in Rome, can finally be brought to bear on the Christians there (12:1–15:13)?[11]

Beker has suggested that the catalyst for the heightened antagonism between Jewish and gentile segments of Christianity was Paul's letter to the Galatians. He argues that Paul's strong presentation of the law-free gospel in Galatians worsened his relations with the church in Jerusalem and that his letter to the Romans is a discussion of the "Jewish question" aimed to "defuse the negative reaction to his Galatian letter."[12] Beker's case is certainly plausible and would help to explain why Paul has to travel to Jerusalem before visiting Rome. But the only evidence Beker can offer for connecting the Galatian and Roman correspondence is the fact that the Galatians are conspicuously absent from the list of contributors to the collection for Jerusalem (15:26), a rather fragile foundation for such a weighty argument.[13] Instead, a more persuasive reason lies closer at hand. At the time in which Paul writes his letter, the mid–fifties or shortly thereafter, the edict of the emperor Claudius, which had evicted the Jews from Rome in 49 A.D., had just been lifted by Nero in 54 A.D. If the evidence from the historian Suetonius is accurate, that Claudius issued the edict because of disturbances in the Jewish synagogue over a "certain Chrestos," and if we are correct in surmising that this reference is to be equated with "Christ," then it is probable, as Wilckens reasons, that the commotion was started because of the appearance in Rome of Jewish-Christian missionaries, the only Christians who would have had access to the synagogue.[14] Claudius dealt with the matter by throwing them all out of Rome. This meant, however, that those Christians left behind in Rome were gentiles, who doubtless distanced themselves from the synagogue and organized themselves into "their own *collegia*," as Wilckens describes it.[15] So when the Jews, and Jewish Christians, began returning to Rome after the ban was lifted, they would have encountered a very different, and probably strong, developing gentile Christianity, and this would have only renewed and

Encounter 33 (1972): 330-332. But cf. Kümmel, who thinks the identity of the "strong" and "weak" is debatable and is of the opinion that 12:1–15:13 says nothing about the composition of the letter (*Introduction*, 310f.).

[11]Victor Furnish, *Theology and Ethics in Paul* (Nashville: Abingdon, 1968), 103 ff. He provides evidence for a strong connection between Romans 1 and 12-15.

[12]Beker, *Paul the Apostle*, 73. His argument is heavily oriented toward the view that Paul's main concern is not in Rome but Jerusalem.

[13]Ibid.

[14]Wilckens, *Römer*, 1:36. See also Marxsen, *Introduction*, 98 ff., and Bartsch, "Historical Situation," 331.

[15]Wilckens, *Römer*, 1:36.

intensified the tension between the two groups.[16] But this is not all we can say from the evidence. If Paul was at the center of a conflict in early Christianity over the relationship of gentile Christians to the Jewish law (Acts 15; Gal. 2:11-21), then the expulsion of Jews from Rome because of a disturbance related to the Christian message cannot help but have strained the already tenuous relationship between Paul and the Jerusalem Church. Paul has to go to Jerusalem to give answer. And it does not require a great deal of imagination to realize that the "Roman problem" would be thrown in his face. Beker's observation, therefore, is exactly on the mark: "Paul's basic apostolic effort—to establish the one church of the Jews and Gentiles—is jeopardized in Rome, where disunity threatens in the factions of the 'weak' and the 'strong.' "[17]

It becomes clearer, at this point, why Paul has chosen this particular time, just prior to his journey to Jerusalem and before his visit to Rome, to send such a lengthy, carefully thought-through epistle. He needs to arrive in Jerusalem able to say that the "Roman problem" is on its way to solution, that he corrected the situation, that the law-free gospel for the gentiles is not incompatible with Jewish piety and law. His letter to the Romans intends to settle the dispute, and, judging by the length and depth of the theology, to settle it permanently.

On the other hand, this presents the apostle with a delicate problem. He has not been to Rome before, has not founded the Christian congregation there, and as a result does not actually have authority over it! This factor leads us to the intriguing and instructive arguments of Klein, arguments which both clarify Paul's dealing with Rome in the letter and at the same time offer further credence to our proposed reconstruction of the circumstances of Romans. Klein has noticed and taken very seriously the tension between Paul's "non–interference clause" in 15:18-20, by which the apostle renounces missionary work in another's territory, and his stated purpose in 1:13-15, that he intends to "preach the gospel" also in Rome and "reap some harvest" there.[18] From this curious fact, together with the fact that "fruit" (*karpos*) is a missionary term and that "to lay a foundation" (*themelion tithenai*) is an express term for apostolic founding (1 Cor. 3:1), Klein concludes that Rome presents Paul with a unique situation. On the one hand they are already Christian "brothers," and yet at the same time missionary objects, because, as Klein suggests, "he does not regard the local Christian community there as having

---

[16]Ibid. Marxsen argues that this shows that 13:1-7 is not a dogmatic statement about governmental authority, but a "demand for loyal conduct in order to avoid a fresh edict" (*Introduction*, 99f.).

[17]Beker, *Paul the Apostle*, 74.

[18]Klein, "Paul's Purpose," 38f.

an apostolic foundation."[19] When this tenuous position on the part of Paul is combined with the delicate but volatile situation of his "Roman problem," it is more easily seen what Paul is trying to do with the letter to Rome. To defuse the Jewish-gentile question among Christians he must act, even though it puts him on a shaky foundation with regard to his non-interference policy (15:20). But he also must exercise his apostolic authority so as not to arouse resentment or suspicion about his motives on the part of Christians he has not met. This is particularly noticeable as Paul tries to maintain a balance between exercising his apostolic authority and respecting the autonomy of the Christians in Rome (1:11–13; cf. 15:14-16!).

At first one may be hesitant to accept Klein's bold proposal, especially since it implies that the gospel has not yet been preached, or fully preached, in Rome. And since the Romans are addressed as Christians, it is only reasonable to conclude that they have received the gospel, which of course means that in some way it must have been preached to them. On the other hand, if Christianity first arrived in Rome via the trade route, it is easily understandable that there might be no apostolic foundation there.[20] If Christianity was started by Jewish-Christian missionaries in the synagogue, who were then expelled by Claudius along with the rest of the Jews, then the gentile Christians in Rome would probably be made up chiefly of "god-fearers" who first heard the gospel in the synagogue, but who now, with the expulsion of the Jews, have been cut loose from the only authoritative Christian structure at hand. When we add to this the fact that, as we have seen, the gospel for Paul is not merely the message of Christ but also the power sphere in which the Christian lives, it becomes comprehensible why Paul must "preach the gospel" in Rome. By doing so, he takes the Roman Christians into the gospel's influence, its power, from which he can then exercise apostolic authority. And by means of that authority he can straighten out the conflicts there, thus presenting a unified structure of Christianity to the mother church in Jerusalem. It is of great importance that Paul's approach to Rome is by way of the "gospel" (1:1!), for it is only as a preacher set apart for the gospel "to the gentiles" (1:5-6, 14) that Paul can extend his authority to Rome.[21]

If this reconstruction is accurate, then Paul's letter to Rome is anything but an abstract theological treatise. The epistle arises in the middle of a lively,

---

[19]Ibid., 44. The argument of Klein, and also of Bartsch ("Historical Situation," 330), which proceeds from the fact that the term *ekklēsia* ("church") does not appear in Romans is not convincing. Too many other ecclesiologically descriptive terms do occur, such as *klētoi hagioi* ("called saints") in 1:7 and *sōma Christou* ("body of Christ") in 12:5, which are employed by Paul with reference to Christians in his other churches (see 1 Cor. 1:1, 12: 1 ff.).

[20]Kümmel believes Christianity first came to Rome "on the streams of world commerce through the instrumentality of the great Jewish Diaspora at Rome" (*Introduction*, 308).

[21]Klein, "Paul's Purpose," 38.

critical situation in the early church. This realization is important for our investigation, for not only does it place the texts to be treated against a background of considerable energy and vitality, but also Paul's theology of preaching becomes foundational for exercising apostolic authority in the form of settling conflicts and restoring unity to the Christian church.

ROMANS 1:1-17

A. The Literary Context

Paul's references to preaching in Romans occur in the very opening words of the letter, 1:1-17. As will be seen, this portion of the work emphasizes his apostolic calling to preach the gospel to all the gentiles and his intention to do precisely that among the Roman Christians, in the confidence that the power of God for salvation is given to all who have faith.

Paul's introductory accent on the power of the gospel, as the exercise of God's righteousness, and its availability to all on the basis of faith, is followed by lengthy descriptions of the gentiles, who are not under the law, and the Jews who are (1:18–3:8). Paul will argue that both groups have access to the knowledge of God, the gentiles by means of the witness of creation and conscience and the Jews by the revelation of God's law, but that has made no difference in their status before God. Both are equally "under sin" (3:9-20). As a result, God's righteousness, described by Paul in terms of his saving power, has been manifested to both Jews and gentiles equally "as a gift" in their "being justified by his grace through the redemption which is in Christ Jesus," a gift of God to "all who believe" (3:21-26). This revelation of God has obliterated all distinctions and all "boasts" before him (3:27-31). Paul documents his argument in 4:1-25, which rounds out the first major section of the letter, by appealing to the Scriptures, specifically to the example of Abraham, the very "father" of Israel. He is, for Paul, the supreme biblical exhibit and human prototype of those who are justified by God on the basis of faith.

B. Exegesis

> Paul, slave of Christ Jesus, a called apostle, set apart for the gospel of God, which he promised beforehand through his prophets in the holy scriptures, (the gospel) concerning his Son, who was begotten of the seed of David according to the flesh (and) appointed Son of God in power according to the Spirit of holiness from the resurrection of the dead, (even) Jesus Christ our Lord, through whom we received grace and apostleship in order to bring about obedience of faith among all the gentiles for the sake of his name, among whom are also you, called of Jesus Christ, to all those who are in

Rome who are beloved of God, called saints: Grace to you and peace from God our father and the Lord Jesus Christ (vv. 1-7).

Paul begins by identifying himself, a most urgent matter since he is dealing with a Christian community he has not before visited. He does so by means of three phrases, all of which, though they are closely connected, are really appositions to *Paulos*.[22] Paul is a "slave of Christ" (*doulos Christou Iēsou*), an "honorific title of the Old Testament men of God" which emphasizes both his election and submission to God's will.[23] He is also a "called apostle" (*klētos apostolos*), his key term stressing the fact of his divine appointment to a position of authority.[24] But more important is the fact that he is "set apart for the gospel of God" (*aphōrismenos eis euaggelion theou*). The emphasis on these latter words is clear both from the length of the third phrase and from the fact that it receives a further elaboration in vv. 3-4. With this expression Paul immediately sends up a clear signal indicating the basis of his address to the Roman Christians. His warrant is the gospel, which emanates from none other than "God" (*theou*).[25] And as we have seen, the gospel implies at once the message of Christ and the sphere of his authority among those who believe.[26]

Paul introduces the phrase "gospel of God" in an absolute sense. The ensuing verses (vv. 5ff.) will clarify the relationship between Paul's apostleship and the Roman Christians which is implied in his exercise of this gospel. But for now it is necessary for Paul to amplify what he means. This is done in two ways, first by the relative clause of v. 2 and then by the declaration of the gospel's content in vv. 3-4.[27] The first, which emphasizes that the gospel originates in the earlier promises of God in the Scriptures, is of prime importance to Paul. The connection of the gospel of Christ with the Old Testament means for Paul that the promises of God recorded there are part of the gospel itself, serving as a "prototype of the gospel," to use Käsemann's apt description.[28] What is more, reference to the Scriptures gives Paul access to proofs for his argument which will be convincing both to gentiles and to Jews.

---

[22]C. E. B. Cranfield, *A Critical and Exegetical Commentary on the Epistle to the Romans* (Edinburgh: Clark, 1975), vol. 1, 53.

[23]Ernst Käsemann, *Commentary on the Romans* (Grand Rapids: Eerdmans, 1980), 5. Cranfield believes it is also intended to stress his "total allegiance" (*Romans*, 50f.).

[24]See our discussion of Paul's call in chapter 3. He describes it in terms similar to that of the Old Testament prophet Jeremiah (Gal. 1:11-16).

[25]The genitive *theou* ("of God") is a genitive of author, according to Käsemann, *Romans*, 8. See also C. K. Barrett, *A Commentary on the Epistle to the Romans* (New York: Harper, 1968), 18.

[26]See our discussion of this key term in chapter 2.

[27]Wilckens, *Römer*, 1:56.

[28]Käsemann, *Romans*, 9. He points to Rom. 4 and Gal. 3 as prime examples. But Cranfield thinks Paul also means to underscore the gospel's trustworthiness (*Romans*, 1:56).

Wilckens explains: "Since the gospel of Christ is already the content of the previously issued promise, the Scripture becomes in the Christian present a 'witness' to which the apostle can appeal (3:21), particularly for the right to preach the righteousness of faith to the Gentiles as well as to Jews (1:17, 4:1ff., Gal. 3:6ff.)."[29]

The second key amplification of the gospel is vv. 3-4. It is opened with the words "concerning his Son" (*peri tou huiou autou*) and concluded with the specific identification "Jesus Christ our Lord" (*Iēsou Christou tou kuriou hēmōn*). In between lies what is probably an early Christian confessional or liturgical formula.[30] This is suggested not only by its parallel structure but also by its non-pauline language and content.[31] The parallelism is striking in the careful balancing of *tou genomenou ek spermatos Dauid kata sarka* ("begotten of the seed of David according to the flesh") with *tou horisthentos huiou theou kata pneuma hagiōsunēs* ("appointed Son of God according to the Spirit of holiness").[32] This isolates *en dunamei* ("in power") and *ek anastaseōs nekrōn* ("from/by resurrection of the dead"), and since they are both Pauline terms, they are likely his own additions and therefore indicate where his emphasis lies.[33]

En dunamei ("in power") is probably adjectival, meaning that Paul regards the resurrection of Christ from the dead not as the point of his becoming Son of God—as in the older, adoptionist Christology of the formula—but of his Sonship now being exercised in the sphere of the power of God.[34] This correlates well with the literary context. Notice that Paul has bracketed the quotation with decisive declarations about the Sonship and Lordship of Jesus Christ (v. 3a, 4b). Also the thrust of the entire prescript of the letter emphasizes the authority of the gospel of God in the exercise of the apostolic office (v. 5).

With this overture of power and lordship in the gospel of Christ Paul finally arrives at the point he really wants to make (v. 5f.). It is from the Lord Jesus Christ, Son of God, as confessed in the creed to which he and his read-

---

[29]Wilckens, *Römer*, 1:64.

[30]Barrett (*Romans*, 18) and Cranfield (*Romans*, 1:57) speak of it as confessional. Käsemann (*Romans*, 11) calls it a liturgical fragment, as does Wilckens (*Römer*, 1:58).

[31]Wilckens, *Römer*, 1:58f. He points to the adoptionist Christology in the formula as opposed to Paul's belief in the pre-existent Son of God (Gal. 4:4). See also Käsemann, who reminds us that "Son of David" and "Spirit of holiness" are cultic terms, which are also uncharacteristic of Paul (*Romans*, 10f.).

[32]Wilckens, *Römer*, 1:58.

[33]Cranfield (*Romans*, 1:62) directs us to 1 Cor. 15:43 and 1 Thess. 1:5 for Paul's usage of the expression *en dunamei* ("in power"). Note that *ek anastaseōs nekrōn* ("from resurrection of the dead") appears in Paul's crucial argument regarding the resurrection in 1 Cor. 15:12 ff.

[34]Barrett, *Romans*, 20. Cranfield, *Romans*, 1:62. However, Cranfield goes too far in taking *kata sarka* ("according to the flesh") as a reference to Christ's human nature (Ibid., 60).

ers together subscribe (vv. 3b-4a), that he derives his apostleship. The mention of "grace and apostleship" (*charin kai apostolēn*) should not mislead us into thinking of two separate aspects of Paul's call; the expression is practically a hendiadys.[35] Thus Paul's accent is that the grace of God came to him specifically in the form of his call to apostleship.[36] As apostle Paul is a divinely authorized representative of the gospel, with the further factor that in his particular case that authority is exercised in a specific area, namely, his commission from God "to bring about the obedience of faith among all the Gentiles" *(eis hupakoēn pisteōs en pasin tois ethnesin)*. This is where the emphasis lies in the opening verses, as Achtemeier has observed.[37] For it is among the gentiles that the Roman Christians live. Therefore they fall within the "action radius of his special mission task," as Wilckens puts its.[38]

This last point brings us to a subtle, but important observation. *En hois* ("in the midst of whom") in reference to the gentiles should not be taken to mean Paul is characterizing his addressees as exclusively gentiles themselves. For if Paul intended to say his readers were entirely from the gentile group, he would have had to use the expression *ex hōn* ("of whom").[39] As a result, Paul sees his authority among the Roman Christians as residing not in their gentile identity but in their gentile *locus*. Why does he approach the Romans so obliquely? Why does Paul not just say, "I have been authorized to preach the gospel to gentiles, and since you are gentiles, I have the right to preach to you people in Rome?" The answer lies in the circumstances we described above. The Christians in Rome are a *mixed* group, Jews as well as gentiles, but Paul's commission is expressly confined to gentiles (Gal. 1:16)! He has no authority, at least in a *prima facie* sense, to exercise authority over the *Jewish* contingent. And yet the nature of the problem in Rome, the conflict between Jewish and gentile Christians, means he must address both groups. By interpreting his apostleship as extending not only to the gentiles in the narrower sense of identity, but also to gentile territory, Paul is able to cast the mantle of his gospel over both groups and so arbitrate the dispute. In this way he can bring about the "obedience of faith" *(hupakoēn pisteōs)* so that Christ's name, his presence and his glory, may be acknowledged among "all the nations."[40]

What does Paul mean by the "obedience of faith" *(hupakoēn pisteōs)*? As Wilckens reminds us, the expression is a technical term of early Christian

[35]Käsemann, *Romans*, 14. Cranfield, *Romans*, 1:65.
[36]Wilckens, *Römer*, 1:66. See also Käsemann, *Romans*, 14.
[37]Paul Achtemeier, *Romans* (Atlanta: John Knox, 1985), 32.
[38]Wilckens, *Römer*, 1:68. See also Cranfield, *Romans*, 1:67f.
[39]Wilckens, *Römer*, 1:67. He follows Schlatter. See also Beker, *Paul the Apostle*, 76.
[40]Cranfield argues that the expression *huper tou onomatos autou* ("for the sake of his name") should be taken to mean that Christ himself may be known and glorified, as opposed to "in his name" or "in his behalf" (*Romans*, 1:67).

missionary language which "describes conversion as subjugation under the gospel (10:16, 15:18; cf. 6:16, 1 Peter 1:22, 2 Thess. 1:8), which in turn means under Christ as Lord (2 Cor. 10:5; 1 Pet. 1:2, 14; Hebr. 5:9)."[41] The genitive *pisteōs* ("of faith") is therefore explicative or epexegetical, meaning, as Cranfield phrases it, "obedience which consists in faith."[42] This implies that obedience is not understood by Paul here in an ethical sense, but rather, as Käsemann stresses, in an eschatological sense.[43] Käsemann goes on to say, "When the revelation of Christ is accepted, the rebellious world submits again to its Lord. This understanding of faith corresponds to the apostle's Kyrios Christology."[44] That Paul understands faith in this way is confirmed by the fact that for Paul faith comprises both confession (*homologia*) and obedience (*hupakoē*) in accepting the kerygma, which Bultmann describes as "subjection to the way of salvation ordained by God and opened up in Christ."[45] In this way Paul, like the early church in general, continues the Old Testament emphasis on faith as trust and hope in God on the basis of his word, but he also goes beyond it in the sense that faith is a historical possibility of existence for all humanity.[46]

This understanding of faith fits perfectly with the historical circumstances of Paul's letter to the Romans. The squabbling Jewish and gentile Christians need to be brought under the power of their Lord, Jesus Christ. They need to apprehend anew that submission to his Lordship which trusts him and his gospel to the extent that each group will relinquish all claims to superiority, every "boast" (*kauchēsis*), and be united in Christian love (see especially 12:1ff.). And this happens when the gospel is proclaimed, which is precisely why Paul intends to arrive in Rome "gospelizing" (v. 15!).

Paul brings his prescript to a close by acknowledging the Roman Christians in terms of several important "primitive Christian self-predications," as Käsemann refers to them.[47] He describes them as "called of Jesus Christ," "beloved of God," and "called saints," all standard expressions for Christian fellow believers, although conspicuously absent is the word "church" (*ekklēsia*).[48] Whether or not this is further evidence, as Klein and Bartsch believe, that Paul does not regard the Roman Christians as constituting a church,

---

[41]Wilckens, *Römer*, 1:66.

[42]Cranfield, *Romans*, 1:66. See also Käsemann, *Romans*, 14f., and Wilckens, *Römer*, 1:67.

[43]Käsemann finds the eschatological linkage of faith and obedience very clear in 2 Cor. 10:4-6 (*Romans*, 15).

[44]Ibid.

[45]Rudolf Bultmann, *TDNT*, 6 (Grand Rapids: Eerdmans, 1968), 217ff.

[46]Ibid., 205-215.

[47]Käsemann, *Romans*, 15.

[48]Ibid. Klein, "Paul's Purpose," 47. Wilckens, *Römer*, 1:68.

since they are without apostolic foundation, may remain an open question.[49] It is clear Paul regards them as fully and completely members of God's elect in Christ and therefore Christ's body (see 12:5). He therefore concludes by pronouncing the blessing of "grace and peace" upon them.[50]

> First of all I give thanks to my God through Jesus Christ for all of you, because your faith is broadcast in all the world. For God is my witness, (the God) to whom I offer worship in my spirit in the gospel of his Son, how unceasingly I make remembrance of you, always in my prayers asking (that) somehow at last I may succeed by the will of God to come to you (vv. 8-10)

Paul expands and Christianizes the stereotypical prayer which customarily begins the *proemium* of hellenistic letters.[51] He assures the Roman Christians that he offers thanks "for all" (*peri pantōn*) of them, particularly because of their "faith" (*pistin*) which is "broadcast" (*kataggelletai*) throughout the world.[52] By phrasing it in this way, Paul keeps before his hearers the key term "faith," which he will be elaborating in his letter in reference to the problem in Rome. That Paul mentions that his prayer is made "through Jesus Christ" (*dia Iēsou Christou*) is, as Käsemann says, "an appeal to the basis and validation of prayer."[53]

Paul's prayer, begun on a broad note of thanksgiving, now gives way to intercession of a specific nature. The importance which the apostle attaches to this point is obvious from the oath formula, "God is my witness" (*martus gar mou estin ho theos*), which begins the sentence.[54] Paul seems to want to emphasize two related points. The first is that his constant intercessory prayer is a part of his apostolic ministry. That is unmistakable from his choice of words in v. 9. Paul calls as witness God, "whom I worship in my spirit in the gospel of his Son" (*hōi latreuō en tōi pneumati mou en tōi euaggeliōi tou huiou autou*). The term *latreuo* can be translated as "service," and therefore it could mean that he serves God by preaching the gospel.[55] However, the word is a cultic term, and this suggests that Paul is thinking of his intercessory

---

[49]Klein ("Paul's Purpose," 47) and Bartsch ("Historical Situation," 330) are convinced this points decisively to the lack of apostolic foundation in Rome, but Käsemann (*Romans*, 15) and Wilckens (*Römer*, 1:68) do not agree with this conclusion.

[50] Käsemann reminds us that it is in fact a blessing, not just a greeting. He thinks Paul's language here is a modification of an oriental Jewish formula (*Romans*, 16).

[51]Achtemeier, *Romans*, 30. Käsemann, *Romans*, 17. Cranfield, *Romans*, 1:74.

[52]Käsemann alerts us to the fact that *kataggelletai* is too strong to be translated merely as "report" (*Romans*, 18). Thus we have translated "broadcast." His suggestion, however, that their faith is known "because it is that of the church in the imperial city" is suspect (Ibid., 17). Paul says something similar about the Thessalonians (1 Thess. 1:8).

[53]Ibid., 17. He points to a similar usage in 12:1. Cf. Cranfield, who regards the phrase as a reference to the risen, exalted Lord who is thus "mediator of the approach to God in worship" (*Romans*, 1:74).

[54]Cranfield, *Romans*, 1:75f.

[55]Barrett, *Romans*, 24.

prayer as an act of worship which is part of his apostolic ministry.[56] This is confirmed by Paul's emphasis that he worships "in spirit" (*en tōi pneumati*), which here is to be taken anthropologically as a reference to his whole inner self.[57] One does not have to go too far in search of a reason for Paul's saying this. The apostle writes as if he owes the Romans a visit, as if they have been expecting him and he must offer an apology for the delay (1:10, 13; 15:22ff.). In view of the conflict in Rome, he intends to exercise his apostolic authority. So it is important for him to indicate clearly at the outset that, although he has not yet personally been able to visit them and proclaim the gospel of Christ, the Romans have nonetheless been part of his apostolic ministry. His apostleship obligates him both to preaching and to intercession. The Romans have been part of the latter, as he stresses by the hyperbole which accompanies his statement, namely, his mention that he prays "unceasingly," "always," for "all."[58]

The second important point is that, although previously prevented, he definitely intends to come to them in Rome. He regards this visit as a solid prospect, a genuine intent, as can be seen from the fact that he brings his plans before God in prayer. Paul uses the expression *euodōthēsomai en tōi thelē-mati* ("that I may succeed by the will of God") in order to indicate that he understands his mission to be directed from heaven and also to suggest why his plans for a visit in Rome have not yet materialized.[59]

With this expanded prayer, therefore, Paul comes across as exceedingly eager to establish a positive relationship with his fellow Christians in Rome. Even though he is a stranger to them, he emphasizes the points of contact between himself and the Romans. Paul wants them to understand that they are embraced by his apostolic office, by prayer if not by any other means.

> For I long to come to you, so that I might share with you some spiritual gift in order that you might be strengthened, that is (to say), to be mutually encouraged together through each other's faith, both yours and mine. For I do not want you to be ignorant, brothers, that frequently I intended to come to you, but was prevented until now, so that I might have some fruit even among you just as (I have) also among the rest of the Gentiles. I am under obligation both to the Greeks and barbarians, to the wise and the unlearned; thus (the) readiness, at least on my part, to preach the gospel also to you who are in Rome. For I am not ashamed of the gospel, for it is the power of God for

---

[56]Wilckens, *Römer*, 1:78. He refers to the fact that such a function characteristically came to prophets and teachers of apocalyptic revelation. In similar fashion Cranfield (following Kuss) argues that Paul is designating his service in the gospel as worship, by which he means the glorification of God (*Romans*, 1:76).

[57]Käsemann, *Romans*, 18. Cf. Barrett, who speaks of the "spiritual side of his nature" (*Romans*, 24). Wilckens (*Römer*, 1:78 n. 77) emphasizes the connection between prayer service (*latreuein*) and spirit (*pneuma*).

[58]Käsemann, *Romans*, 18. Elsewhere in Paul see 1 Thess. 1:2 for similar hyperbole in connection with the context of intercessory prayer.

[59]Wilckens, *Römer*, 1:79.

salvation to all who believe, to the Jew first and then to the Greek; for in it the righteousness of God is revealed from faith to faith, just as it is written, "He who is righteous by faith will live" (vv. 11-17).

With these verses Paul has come to the point of revealing his intention in coming to Rome. His thought process at this point is striking, because it takes a rather circuitous route until it reaches the thematic climax of vv. 15-17. In fact, there is a tension between the apostle's real motives, as revealed in 1:5, 9, 14ff. and 15: 18ff., and his apparent hesitancy in vv. 11-13.[60] Paul strikes the note of mutuality.[61] In v. 11 he wants to "share some spiritual gift" (*ti metadō charisma humin pneumatikon*) for their "strengthening" (*stērichthēnai*), a gift that remains unspecified. Then in v. 12 Paul immediately qualifies this statement by emphasizing that what he has in mind is a mutual encouragement by means of "each other's faith" (*dia tēs en allēlois pisteōs*). Then in v. 13 he assures the Romans of his firm resolve over a long period of time to visit them, adding as his purpose that he might "have some fruit" (*tina karpon schō*) from them. Still, he hastens to assure them that the reason he has not yet appeared is due to circumstances beyond his control. His reference to being "prevented" probably means by God.[62] And quite noticeably his word "fruit" is qualified by "some" (*tina*), again leaving the matter indefinite.

Why this vagueness and apparent hesitancy on the part of an apostle who is customarily anything but reticent? Is he embarrassed because his "plans are anomalous," as Barrett thinks?[63] Or, as Käsemann believes, is the apostle anxious to avoid any claims to authority in a congregation not founded by him, so as to leave his visit "divested of any official character?"[64]Or is Cranfield more accurate in saying Paul's approach in these verses is an expression of the apostle's humility?[65]

Actually, all of these are equally unsatisfactory explanations for the simple reason that they do not take seriously enough the language of the text and context. Paul clearly intends to preach the gospel as an exercise of his apostolic office (1:5f., 14f.)! His plans are not in the least anomalous, and his visit is anything but unofficial. One need only point to the key term *karpon* ("fruit"), which dominates the apostle's thought at the end of v. 13. This is

---

[60]Ibid.

[61]Barrett, *Romans*, 25.

[62]Ibid., 26. Cranfield, *Romans*, 1:82. Both point to Paul's references to his work in the east (15:18f., 22f.).

[63]Barrett, *Romans*, 25.

[64]Käsemann, *Romans*, 19. In a similar vein, Wilckens is of the opinion that Paul knows himself to be apostle to the gentiles, yet respects their autonomy, the result being that he assiduously avoids any claim of one-sided authority (*Römer*, 1:79f.).

[65]Cranfield, *Romans*, 80. He flatly rejects any suggestion of embarrassment on Paul's part (against Barrett).

a missionary term for making new converts, and it will not do to weaken the emphasis by trying to expand the term to embrace apostolic "edification" as well.[66] It is true that "fruit" can be used as descriptive of Christian edification, as when the apostle speaks of "fruit of the Spirit," but in those cases the "fruit" is never something he speaks of himself "having" personally.[67] Even more important, however, is the fact that if *karpon* here meant only edification, the apostle would hardly have had to qualify the word with "some" (*tina*).[68] Finally, that for Paul "fruit" means apostolic missionary work becomes quite clear when one takes into consideration the concluding phrases of v. 13, "also among you just as among the rest of the Gentiles" (*kai en humin kathōs kai en tois loipois ethnesin*). For this can only be a reference to his missionary work in Asia, Macedonia and Achaia.[69]

More likely, therefore, Paul's caution is connected with his intention to exercise apostolic authority in order to resolve the problem of the conflict between Jewish and gentile Christians in that city. Since they do not know him, and since he has not established the congregation, he must make his case very carefully. Wilckens is doubtless correct in arguing that Paul does not want to arouse their anxieties or apprehensions nor have his motives misunderstood as he tries to "subordinate to his apostolic authority a congregation not founded by him."[70] It is important, especially if the situation in Rome is as full of tension as we believe, that his approach to the Roman Christians not be dismissed at the outset as outside interference. Paul's letter, then, begins on a note of mutuality which is aimed to gain the confidence of the Roman Christians by demonstrating his respect for their present standing in the gospel, which means that his exercise of authority as an apostle of the gospel is meant to be a blessing, a "gift" (*charisma*), which he shares with them.

Having attempted to allay the misgivings of his Roman fellow Christians and having expressed his long–standing intent to come to them, Paul now reveals the basis for his approach in v. 14. He is under obligation, a "debtor" (*opheiletēs*) to them, a reference to the divine compulsion of his commission.[71] Furthermore, his obligation in the gospel reaches across cultural distinctions and conventions. His reference to "Greeks and barbarians, wise and ignorant" (*Hellēsin te kai barbarois, sophois te kai anoētois*), a reference to the cultured and uncultured of the Graeco-Roman world, the educated and

---

[66]As Barrett (*Romans*, 26), Cranfield (*Romans*, 1:82), and Käsemann (*Romans*, 20) all try to do. Cf. Klein, "Paul's Purpose," 38, and Wilckens, *Römer*, 1:79f. See also Phil. 1:22.

[67]See Gal. 5:22 ff. Cf. Phil. 4:17.

[68]Any explanation based on Paul's humility at this point represents merely a projection of piety, not exegesis.

[69]Wilckens, *Römer*, 1:79.

[70]Ibid., 79f.

[71]Käsemann, *Romans*, 20. See 1 Cor. 9:16.

uneducated, makes this manifest.[72] In this way Paul takes in the "sum of Gentile mankind."[73] This implies that Paul understands himself to have a divine obligation to preach the same gospel, the same word, without distinctions among peoples and without respect of persons.[74] If Paul's intent is to bring harmony to a divided Christian community, this note of universality in the gospel has an obvious purpose. As Wilckens notes, "Thus" (*houtōs*!) Paul wants to preach the gospel in Rome.[75] His "gospeling" activity, since it originates in the Christ whose work makes obsolete all distinctions and is universally available to all who believe, is aimed to reunify the Roman Christians. His apostolic preaching will function in Rome as an "equalizing" force, as he will spell out in the remainder of his letter by pointing to the universality of sin (3:9) and the universality of God's power of salvation to "every one who believes" (1:16). Preaching the gospel, as far as Paul is concerned, has as part of its purpose to sweep away all obstacles to human unity, whether cultural, religious, or pretensions of self-superiority, so that one's only claim is in the righteousness of God (1:16).

And with that observation we arrive at the crucial and heavily-laden thrust of vv. 16ff., which are intended, by virtue of the "for" (*gar*) which begins each sentence, to form a chain of subordinate clauses providing a foundation for his desire to "thus preach the gospel" in Rome (1:15).[76] These verses are so filled with key concepts which are important for the rest of the letter that it has been standard practice to regard them as thematic for Romans as a whole.[77] However, we are well advised by Achtemeier not to press this so far that we exclude v. 15, for as the subordinate structure of vv. 16-17 and the connecting words "gospelize" and "gospel" (*euaggeslisasthai, euaggelion*) bear witness, the real theme note of the epistle is the gospel![78] In fact, Paul begins v. 16 with a confessional formula, "For I am not ashamed" (*ou gar epaischunomai*) of the gospel.[79] Stated in the form of an emphatic negative, the assertion expresses boldly and vividly the apostle's confidence in

---

[72]Wilckens *Römer*, 1:81. Cranfield, *Romans*, 1:83f.

[73]Cranfield, *Romans*, 1:83.

[74]Wilckens, *Römer*, 1:81.

[75]Ibid.

[76]Achtemeier, *Romans*, 35. He particularly emphasizes the grammatical structure of vv. 16 ff., which shows that v. 15 is dominant. He therefore questions the logic of many who regard vv. 16-17 as the theme of the entire letter to the Romans. His argument is persuasive and makes highly questionable Käsemann's contention that *euaggelisasthai* ("to preach the gospel") was introduced in v. 15 simply to make a transition to vv. 16ff. (*Romans*, 20).

[77]Käsemann, *Romans*, 21ff. Cranfield, *Romans*, 1:86. Barrett, *Romans*, 17. Barrett even goes so far as to refer to the verses as the "text" for the letter.

[78]Achtemeier, *Romans*, 35 ff.

[79]Käsemann, *Romans*, 22. See also Peter Stuhlmacher, *Gerechtigkeit Gottes bei Paulus* (Göttingen: Vandenhoeck & Rupprecht, 1966), 78f. Wilckens, *Römer*, 1:82. The term is not psychological but is equivalent to *homologein* ("to confess").

the preaching of the gospel.[80] It is in fact much more than a message. It is the "power of God" (*dunamis theou*). By expressing it negatively there is also a further nuance, noticed by Wilckens, that the preaching of the gospel by its very nature invites a negative reaction and places its confessor/preacher in a precarious position. He states:

> Whoever confesses the gospel is conscious that he represents something which does not conform to the interests and standards of the surrounding world, by whom it is dismissed as "nonsense" and an "annoyance" (1 Cor. 1:22) and frequently is embattled and persecuted (1 Thess. 2:14-16). Whoever preaches the gospel is thus exposed to a pressure of social contempt and enmity, so that his "not to be ashamed" requires a special courage.[81]

Paul's special courage, then, is revealed precisely at this point in his apostolic ministry where the problem at Rome threatens to undo all his previous work and his efforts to preserve the unity of the Christian church. Paul's proclamation of the gospel has proven strong enough to found congregations, settle internal problems, and make converts. But is it powerful enough to restore a Christian church badly divided by the Jewish-gentile issue, with each side certain of its own claims and superiority? Paul is sure it does! For he sees the gospel as the "epiphany of God's eschatological power," to borrow Käsemann's phrase.[82] This perspective is borne out in vv. 16b-17, where the apostle stresses, though admittedly in a compact form, the eschatological nature and character of the gospel's strength.

The eschatological character of Paul's argument emerges in the reference to "salvation" (*sōtērian*). The term originated among the Jews as a designation for a future time in which God would vindicate his elect, the faithful, in the final judgment of the world.[83] For Paul the term has some added features. One is the fact that "salvation" has both a negative and positive content, the negative being that salvation is deliverance from the wrath of God (Rom. 5:9; 1 Cor. 3:15, 5:5; 1 Thess. 5:9) and the positive being the restoration of sinful humanity to divine glory (Rom. 3:23, 8:29).[84] A second feature is that while the future expectation is maintained by Paul, "salvation" has already now become a present reality through God's action in Christ (see Rom. 8:24; 2 Cor. 6:2).[85] It is not that salvation has already arrived, but that

---

[80]Käsemann, *Romans*, 22.

[81]Wilckens, *Römer*, 1:82.

[82]Käsemann, *Romans*, 22. Wilckens reminds us that *dikaiosunē theou* ("righteousness of God") refers to God's power demonstrated in acts of salvation, and he suggests that Paul here may be thinking specifically of the resurrection of Jesus (*Römer*, 1:82).

[83]Käsemann, *Romans*, 22. Barrett, *Romans*, 27f.

[84]Werner Foerster, *TDNT*, 7 (Grand Rapids: Eerdmans, 1971), 992 ff. See also Cranfield, *Romans*, 1:89.

[85]Käsemann, *Romans*, 22. Barrett, *Romans*, 27f. Cranfield, *Romans*, 1:89. Foerster, *TDNT*, 7:993f.

the expected deliverance has already begun for "every person who believes" (*panti tōi pisteuonti*).

Once again Paul has brought "faith" to our attention. Salvation is oriented to faith. Just as we saw in 1:5, this faith means "believing obedience," to quote Barrett.[86] Faith is both trust in God, in the Old Testament sense, and also the reception of the gospel.[87] But for Paul and the early Christians faith in God now means faith in the God who raised Jesus Christ from the dead.[88] In v. 16 Paul has oriented the term so as to disclose the universal availability of God's salvation. That is noticeable from the added modifying phrase "to the Jew first and also the Greek" (*Ioudaiōi te prōton kai Hellēni*). The implications of this are important for Paul. Since the gospel is God's eschatological saving event for the whole world, it is imperative that it be made available on a universal basis. And that single response to God which is at hand for every person—note the emphasis on the individual in "everyone who has faith" (*panti tōi pisteuonti*)—is faith.[89] Faith is universal.

On the other hand, there is yet another implication which surfaces in the word "first" (*prōton*). This word must not be weakened, Käsemann warns, for it testifies to the priority of the Jews in God's plan of salvation.[90] This does not mean Paul harbors any idea of the precedence of the Jews as such.[91] Rather, as Cranfield sees, there is a paradox in the epistle in that Paul understands all humanity as appearing before God without "distinction" (*diastolē*), yet the continuing validity of the "Jew first" in God's plan of salvation is maintained.[92] This is important for Paul, since he is trying to persuade Jew and gentile alike with regard to the universal validity and claim of the gospel. For Jews it is important for Paul to stress that God has not reneged on his promises, his elective activity in the past (3:1-4! and especially chapters 9-11). For the gentiles, who are the "strong" in Rome and claim the superiority of culture, Paul must stress that it is "Jew first." Thus at this point, albeit subtly, Paul has introduced his description of salvation on the universal basis of faith so as to provide neither Jewish nor gentile Christian in Rome a basis for "boasting" (3:27ff.).

Paul's claim that the gospel is the "power of God for salvation," available to humankind on the universal basis of faith, is now developed further in v. 17. Thus the two key terms, salvation and faith, are undergirded. Verse 17 answers two questions: how can the preaching of the gospel bring about

---

[86]Barrett, *Romans*, 28.

[87]Käsemann, *Romans*, 23. Bultmann, *TDNT*, 6 (Grand Rapids: Eerdmans, 1968), 215.

[88]Wilckens, *Römer*, 1:85.

[89]Käsemann calls attention to the stress on the individual (*Romans*, 23).

[90]Ibid. Wilckens, *Römer*, 1:86. See also Cranfield, *Romans*, 1:91.

[91]Wilckens, *Römer*, 1:96.

[92]Cranfield, *Romans*, 1:91.

salvation, and how does it come about that God offers his salvation on the basis of faith?

The answer to the first question comes with Paul's words "for in it the righteousness of God is revealed" (*dikaisosunē gar theou en autōi apokaluptetai*). That much is clear. What is not clear is precisely what Paul means by the pregnant expression *dikaiosunē theou* ("righteousness of God"). This issue has generated fervent debate among scholars, and there is at present no consensus. According to Williams, most scholars agree that "righteousness" does not refer to a static attribute of God, but that it "designates conduct or activity appropriate to a relationship."[93] Beyond that, scholars divide into three main streams: those who take the term as referring to a human righteousness which counts in God's eyes (*theou* as an objective genitive); those who believe it refers to God's own saving activity or power (*theou* as a subjective genitive); and those who see it as meaning God's gift of righteousness (*theou* as a genitive of origin).[94] None of these, however, is altogether satisfactory. The first is suspect on its face, for it attributes too much to human initiative, while Paul emphatically argues that one is "put right" (*dikaioumenoi*, Rom. 3:24, a passive!) by God. The second, that righteousness is a power, does not square with the line of argument here. Paul says the *gospel* is the power, for God's righteousness is revealed "in it" (*en autōi*), not that God's righteousness is itself the power.[95] The third alternative, righteousness as gift, is doubtful too. To be sure, in Phil. 3:9 Paul does speak of the divine righteousness which he has received, but there he describes it as the righteousness "from God" (*ek theou*). If Paul intended that meaning here, at such a crucial point in his early discussion in Romans, it seems unlikely that he would not have taken care to remove any traces of ambiguity by using the word *ek* ("from").[96] And even the careful analysis of Käsemann, which understands God's righteousness to embrace both power and gift, does not account adequately for Paul's ambiguity.[97]

How, then, are we to understand Paul's expression "the righteousness of God?" Several clues lead us in the direction of a solution. The first is in the

---

[93]Williams, " 'Righteousness of God' ," 241. Williams offers a very useful summary of the debate (Ibid., 241-245). See also the careful review of the alternative interpretations in Achtemeier, *Romans*, 61 ff.

[94]Williams, " 'Righteousness of God'," 242f.

[95]Ibid., 258.

[96]Ibid., 258f.

[97]Ernst Käsemann, " 'The Righteousness of God' in Paul," in *New Testament Questions of Today* (Philadelphia: Fortress, 1969), 168-182. He regards the phrase as having a "double bearing," so that at no time can the gift be separated from the giver. He believes helpful analogies are to be found in Paul's similar treatments of such key concepts as Spirit, grace, gospel, and Christ. In sum, "*Dikaiosunē theou* is for Paul God's sovereignty over the world revealing itself eschatologically in Jesus" (Ibid., 180). See also Käsemann's treatment in *Romans*, 23-30.

answer to the question, How can Paul tolerate ambiguity in this crucial verse? With penetrating insight William answers, "Paul must have expected his readers to be familiar with the term."[98] That must mean the term is understood on the basis of the Scriptures, the Old Testament usage.[99] Williams then investigates the Old Testament for further evidence. He finds the expression "righteousness of God" used particularly in Second Isaiah and Psalms; in both works it refers to the faithfulness and constancy of God, thus "characterizing the being of God who makes himself known in deeds."[100] And the deeds of God most often associated with his righteousness are deeds of salvation and deliverance.[101] There is, however, the added factor that God acts in fidelity within his covenant relationship so that "God persists in willing and doing that which is right and fitting in the context of his relationship with those who obey his will."[102] Paul can assume, therefore, that the Christians in Rome understand this term similarly.

The second clue comes from the observation that *dikaiosunē theou* ("righteousness of God") must be taken together with *apokaluptetai* ("is revealed"). This arises from a comparison with the parallel expression *apokaluptetai gar orgē theou* ("for the wrath of God is revealed") which begins v. 18. The fact that both God's righteousness and wrath are "revealed" indicate that we are here dealing with eschatological terms.[103] Since "righteousness of God" is intended in v. 17 to further clarify the "salvation" spoken of in v. 16, this should come as no surprise, though it seems to be continually overlooked by scholars. The Jewish eschatological expectation, as we saw with *sōtērian* ("salvation"), involved God's final end-time vindication of his faithful and punishment of those who hate and oppose him. Presupposed in this expectation is that God will act in this way at the last because he has so promised, that he is faithful to his word and to his people whom he has created. The covenant faithfulness of God as Creator is thus underscored in the expression "righteousness of God."

The third clue comes in the close parallel between v. 17 and Rom. 3:21ff. Here again we find tinges of apocalyptic coloring. For in 3:21 Paul says of the righteousness of God that it "has been manifested" (*pephanerōtai*), and both *apokaluptein* ("to reveal") and *phaneroun* ("to make manifest") are

---

[98]Williams, " 'Righteousness of God' ," 260.

[99]Ibid.

[100]Ibid., 261.

[101]Ibid. See also Barrett, *Romans*, 29f.

[102]Williams, " 'Righteousness of God,' " 262. He finds this approach confirmed particularly in Rom. 3, and especially in 3:1-7.

[103]Stuhlmacher, *Gerechtigkeit*, 79f. He emphasizes that *apokaluptein* is an eschatological technical term.

nearly synonymous terms in the apocalyptic tradition.[104] The reference is to "the disclosure of end-time events prepared in heaven but hidden to earthly, human view," a special revelation of divine secrets to especially chosen seers.[105] In Rom. 3:21ff. that special revelation is that God's righteousness is manifest in his justification of sinners as a gift in Jesus Christ, offered on the basis of faith.

When these pieces are drawn together and assembled, then, what does Paul seem to be saying with the term "righteousness of God" in v. 17? And how does this relate to God's power of salvation in the preaching of the gospel? As Wilckens so succinctly puts it:

> When Paul puts forth the thesis that God's righteousness is 'revealed' *in the gospel*, it signifies, on the background of this [apocalyptic] tradition, the claim that already now (*apokaluptetai* is present tense!) the hidden reality of the eschatological saving act of God is being brought to effect in the *dunamis* ["power"] of his preaching of Christ— plainly for 'everyone who believes': a fundamental antithesis over against the revelatory claim of the Torah!"[106]

What this signifies is that in preaching a new age dawns, and new realities inform the lives of those who have faith in God and expect the consummation of his saving promises. In preaching the new age comes to expression (see 2 Cor. 5:17-21).[107] In the gospel of Christ God has proven faithful to his creation in offering salvation as a present reality on the universal basis of faith.

With this conception of God's power of salvation in the gospel Paul answers the second question, How has it come about that God offers salvation on the basis of faith? In so doing Paul arrives at his emphatic final point in v. 17, a claim which becomes the pivot to the extended discussion which ensues in v. 18ff. It is not just that God's righteousness is revealed in the gospel to everyone who has faith, but it is revealed "from faith to faith" (*ek pisteōs eis pistin*). The importance of this point is punctuated by the citation of Hab. 2:4 as biblical proof.

What does Paul mean by this compact phrase, "from faith to faith?" As with the term "righteousness of God," so also this phrase has received a variety of interpretations.[108] For example, Barrett speaks of it meaning "on the basis of faith from start to finish."[109] Käsemann, though, emphasizes the phrase's character as semitic rhetoric, an expression for indicating the " 'unbroken continuity' " of faith, which he explains by saying, "The revelation of God's righteousness, because it is bound to the gospel, takes place only in

---

[104]Wilckens, *Römer*, 1:86.
[105]Ibid.
[106]Ibid., 88.
[107]Stuhlmacher, *Gerechtigkeit*, 83f.
[108]For a complete description of the alternatives see Cranfield, *Romans*, 1:99f.
[109]Barrett, *Romans*, 21.

the sphere of faith.''[110] And Cranfield similarly takes the term as having "much the same effect as the 'sola' of 'sola fide.' ''[111] These interpretations are no doubt correct in pointing us in the direction of continuity. But there is more one can say at this point to clarify Paul's meaning. That meaning surfaces when we consider the Old Testament text the apostle uses as his proof, Hab. 2:4: "He who is just by faith shall live" (*Ho de dikaios ek pisteōs zēsetai*).

Two aspects of Paul's quotation are striking. The first is that only the phrase *ek pisteōs* is repeated, and this surely suggests that Paul's emphasis is precisely at that point.[112] Pertinent in this connection is Käsemann's observation that the passage probably was used in the Jewish–Christian mission as a proof from prophecy that salvation was by faith in the Messiah.[113] It might also be added, as Cranfield notes, that the context requires *ek pisteōs* ("by faith") to be connected adjectivally with *dikaios* ("righteous") rather than adverbially with *zēsetai* ("shall live"), since there is no other emphasis in the context on "living by faith.''[114]

The second striking feature is that Paul quotes neither from the Hebrew Text, which has "by his faith," nor from the Septuagint, which reads "by my faith.''[115] By dropping the pronouns in the quotation Paul not only intends to stress *ek pisteōs* ("by faith"), but he appears intent on divesting the term of any suggestion about whose faith is involved, whether God's or his people's. Rather, Paul seems to want to focus on the faith as such, as an entity or sphere of activity. This would correspond to the apostle's occasional reference to faith as a power sphere (see Gal. 3:23). As a result, Paul appears to understand the prophecy as a reference to salvation coming to the person who is righteous in the sphere of faith, where faith holds sway. And since every person is sinful and therefore must be "made righteous" by the power of God in Christ, offered to those who believe, faith as a power sphere clearly emerges as the point of interaction between God and his people (Rom. 3:21-25). This claim will be made even more boldly when the apostle offers his chief exhibit from the Old Testament, the example of Abraham (Rom. 4).

Paul's point is actually a very simple one, despite the difficulty in interpreting the words of v. 17. The apostle is claiming that the revelation of God's

---

[110]Käsemann, *Romans*, 31. His quoted words are from Fridrichsen. By way of semitic parallels he points to Jer. 9:2 and Ps. 83:8 in the Old Testament. He also finds similar Pauline examples in 2 Cor. 2:16, 3:18, and 4:17. This leads him to believe the expression has the sense of *sola fide*.

[111]Cranfield, *Romans*, 100.

[112]Wilckens, *Römer*, 1:88. He finds this confirmed in 3:26, 28; 4:5, 16; 5:1; 10:4-6.

[113]Käsemann, *Romans*, 31.

[114]Cranfield, *Romans*, 1:102. He also refers to the further discussion in the epistle. See also Wilckens, *Römer*, 1:89f.

[115]Barrett, *Romans*, 31.

righteousness, as a power of salvation offered to every person who believes, is not a novel idea. For his fellow Jewish Christians, who are dissatisfied with what they see as Paul's abandonment of the Torah, Paul is emphasizing his continuity with the Old Testament. Paul argues that God's righteousness revealed "to faith" (*eis pistin*) is no different from the way God has dealt with his people all along. God has always revealed his saving faithfulness to those who believe, on the basis of faith, or "from faith" (*ek pisteōs*). It should be no surprise to Jewish Christians, Paul implies, that God has made his end-time salvation in Christ available to all the gentiles on the basis of faith, "apart from the Torah" (*chōris nomou*), Rom. 3:21. God's biblical track record is such that he always deals with his people on the foundation of faith. God's righteousness, his covenant faithfulness as creator of the entire world (Rom. 3:29f.), is received, appropriately, by faith. And that applies to every individual who trusts his promises.

C. Preliminary Observations

This text is important for our investigation of Paul's theology of preaching, for not only does it confirm our previous conclusions about the gospel as a power structure brought to effect in preaching, but it also reveals the precise goal of the gospel. The proclamation of the gospel aims at faith. It proclaims that God has kept faith with his people in the event of Jesus Christ, and, on the basis of God's revelation of himself in the crucified and risen Christ, the preaching of the gospel calls upon the hearer to keep faith with God.

ROMANS 10:14-17

A. The Literary Context

Romans 9-11 form the context of the final passage of our exegetical investigation. As Käsemann remarks, "Apart from chapter 16, no part of the epistle is so self-contained as this."[116] And yet there is an observable connection between this section and what has preceded. That continuity is located in God. Paul argued that both Jews and gentiles are under sin and that both are justified by God's grace as a gift to be received by faith, his chief exhibit being the faith of Abraham (Rom. 1:8–4:25). The apostle then turned his attention to the benefits of being justified by faith (Rom. 5), following that up with a discussion of the basis for righteousness (the in-dwelling Spirit)

---

[116]Käsemann, *Romans*, 253.

and the weakness of the law to effect the righteousness it requires (Rom. 6-7). Paul brought his argument to a conclusion by announcing, ''There is therefore now no condemnation for those who are in Christ Jesus'' (8:1). The basis for that bold pronouncement is the fact that ''God has done what the law, weakened by flesh, could not do'' (8:3a) in sending his Son to''condemn sin in the flesh'' (8:3b), in order that the law's requirement might be fulfilled in our walking ''according to the Spirit'' (8:4). Paul calls the Christians in Rome to live, therefore, according to the Spirit and to stand firm in the faith until the time of the consummation of God's glory, since ''all who are led by the Spirit are sons of God'' (8:5) and therefore his ''heirs'' (8:17). This universal emphasis is intended to reduce the tensions between the Jewish and gentile Christians in Rome. But that leaves unanswered the question about the Jews, about Israel. If all, Jews and gentiles, are the same before God, then has God reneged on his election of Israel? What is the relation now between gentile Christians and Jews? If, as Paul has argued, there is no ''distinction'' (*diastolē*), have the lines between Jews and gentiles been altogether obliterated? To these questions Paul turns in chapters 9-11. The connection, then, has to do with God. In chapters 1-8 the focus is, as Barrett says, on the ''character and deeds of God who is the source of salvation,'' while in chapters 9-11 the concern is ''with the character and deeds of God who elected Israel and now calls the gentiles.''[117]

As a result, chapters 9-11 deal with a delicate issue which is crucial both to a solution of the problem in Rome and to Paul's being able to offer a credible defense of the law-free gospel when he arrives in Jerusalem. The large number of Old Testament citations which the apostle employs to shore up his presentation shows how important this argument is. The key problem, as Achtemeier says, is ''the persistent unbelief of God's chosen people.''[118] What is one to make of that? Does it mean God has rejected them, so that gentiles in Rome are justified in abusing the returning Jews? Or, does Israel's rejection mean that God's redemptive work has been thwarted, that grace is not quite so divinely empowered as Paul has been arguing?[119]

Paul begins with a lament in behalf of his fellow Jews, his ''kinsmen by race'' (9:1-3). They have had all the advantages of election by God yet have failed to accept the Christ who is ''of their race, according to the flesh'' (9:5). Still, Paul insists, that does not mean God's word has failed (v. 6). This is the key point of his opening discussion, and it is based on the argument (resumed from 2:28 f.) that the true Israel is not a matter of racial descent but of the sovereign call of God (9:7-13).[120] Paul explains this further in 9:14-19. It

[117]Barrett, *Romans,* 175.
[118]Achtemeier, *Romans,* 153.
[119]Ibid.
[120]Ibid., 155f.

is not that God has been unfair to his chosen people, but he has now expanded the people of promise to include gentiles (9:24!).[121] In so doing he has created a new people, to be sure, but God has done so in a way "consistent with his original choice of Israel as chosen people."[122] That is to say, God has acted as creator and Lord of history, as the God of mercy.[123]

In 9:30–10:21, which forms the immediate framework for the text we will be treating, Paul draws out the implications of what he has been arguing. There is a certain irony, Paul points out, in that the gentiles have attained God's righteousness while Israel did not, even though the latter had the advantage of the divine law (9:30-31). The reason is that the latter "did not pursue it through faith, but as if it were based on works" (9:32). In trying to establish their own righteousness they did not submit to God's, so that, for all their zealousness to be godly, theirs in not an "enlightened" righteousness (10:1-3). The apostle concludes with a fundamental assertion, "for Christ is the end of the law, that everyone who has faith may be justified" (10:4).

What does Paul mean that "Christ is the end of the law?" The word *telos* ("end") can mean either the goal or the termination. In the context Paul seems to mean both. For 10:5-13 shows how Christ has fulfilled the law and embodied its reality, which is precisely the point of the gospel he preaches (10:8b).[124] In vv. 14-21 Paul takes up the other thrust, that Christ is the termination of the law as a means of salvation, since faith arises out of the preaching of Christ (v. 17), and since also the gospel has been proclaimed, heard, and understood by Israel, Israel is without excuse when it rejects Christ.[125]

Chapter 11 climaxes Paul's discussion, begun already back in the first chapter. Achtemeier's comment is apt: "Since the story of the rescue of God's creation began with Israel, the chosen people, it will also conclude with them," the difference being that now the basis is trust in Christ.[126] The crucial question is, "Has God rejected his people?" (11:1). Paul's answer is a resounding "No!" Paul refers to himself and to Elijah as premier exhibits of that fact (11:1b-4). He points out that there is a "remnant, chosen by grace" (11:5). As for the rest, God has hardened them so as to make room for the gentiles, an act of mercy that will one day come full circle to embrace Israel once again (11:6-12). Then, after he has specifically warned the gentiles, in the figure of the olive tree, not to presume upon God's grace and to boast over the Jews (11:13-14), the apostle closes by revealing a "mystery." This mys-

---

[121]Ibid., 160.
[122]Ibid.
[123]Ibid., 161f.
[124]Ibid., 168f.
[125]Ibid., 173 ff.
[126]Ibid., 177.

tery turns out to be the hardening of part of Israel for the sake of the gentiles
(11:25, 28). The climax is in v. 32: "For God has consigned all men to disobedience, that he may have mercy upon all."[127] God does not renege on his
promises, but in the paradox of his mercy he hardens the very people he intends to save (11:29, 31), so that even the sin and disobedience of humanity
plays its part in God's redemptive work. In the end God's grace reigns supreme. Grace cannot be thwarted. And to this Paul can only conclude with a
doxology in praise of the knowledge and saving power of God (11:33-36).

B. Exegesis

> How, then, can they call upon one in whom they have not believed? And how can they
> believe him whom they have not heard? And how can they hear without someone to
> preach? And how can they preach unless they are sent? As it is written, "How beautiful
> are the feet of those who preach good things." But not all obeyed the gospel; for Isaiah
> says, "Lord, who believed our message?" So then faith is from the message heard,
> (and) the message heard is through the word of Christ (vv. 14-17).

Having demonstrated that "Christ is the end of the law" (10:4) by
showing that he is the fulfillment, the goal, of the Mosaic law and its righteousness (10:5-8), Paul asserts that salvation is exclusively a matter of
faith (10:9-13). Two biblical promises undergird this claim, the fact that
"No one who believes in him will be put to shame" (v. 11) and the parallel
concluding statement that "every one who calls upon the name of the Lord
will be saved" (v. 13). Paul's reference to the Lord here certainly refers
to Christ (cf. v. 9).[128] Thus, Christ is the end of the law as the means of
salvation. Christ spells the demise of anyone's making a claim on God
based on works of law (see 3:27). This means that for Jews and gentiles
alike salvation consists in the fact that God "bestows riches on all who call
upon him" (v. 12).

In the section that begins with v. 14 the apostle now turns his attention to
the question of the fate of Israel. For Israel has rejected the Lord, who Paul
has claimed vigorously is the universal savior of humankind on the basis of
faith. Does that mean that Israel is now rejected by God, that the people of
promise and blessing have made themselves accursed? In the context of the
Roman situation would that then mean that the Jews are of no account or matter of responsibility to gentile Christians in Rome, that the returning Jews can
be treated with scorn and abuse? Paul will answer that question negatively
(11:1ff.) But before he can deal with that issue, he must first establish that
Israel does not constitute an exceptional case. He must show that Israel does

---

[127]Ibid., 178.
[128]Barrett, *Romans*, 203.

not have any excuse which makes them exempt from having to confess Christ as Lord.

Paul begins in vv. 14-15a with four parallel questions. They provide the basic presuppositions which will establish conclusively that instead of Israel having an excuse, of their being a special case, it is rather the case that "not all obeyed the gospel" (v. 16).[129] The "not all" he has in mind is obviously Israel (vv. 18-19). These questions are connected to the preceding section through the repetition of *epikalesōntai* ("call upon"), which provides the point of departure for Paul's claim.[130] The questions form a chain of key terms which, linked together, show the progression by which God's action in Christ, as present in the gospel, puts people in such a position that "calling upon" God becomes a possibility for them and thereby the source of salvation. To be able to "call upon" the Lord, one must have faith in him, which presupposes that one has heard him, which in turn presupposes someone to proclaim the message in the Lord's behalf, which finally must rest on divine authorization, the fact of the preacher's having been "sent" (*apostalōsin*).[131] This progression sets up the necessary conditions for faith, which apply to Israel just as with all the gentiles. Simultaneously the progression indicates the precise points at which excuses might be offered which could exonerate Israel for its rejection of Christ.[132] If any of these conditions have not been met, then Israel cannot be held responsible for rejection. Paul intends to show, however, that the conditions have been met, and therefore Israel is without excuse, that its rejection stems from the fact that it is a "disobedient and contrary people" (10:21).

Paul's chain of questions concludes in v. 15b with his quotation of Is. 52:7, "How beautiful the feet of those who preach good things" (*hōs hōraioi hoi podes tōn euaggelizomenōn ta agatha*). This passage was, as Käsemann reminds us, "almost always related by the rabbis to the messianic age" and understood as a reference to those who were bearers of the divine gospel.[133] Paul is surely reflecting here his own apostolic experience against the backdrop of biblical prophecy. He and his fellow apostles, missionaries of the gospel, know themselves to be divinely commissioned for the

[219]Ulrich Wilckens, *Der Brief an die Römer*, vol. 2 (Zürich, Einsiedeln, Köln: Benziger/Neukirchener Verlag, 1980), 218.

[130]Ibid. Käseman, however, denies that there is a connection with what precedes (*Romans*, 293).

[131]See the logical chain linkage worked out by C. E. B. Cranfield, *A Critical and Exegetical Commentary on the Epistle to the Romans*, vol. 2 (Edinburgh: Clark, 1979), 533.f. See also Barrett, *Romans*, 204.

[132]It is true that the third person plural of the verb forms can be indefinite and thus be understood as a general reference, meaning "anyone," but in view of the context, as Cranfield indicates, Paul surely means the Jews (*Romans*, 2:533). But cf. Käsemann, *Romans*, 294.

[133]Käsemann, *Romans*, 294.

sake of the gospel (see again Gal. 1:15f.), and therefore Paul sees the
Christian apostles as the fulfillment of Isaiah's prophecy. The final era has
dawned, since God has sent authorized preachers, in conformity with the
Isaianic prophecy.[134] As a result, two conditions have been met: there are
preachers of good news, and they are divinely sent.[135] The preconditions
for hearing and faith are a reality, and a universal reality at that (note Paul's
quotation of Ps. 19:4 in v. 18!).

It cannot be the case, therefore, that God has failed his chosen people. He
has sent preachers with good news to the whole world. The fault lies in the
fact that for some "their *akouein* ["hearing"] has not become *hupakouein*
["obeying"]."[136] What is missing is the response of the hearers in "obedience of faith" (1:5). Or, as Barrett aptly phrases it, "The break in the chain
occurs at the link of faith."[137] This is likewise supported by Paul with a reference to the prophetic Scriptures, Isaiah's lament, "Lord, who believed our
message?"[138] By *akoē* Paul does not mean the faculty of "hearing" but the
"message which is heard."[139] And the message he has in mind is the gospel
of Christ, the result being, as Käsemann emphasizes, that "Israel has become
guilty in relation to the gospel."[140]

Paul now draws out the inferences of what he has been saying, as is plain
from the first word *ara* ("so then"). Verse 17 is therefore both a summary
of vv. 14f. and a transition to the questions of vv. 18ff.[141] As such, in its formulaic expression it is, as Schütz says, "paradigmatic: word of Christ—
hearing—faith."[142] However, in order to appreciate the exact force of this
passage, especially for our investigation of Paul's theology of preaching, it
is necessary to understand what the apostle means by the word *akoē* ("hearing") and the expression "through the word of Christ" (*dia hrēmatos Christou*).

It is important to stress that by *akoē* Paul does not refer to the biological
sense of hearing. This is not a general philosophical statement, a phenomenology of faith. Rather, just as it stands in the Isaianic citation (v. 16b) for
the "message that is heard," so also here Paul means the message of the gos-

---

[134]Barrett, *Romans*, 204.

[135]Cranfield, *Romans*, 2:535. But Wilckens believes the citation is intended to support the
"whole event of preaching," as described in vv. 14f. (*Römer*, 2:228).

[136]Wilckens, *Römer*, 2:229. Cranfield, *Romans*, 2:535.

[137]Barrett, *Romans*, 204.

[138]This quotation shows clearly that Paul understands obedience in v. 16a to mean faith,
as Barrett sees (*Romans*, 205). See also Cranfield, *Romans*, 2:536.

[139]Käsemann, *Romans*, 295.

[140]Ibid.

[141]Wilckens, *Römer*, 2:218. The linkage is in the words *akoē* ("hearing") in v. 17 and
ēkousan ("they heard") in v. 18.

[142]Schütz, *Anatomy*, 61.

pel.[143] The fact that *akoē* ("hearing") is linked in v. 17b to the expression "word of Christ" (*hrēmatos Christou*) also shows that this is Paul's meaning.[144]

The expression *dia hrēmatos Christou* ("through the word of Christ") takes us back to 10:8. There Paul had interpreted Deut. 30:12-14 as referring to Christ, even though Moses specifically refers to the law in that passage. This is justified because Paul regards Christ as the fulfillment of the law, as the law's embodiment and essence. As a result, Paul can say with Moses, "The word is near you" (v. 8a), which he interprets as "the word of faith which we preach" (*to hrēma tēs pisteōs ho kērussomen*). By "word of faith" the apostle does not mean "the word which has faith as its content, but in which faith itself comes to expression."[145] And since in the very next verse Paul spells this out in terms of the early Christian confessional formula "Jesus is Lord" (*kurion Iēsoun*) and the traditional formula "that God raised him from the dead" (*hoti ho theos auton ēgeiren ek nekrōn*), there is no doubt that Paul understands *rhēma* ("word") to mean the gospel which he, as a Christian apostle, preaches.[146] The upshot of v. 17b, then, is, as Wilckens explains, "In the word of faith Christ himself speaks and acts, as in the word of the prophets God himself acts."[147]

C. Preliminary Observations

This text advances our thinking about Paul's theology of preaching. It makes specific the linkage between the divinely authorized word of Christ, the office of preaching, the message which is heard, and the resulting faith which makes possible one's "calling upon the Lord." The goal of faith in the act of preaching is for the final time emphatically stressed. And in view of the apostle's further point in v. 18ff., that Israel nevertheless rejected the gospel and therefore must bear responsibility before God, an ominous note has been struck. The word proclaimed is in fact the power not only of salvation but also of destruction. As Käsemann puts it, "Faith and unbelief are not arbitrary human decisions. As obedience or disobedience they are a response to God's prevenient grace. The word that has come near simultaneously establishes the possibility of perdition."[148]

---

[143]Barrett, *Romans*, 205. Wilckens, *Römer*, 2:229. But cf. Cranfield (*Romans*, 2:537 n. 1), who thinks it does carry here the simple meaning "hearing."

[144]Wilckens, *Römer*, 2:229.

[145]Ibid., 227.

[146]Ibid., 229.

[147]Ibid.

[148]Käsemann, *Romans*, 293.

CONCLUSIONS

If Paul's purpose in writing to the Romans is, as we believe, to disclose his intention to "preach the gospel" and so bring the Roman Christians under his apostolic authority, then it is patent that for Paul preaching functions as the exercise of authority, of the power of God. In view of our previous exegetical studies, this is not surprising. It simply indicates how consistently Paul connects preaching and authority. What is new in his discussion in Romans is that preaching the gospel is the implementation of the "righteousness of God." Through the preaching of the gospel of Christ, God in his covenant faithfulness as creator and sovereign Lord of human history acts in good faith, exercising his power for salvation on the universal basis of faith. And since the "righteousness of God" is a covenant term, and is thus relational, then preaching as the implementation of the "righteousness of God" is also relational. It is the personal exercise of a restoration process. Through the preaching of the gospel of Christ God puts people back into a right relationship with himself, and that is the essence of salvation.

It should be obvious why such an approach is decisive for Paul's dealing with the Christians at Rome, both Jewish and gentile. His understanding of the church will not permit any potential fracturing of the body of Christ to stand uncorrected. Paul intends to preach the gospel in Rome, in person as well as by his advance letter, so as to bring about the restoration of the unity of the Christian community there. This corresponds to the apostle's call for reconciliation in 2 Cor. 5:17–6:2, the difference being that there he called the Corinthians to reconciliation with God and himself while in Rome the reconciliation is between Jewish and gentile fellow Christians. This explains why the apostle's imagery changes from reconciliation to "righteousness of God." The latter term embraces both Jews and gentiles alike, since God as creator is faithful to his whole creation (see 3:29-30).

But if preaching is the exercise of God's power and consequently has the character of authority, that authority in part is intended to be used as the means of unity for the church. Paul's logic runs along the lines that since God is universal Lord, Christ is God's universal redeemer, and universal redemption is available in the gospel of Christ. The preaching of the gospel is therefore the universal means of a unified Christian front, gentiles and Jews together in the church. Since the gospel recognizes no distinctions, neither does preaching. Since the gospel is for all, so is preaching. Preaching the gospel is God's great equalizer. Preaching strips away all divisions and every pretense. For in the preaching of the gospel every person alike is brought face to face with the universal grace of God.

Such preaching calls for a specific response, the "obedience of faith." Faith is submission on the part of the subject, the creature, to the sovereign

Lord, the creator, who in preaching announces the merciful terms of life in his world. The response of faith is at the end of a divine process, represented by an ordained chain of grace. God authorizes the gospel message in Christ, appoints preachers to bear his good news, brings human beings into a hearing relation to the gospel, and calls them to faith in the gospel so as to create the possibility of their calling upon him for deliverance.

On the other hand, just because the preaching of the gospel is aimed at universal faith does not mean the gospel will meet with universal acceptance. Faith is an act of submission, of obedience to a sovereign God. It means divesting oneself of every claim before that sovereign Lord, whether it is a claim based on culture, race, or religion. And "not all" are willing to do that by any means. The gospel is resisted. The preacher, therefore, must expect to invite anger and abuse upon herself/himself and upon the message, for it does not meet the world's standards. At the same time, those who do reject the gospel stand in jeopardy before God. If faith is an act of obedience, then unbelief is an act of disobedience in the face of a gracious and merciful Lord. Such rejection has destructive consequences.

For Paul's fellow Christians in Rome, Jews and gentiles, this all means they are being called, in the gospel which Paul is divinely authorized to preach, to close ranks in mutual recognition and respect. In faith toward God, in making the confession "Jesus is Lord," Jewish and gentile believer alike is committed to giving up every claim, every presumption, over against God and, importantly, over against each other. If they are to outdo each other at all, it must be that they "outdo one another in showing honor" (12:10). To Jews and gentiles in Christ who are confronting each other at Rome, in the aftermath of the tension created by Claudius' edict of expulsion, Paul appeals:

> May the God of steadfastness and encouragement grant you to live in such harmony with one another, in accord with Christ Jesus, that together you may with one voice glorify the God and Father of our Lord Jesus Christ.
> Welcome one another, therefore, as Christ has welcomed you, for the glory of God. For I tell you that Christ became a servant to the circumcised to show God's truthfulness, in order to confirm the promises given to the patriarchs, and in order that the Gentiles might glorify God for his mercy (15:5-10).

CHAPTER 6

CONCLUSION: PAUL'S THEOLOGY OF PREACHING AND MODERN PROCLAMATION

The Pauline texts that have been examined in this investigation provide instructive insights into Paul's theology of preaching. Now it becomes our task to draw the results of our exegetical study into an organized pattern. Simply put, we want to describe and understand Paul's theology of preaching as a whole. Once we have arrived at that point, we can compare Paul's theology of preaching with that of the representative theologians we selected in the opening chapter, and we can indicate how Paul's theology of preaching might have a beneficial impact on contemporary preaching.

PAUL'S THEOLOGY OF PREACHING

Inquiring into Paul's theology of preaching we set for ourselves several key questions which were the leading edge of our research. We examined the Pauline texts to discover the theological origin and definition of preaching. We sought to know what Paul regarded as the function of preaching. We were concerned with the nature and character of preaching. And we wanted to know the expected results, the outcome, of the preaching task, according to Paul. These questions form a useful outline as we now clarify Paul's theology of preaching.

There is no question that for Paul preaching arises in the orbit of the word of God and the gospel (1 Thess. 1:4-10; 2:13). These two key concepts are connected to Paul's soteriology. Together the word of God and the gospel bring the hearer into a relationship with God's salvation, which historically is located in the death and resurrection of Jesus Christ. The word of God, as we saw, is understood by the apostle to refer to the creative power of God. It is a word which is "at work" in believers (1 Thess. 2:13). The gospel, on the other hand, is at one and the same time a threefold phenomenon: a message which is proclaimed, with the Christ event as its heart and content; a saving event; and also a saving, dynamic environment in which God's people live. As the message of salvation, the gospel finds its warrant in the fact that God raised Jesus "from the dead" (1 Cor. 15:12-15; Rom. 1:4f.) The gospel is the gospel of Christ, the revelation of God in his Son (Gal. 1:11f.). As a saving event the gospel of Christ liberates people from the sphere of sin, death and wrath, and it incorporates them into the sphere of God's power (1 Thess. 1:9-10; Rom. 1:15-17). As a saving environment it is the area of time and space in which the power of God holds sway, the environment of the community of believers (1 Thess. 1:4-5; 1 Cor. 1:26–2:5). It is these two closely related key terms, word and gospel, that form the matrix for Paul's conception of the preaching task.

But how are word and gospel related? And how does preaching fit into this word-gospel structure? It appears that for Paul preaching is the mediating term between word of God and gospel.[1] That is to say, the word of God is God's creative power at work in the world, while the gospel is the word of God in a specific shape and form. Word of God is broadly understood, a term tailored to the created universe, since from the start God is understood as creating by means of his word (Gen. 1:1ff.). Gospel is understood more narrowly as the specific mode of the word of God in human history. Thus the creative word of God becomes the gospel in the mediating activity of preaching.[2] It is as if in a wilderness of hostile forces God has created an oasis, an area in time and space in which there is refuge and refreshment. That oasis is the gospel. It is called into being by the word of God issued in the act of preaching.

From this dynamic structure of word and gospel, then, Paul's definition of preaching emerges. For the apostle Paul preaching the gospel is the direct, vocal activity of the creative word of God in time and space.[3] Note that preaching is not separate from the gospel. For Paul there is no preaching

---

[1]See the discussion regarding the relationship of preaching to the gospel and word of God in the first chapter, pages 27f., 53-55.

[2]This was made particularly clear in our examination of 1 Thess. 1:9-13. See pages 51-54.

[3]See pages 54, 56-57.

without the gospel (1 Thess. 1:4f., 2:9-13; Gal. 1:8ff.; Rom. 10:14-17). That is why Paul can use *euaggelizesthai* ("to gospelize") interchangeably with *kērussein* ("to preach"). In fact, in order to bring out the spatial framework of the gospel one could almost translate *euaggelizesthai* as "*en*-gospel." Preaching is the voice by which the word of God brings the gospel to exist and sustains it as a salvific territory.

Having determined the theological origin and definition of preaching, according to Paul, it is now possible to describe the way in which preaching functions. How does preaching the gospel work? Here the overarching model is that of the herald in the ancient world.[4] It is no mere coincidence that the apostle uses *kērussein* ("to preach/proclaim") repeatedly. The work of the herald was to speak in behalf of a recognized authority.[5] In so doing, by making public proclamation the herald enacted the will of the king or conqueror who had sent him. Thus for Paul the function of preaching the gospel is to enact, by spoken public proclamation, the will of God as the creator and supreme cosmocrator. By declaring that the crucified Jesus has been raised from the dead to be Lord, the preacher establishes a new, redemptive world and lays down the terms and conditions of new existence (1 Cor. 1:18ff., 15:3ff., 12; 2 Cor. 4:5, 5:17ff.; Rom. 1:1ff.). In the case of the gospel this means peace with God (2 Cor. 5:18-21), a new calling and status with God (1 Cor. 1:26ff.), and a new life that is lived no longer according to human standards but with God as its source (1 Cor. 1:22-31). The preaching of the gospel does not, however, announce a new power structure for life and then abandon the project. Preaching has an important continuing role of interpretation. The preaching of the gospel directs and controls the way in which the gospel is appropriated and lived out, as can be seen in Paul's controversy with the Corinthians (1 Cor. 15:3-12).[6]

Fundamental to this conception of preaching is the belief in God's sovereign authority. The message of the herald is only as good as the authority of the one who sends him. For Paul there is no higher authority than God's, and it is God who sends the preacher of the gospel and so authenticates the power of the gospel (Rom. 10:14-17). Preaching is therefore an exercise of divine authority. The preaching of the gospel of Christ announces the paradox that human beings are liberated from the power of sin and death precisely through one who fell victim to these hostile forces (Gal. 1:4; 1 Cor. 15:3). God has proved true to himself and faithful to his created order by restoring human beings to a right relation with himself through the crucified and risen Christ (Rom. 1:16-17, 3:21-30). This means that freedom does not exist as

---

[4]See pages 103f., 118.

[5]See page 104.

[6]See the discussion of the interpretive function of preaching, pages 124-126, 131-133, 135f.

an independent commodity. Rather, freedom is in relationship to God, so that liberation from the destructive power of sin means incorporation into the sphere of God's saving power, the environment of the gospel (Gal. 1:4, 10; 2 Cor. 5:17ff.). The authoritative preaching of the gospel creates the church (1 Thess. 1:6-8, 2:13f.; Rom. 1:14-17). And once the church is created, when the people of God are thus embraced by the gospel, the authoritative preaching of the gospel maintains unity and peace among them as a believing community (Rom. 1:14-16, 12:1–15:13; 1 Cor. 1:10-17). In every instance the preaching of the gospel constitutes an authoritative divine call to accept and conform one's life to the new world opened up in the eschatological act of God's revelation of his Son, Jesus Christ (Gal. 1:12; 2 Cor. 4:5f., 5:17-19). Preaching the gospel does not describe what might be; it declares what is!

Such an understanding of preaching on Paul's part leads to a wide range of implications which fill in the picture of the character and nature of preaching. The first flows from the observation that for Paul there is no preaching without the gospel. This means the gospel is the authoritative norm of all preaching, and as such it constitutes the highest authority (Gal. 1:6-9). Because it originates in the revelation of God's Son, for Paul the gospel is the source for all other authority in the church (Gal. 1:11f., 2:5). So then, just as there is no preaching without the gospel, so also there is no authority without the preaching of the gospel.[7]

A second characteristic flows from the fact that the preaching of the gospel is the enactment of the creative word of God. Since the word of God is dynamic, the medium of God's word correspondly must be alive, creative and dynamic. As a result, for Paul the word of preaching is by nature oral. It is the spoken word which has the immediacy and directness of personal address (1 Thess. 2:2-12). As a corollary, if the oral preaching of the gospel constitutes an authoritative, dynamic call from God, then it requires a living, personal agent. The preacher is, therefore, the personal, living voice of the gospel, which constitutes the call of God (Gal. 1:11-16).

The personal, direct and oral character of the preaching of the gospel has yet another important consequence. The preaching of the gospel, understood in this way, means that the gospel becomes distinctive for each preacher, each congregation. Paul makes that explicit when he refers to God's having called him to preach the gospel by revealing his Son "in me" (Gal. 1:16).[8] It is equally clear when Paul makes reference to "our" gospel, which, as our exegesis showed, means his own personally (1 Thess.

---

[7]This is especially clear in Paul's treatment of the sensitive situation in Rome, where Paul wants to extend his authority on the basis of his commission to preach to the gentiles. See pages 171-175.

[8]See how Paul personalizes the gospel in Gal. 1:12ff. See pages 74-80.

1:4).[9] And it also manifests itself in the fact that for Paul the gospel is cumulative, that the mutual experience in the gospel on the part of himself and the congregation to whom he preaches becomes the "text" for further proclamation of the gospel (1 Thess. 1:8, 3:6).[10] Since the gospel shapes the destiny and character of the church in the interrelationship between preacher and people of God, the gospel becomes a living, unique experience in each place where it is proclaimed. Since the gospel incorporates those who hear and accept it into the sphere of influence of Christ, it is relational. The preaching of the gospel implies an on-going experience which happens in the relationship between the gospel's preacher and hearers.

It is no great surprise, then, that Paul understands the character of the preacher to be shaped by the dynamic of the gospel. Since the gospel is rooted in the grace of God, preaching is by grace. It is the free gift of God. At the same time it is the free, sovereign act of God. As a consequence, preaching, as Paul knows it, never focuses on itself, is neither underhanded nor manipulative (2 Cor. 2:17, 4:2!; cf. 1 Thess. 2:3ff.). Preaching is a service, and the paradigm of the preacher is that of servant (2 Cor. 4:7-12). In fact, in the case of the preacher of the gospel, the paradigm of the servant is the fate of the master, so that the preacher is always "carrying in the body the death of Jesus" (2 Cor. 4:10). From Paul's point of view the preacher of the gospel is a slave entrusted with a sacred commission to proclaim the message ordained by God within the limits imposed by that commission (1 Cor. 9:15-19; 2 Cor. 2:17, 5:18f.).

As a result, preaching is not the niche for the power hungry or those who seek personal glory. In fact, preaching by its very nature is a weak, vulnerable medium.[11] It is a divine paradox that the preaching of the gospel, both in its content and form, is scandalous (1 Cor. 1:17ff.) The gospel proclaims universal salvation through one who was destroyed, and it is made available to human beings through the vulnerability of preaching. For proclamation presupposes a recognized authority, and the world is not eager to recognize the authority of God (1 Cor. 1:22-25; Rom. 1:18ff.). The preaching of the gospel, therefore, invites resistance and abuse.[12]

This does not imply, though, that Paul has a weak view of preaching. To the contrary, for Paul the preaching of the gospel is the "power of God for salvation to every one who believes" (Rom. 1:16). That power shows up in

---

[9]See pages 36f., 57.

[10]See pages 42-44, 57f.

[11]See the discussion on this in the section on 1 Cor. 1:17ff., pages 103-104.

[12]See also this discussion in the section on 1 Cor. 9:14-18, pages 120-122. See also pages 106-108.

the creation of the Christian community (1 Cor. 2:1-5). That is its positive manifestation. The negative manifestation is in the fact that the gospel is destructive. It breaks down the old world order so that space can be created for the coming of the new creation (1 Cor. 1:19-20, 28-29; cf. 2 Cor. 10:3ff.). The preaching of the gospel has a decidedly polemical thrust. It is no wonder that Paul recognizes no other gospel (Gal. 1:6ff.). In the new age, inaugurated by the preaching of the gospel of Christ, no rivals from the old age, which is passing away, can be tolerated.

Finally, Paul understands the nature and character of preaching to be universal.[13] It is the medium of God in his saving work for all humankind (Rom. 1:14ff.). Preaching the gospel addresses all human beings at the same fundamental level, the universal sense of hearing, and preaching calls for the universal response of faith (Rom. 10:14ff.). It is consequently the means for the unity of the human social order.[14]

What results does the apostle Paul expect from such preaching of the gospel? On the individual level he expects the "obedience of faith" (Rom. 1:5). On the corporate level he expects a community of believers, called and gathered within the sphere of God's power, the saving environment of the gospel. That is to say, Paul expects the Christian church to be created and sustained by the power of preaching the gospel (1 Thess. 1:2-8; 1 Cor. 1:26–2:5).[15]

It appears to have been important for Paul to describe the human response to the gospel as the "obedience of faith." The emphasis is on both words. Obedience consists in faith. And faith is an act of obedience. Why such a description? The answer seems to lie in the nature of the gospel which is preached. The preaching of the gospel, as we have observed, consists in the enactment by public proclamation of the new existence, the new creation, authored by God and accomplished in Jesus Christ. This means specifically preaching that "Jesus Christ is Lord" (2 Cor. 4:5). If Christ is Lord, the plenipotentiary of God in his created world, then those who are called into his circle of salvation are related to him as subjects.[16] And from subjects the master expects loyal obedience. At the same time, in the case of God's gospel, precisely because it announces that sinners are "justified by his grace as a gift" (Rom. 3:24), obedience takes the form of faith. Such faith means accepting the gospel as in fact laying down the new terms and conditions for life. It means submitting oneself to the lordship of Christ in trust and confi-

---

[13]This accent is struck in Rom. 1:14-17. See pages 175f., 179-181.
[14]This is plain from Paul's argument that the preaching of the gospel brings together Jews and gentiles. See pages 175, 181.
[15]See especially pages 35-38, 108-118.
[16]See pages 148-150, 153.

dence. As hearing is universal, so is faith. Faith is therefore the potential response of every human being so that the preaching of the gospel is the salvation of the world, the restoration and new life for "everyone who has faith" (Rom. 1:16f.).

Now that human beings are called by the universal preaching of the gospel through the universal capacity of hearing to the universal response of faith, there is the possibility of a new humanity. This corporate structure is the church, whose existence breaks through the political, cultural, and socio-economic barriers of sinful human beings (1 Cor. 1:26ff.; 2 Cor. 5:17ff.; Rom. 1:14-17, 3:27-30; Gal. 3:26-29). It is within this community of faith that Christ is the source of life, since he is "our wisdom, our righteousness and sanctification and redemption" (1 Cor. 1:30). And this community of believers is created and sustained by the power of God which is at work in the preaching of the gospel (1 Cor. 2:1-5).

Equipped with this understanding of Paul's theology of preaching, we are now able to answer the important question we posed for ourselves at the start of our investigation. That is the question, Why preach? Why is preaching the indispensable form of the gospel's dissemination? From Paul's perspective the answer is that this medium is required precisely because it corresponds to the unique character of the gospel. Because the gospel is the manifestation of the creative word of God enacting a new reality, a new creation, it requires a declaratory voice, as we saw in Paul's characterization of word and gospel in his address to the Thessalonians (1:6-8, 2:13). That is to say, it requires a medium that has the directness of living, personal speech.[17] It requires a medium that by its nature does not interfere with the power that the gospel is, that does not draw its strength from human potential.[18] It requires a medium which extends the word of God as gospel in time and space by drawing together a circle of hearers.[19] It requires a medium which will both enact the reality of the gospel and sustain it by continual interpretation.[20] It requires a medium that is personal, a life that itself lives within the sphere of the gospel's power.[21] In short, the gospel requires the human voice of preaching. Preaching is the medium uniquely suited to the deliverance of the creative word of God in the form of the gospel. If it is true that for Paul there is no preaching without the gospel, then it is not too much to say that for Paul there is no gospel without preaching.

---

[17]See pages 40-42, 54. See also the discussion on the preacher as herald, pages 103f.
[18]See the discussion on the preacher as slave, pages 120-122, 148f.
[19]See on Rom. 10:14, pages 185-187.
[20]See on 1 Cor. 15:12ff., pages 133-135.
[21]See on Gal. 1:10-16, pages 73-83, and on 1 Cor. 9:14-18, pages 118-122.

PAUL'S THEOLOGY OF PREACHING AND MODERN SCHOLARSHIP

It should be obvious to the reader that there are some important points of correpondence between Paul's theology of preaching and that of the scholars whom we reviewed in the introductory chapter. We now need to indicate where the points of contact are. In doing so, the reader should be alerted that it is not the intention here to discuss all of these theologies of preaching in minute detail. Rather, we want to understand Paul's theology of preaching in relation to the broader aspects of the theologies we explored earlier.

We begin by observing that Barth, Bultmann and those who followed in their footsteps all take as their starting point the word of God as an event, God's act of revealing his salvation in Christ.[22] They understand this word of God as encountering human beings in the form of a call which addresses them personally and lays claim to their lives. The expected response is personal faith, and the corporate result of preaching is the gathering of believers in the church. Such preaching is also uniformly seen as the deliverance of the re-velatory message of God, the gospel, although thc scholars we dealt with differed considerably on how this happens.

Paul also certainly regards the word of God as revelatory, as a personal call, as an event of the gospel. He too conceives of the gospel as a message whose heart and center is God's saving work in Christ. And he also expects the response of faith and the creation of the church. But there are at the same time some subtle, but important, differences in the way Paul construes these key concepts. As we have seen, for Paul the word of God is essentially God's creative power in action. The accent for him falls on the image of creation. When the Thessalonians are said to have received the gospel as the word of God, in the context of Paul's discussion he means that they have been incor-porated into the community of the gospel where the word is "at work" in them (1 Thess. 2:13). It is not so much a case of the word of God commu-nicating a message, but of its having created a congregation of believers.

By the same token, while the gospel is for Paul the message of Christ, it is simultaneously understood as referring to the location in time and space where the gospel exercises its influence in the hearing of God's people. The gospel is therefore both temporal and spatial. Paul's temporal-spatial con-ception of the gospel clearly transcends the thinking of the scholars we ex-amined, with perhaps the one exception of Fuchs, who speaks of preaching as the translation of the text so as to "create the same sphere which the text meant to create when the spirit spoke in it."[23]

---

[22]For the summary of the common accents that appear among the word of God theologians, see page 19.

[23]Fuchs, *Studies,* 195.

Similarly, when Paul thinks of the results of preaching, although he too thinks both of the obedience of faith on the part of the individual and of the church as the corporate manifestation of the gospel's power, his emphasis falls on the church. Most of the scholars we reviewed were primarily oriented to the response of the individual, the response of faith, particularly those in the Bultmannian tradition. Only Barth appears to have reserved space for the intimate connection between the preaching of the gospel and the creation of the Christian church, but even he tends to be more concerned with the church in terms of its acting as a body of individual believers gathered at the point of its commission to preach the word of God.[24] For our rethinking of the theology of preaching this has important consequences. Paul's conception of the theological origins of preaching alerts us to some key elements that can be easily overlooked. His theology of preaching invites us to maintain a balance between word of God as revelation and as creation, between the gospel as message and as power sphere, and between the expected response as individual faith and as incorporation within the church.

But perhaps the most striking difference between Paul and modern scholarship, as regards the theological origin of preaching, occurs at the point of intersection between word of God and gospel. For Paul, as for modern scholars, the two key terms, word and gospel, are closely aligned. But because the scholars we have examined conceive of the word of God as primarily revelatory and think of the gospel as essentially a message (even if they redefine it dynamically as an event of personal address), the tendency is to draw the two terms so closely together that they almost merge into one. So, for example, Barth describes God's word as his revelation of himself, which took place historically in Christ who is the "word become flesh."[25] As a result, for Barth Christian preaching means preaching the gospel, which is the same as "speaking the word of God."[26] Or consider Bultmann. For him the word of God is equated with the kerygma, whose content is the death and resurrection of Christ. The gospel therefore constitutes the call of God to give up one's previous self-understanding and accept authentic life as a gift, with the result that preaching the gospel means the living voice of the word of God in the present.[27] Practically speaking, for Bultmann and his followers word of God and gospel almost coalesce. But for Paul that is not the case. Paul knows that the gospel is coextensive with the word of God, but his fundamental presupposition is that the word of God is a creation term, and that makes all the

---

[24]Barth, *Church Dogmatics*, Vol. 1, Part Two, 743.
[25]Barth, *The Preaching of the Gospel*, 16-18.
[26]Barth, *Word of God*, 124.
[27]Schmithals, *Theology of Bultmann*, 177f. Bultmann, *Theology of the New Testament*, 1:30f. This interpretive accent is also found in the works of Ebeling and Fuchs, although they understand it as residing in language.

difference. Since word of God is conceived by Paul as God's activity in creation, the gospel can be conceived as the territory which the word creates by the declaration of the saving event of Christ. Thus, for Barth, Bultmann, and those scholars influenced by them, preaching is a case of delivering a message from God in the form of the gospel. But for Paul preaching is the mediating voice by which the word of God becomes the gospel, both in the sense of a message heard and a dynamic sphere of influence. If Barth could say that the Scriptures become the word of God in the event of proclamation, in the event by which God reveals himself and speaks through them, then Paul can reverse the direction and say that the word of God becomes the gospel when it is preached.[28] Until then, if we may borrow an analogy from the physical world, the gospel as the message of the historical event of Christ exists as potential energy; it is in preaching that its power is released and it becomes the force it was meant to be. Preaching acts as catalyst.

This difference in conceiving the theological origin of preaching explains why for Paul faith in the gospel necessarily implies incorporation into the church. In like manner, it explains why Paul places his emphasis on the church as the gospel sphere, the saving environment created by the word of God. For preaching the gospel redefines reality, setting in motion the terms and conditions of existence under God. It is a new creation, a new social order. The hearer is invited to believe the gospel in the sense that one is joined to and lives out of that power structure.

When it comes to the function of preaching, Paul's conception of proclamation as the authoritative enactment of the gospel finds its closest parallel among modern scholars in Gerhard Ebeling, who describes the activity of preaching as ''the execution'' of the biblical text, which he conceives in analogy to legal precedent.[29] Paul too sees the preacher acting much as an executor of the gospel's estate. As we have seen, Paul's essential model is that of the herald in the ancient world. However, he does not regard that model as implying a distance between preacher and congregation, which Steimle understands that word to suggest.[30] Instead, the herald remains on location as the resident interpreter of the gospel, working as servant of the Lord. In this respect Paul's model of preaching is probably closest to that of Bultmann, who understands preaching to function kerygmatically and interpretively, but with the added dimension of the personal relationship between preacher and hearers, such as that envisioned by Farmer. Perhaps this is why Paul never identifies himself specifically as a *kērux* (''herald''), but always as an *apos-*

---

[28]Barth, *Church Dogmatics*, 1, One: 109f.

[29]Ebeling, *Word and Faith*, 331.

[30]Edmund Steimle, ''Preaching the Biblical Story of Good and Evil,'' *Union Seminary Quarterly Review* 31 (Spring, 1976): 199.

tolos ("apostle"). For in his letters the term "apostle" seems to function broadly enough to embrace simultaneously the kerygmatic, authoritative, interpretive and relational characteristics which he understands the preaching of the gospel to embrace.

So far it is possible to see that Paul works with a conception of preaching that is more comprehensive in scope than that of any of the scholars in the field of the theology of preaching. For that reason Paul's understanding of the nature and character of preaching also has a broad sweep, so that many of his accents are found represented in some form within the insights of the modern scholars we have dealt with. At the same time, none of these theologians draws together into a single coherent structure all the elements which Paul includes.

To begin with, Paul knows the word of God to require the living voice. Preaching is decidedly oral and thus direct and immediate. This accent in the preaching task is reflected in Herbert H. Farmer, who describes the personal encounter of God and the human being as occurring in human speech, in what he calls the "spontaneous directness of serious private conversation."[31] It is also to be found, although to a lesser extent, in the work of Paul Scherer, who believes that for the gospel to be heard it must be proclaimed with a sense of immediacy.[32] Also, Steimle's conception of preaching as re-enacting the biblical story presupposes the dialogical, participatory nature of oral speech.[33]

Secondly, there is Paul's emphasis on the gospel as a living entity in which preacher and congregation grow together in a distinctive way. The preacher and hearers experience the gospel together and become part of it, so that in every place where the Christian community exists the gospel takes on a unique shape and quality. This important aspect of preaching surfaces among modern scholars only in Farmer, who locates the activity of preaching within the structure of a living, personal relationship between God and people, which brings them together in a "community of insight and understanding," of "shared meaning."[34] On the other hand, none of these modern theologians has seen the cumulative nature of the gospel which is so fundamental to Paul as he holds his congregations up to each other as examples. For Paul, as we noted, the experience of believers with the gospel becomes part of the gospel itself.

Paul's conception that preaching the gospel implies a servant role would doubtless be agreed on by all those theologians we considered, though Barth probably takes this up most self-consciously into his theology of preaching.[35]

---

[31] Farmer, *The Servant of the Word,* 33, 39. The quotation is from page 39.
[32] Scherer, *The Word God Sent,* 34.
[33] Steimle, "Preaching the Biblical Story," 199ff.
[34] Farmer, *The Servant of the Word,* 26-28.
[35] See especially Barth's discussion of the relation of the preacher to the word of God in act of proclamation, *The Preaching of the Gospel,* 12ff. Note also his review of the marks of authentic ministry (Ibid., 34-37).

In addition, none of these scholars would deny Paul's fundamental presupposition that there is no preaching without the gospel, that the gospel is the norm. That the preaching of the gospel is the exercise of the "power of God for salvation" would likewise be hailed by one and all, though Paul's thrust that preaching the gospel functions negatively to destroy the old order is not picked up quite so frequently. Barth appears to be conscious of it in his observation that the Scripture, which forms the basis of preaching, is polemical in its rejection of human piety and in its being directed precisely "against the *religious world.*"[36] It is, however, Scherer who is most keenly concerned with the gospel as a scandal, as a destructive force which has to disturb human beings in order to get at the root of the human problem and open them up to participate in God's redemptive purposes.[37] Also unanimously accepted by modern theologians would be Paul's view that the preaching of the gospel is a universal medium, which makes the power of God available to all who hear and come to faith. And finally, all our scholars would stand with Paul in saying that the exercise of preaching is by the grace of God, though it is probably Caemmerer more than any other who consistently understands preaching as a means of grace.[38]

Then again, Paul's insight that the power of the preaching of the gospel resides paradoxically in the fact that the act of preaching is itself weak and vulnerable, in conformity with the cross of Christ, finds little parallel among our selection of theologians. In fairness, though, it must be said that this is sensed by those scholars who see the contrast between the power of the word of God as over against the weakness of human speech.[39] It is only Barth who specifically thinks of preaching as an exercise of the *"theologia crucis"* ("theology of the cross").[40]

This raises an important question. Does this mean that those who conceive of preaching in the mode of the powerful vehicle of language are on the wrong track, so far as Paul is concerned? Browne thinks of the preacher as an artist, a poet. Steimle envisions a story-teller. Ebeling and Fuchs think preaching draws power from the linguisticality of existence. These all are conceptualizations of human language that are by nature strong. How do these stand up against Paul's conception of preaching as eminating from the weak and vulnerable medium of herald? That question is answered by observing, first, that if we are to go by his letters, Paul himself was not only aware of

---

[36]Barth, *Word of God,* 70.

[37]Scherer, *The Word God Sent,* 70-87. See also Browne, *The Ministry of the Word,* 81.

[38]Caemmerer, *Preaching for the Church,* 1-32. See also Caemmerer, "In Many, Much," 654f.

[39]Barth, *Church Dogmatics,* 1, Two:750f., and *Word of God,* 98-127. See also Caemmerer, "In Many, Much," 654.

[40]Barth, *Word of God,* 127.

the power of language, but made use of powerful metaphors and rhetorical devices.[41] So we must not suppose that the work of heralding the terms of God's new creation in the gospel precludes powerful language. The weakness inherent in preaching stems not from its stylistic form, but from the position and posture of its spokesperson over against the hearers. Whatever linguistic or artistic style is employed, the heralding of the gospel is still based on the authority of God and nothing else. The preaching of the gospel, from Paul's perspective, is weakness precisely because the power of God is not evident in self-understood ways that accord with the standards of the world. At the same time, the fact that Paul does locate the power of God in the paradox of the weakness of preaching does suggest a serious word of caution. Whatever the mode of address, whatever the art or style of the preacher, from Paul's point of view preaching does not proceed from the power resident in the language or style of itself. In fact, if preaching proceeds from the fact of linguistic potency, then such preaching subverts the very gospel it proposes to preach, because in that case it would no longer require the power of God (1 Cor. 1:18-25). The power resident in the various forms of human linguistic expression still must conform to the gospel, as the servant to the master, just as Browne, Steimle, Ebeling and Fuchs all emphatically insist.[42]

From our comparative examination it is plain that the diversity of accents which surface among modern theologians of preaching find familiar ground in Paul's theology of preaching. Or, to say it the other way around, the breadth of the character of Paul's theology of preaching manifests itself in the diversity of the insights of modern scholars. This seems to suggest, therefore, that Paul's theology of preaching offers an important structure into which many, if not most, of these diverse insights can be brought to form a coherent whole.

PAUL'S THEOLOGY OF PREACHING AND OUR OWN

Now that we have come to an understanding of Paul's theology of preaching and have placed it in conversation with modern scholarship, it remains for us to suggest some ways in which our present experience of preaching

---

[41]For example, see 2 Cor. 2:14f. In chapter two we already noted the strong similarity between Paul's argument and language in 1 Thess. 2:3-8 and that of Cynic rhetoric. See pages 46-50.

[42]See Steimle, "Preaching the Biblical Story," 205. Browne speaks of the proclamation of the gospel as always having a "definite indefiniteness about it" and calls preachers to resist every temptation to practice coercion (*The Ministry of the Word,* 29). Ebeling argues vigorously that preaching must be in accord with the Christological kerygma from the past so that that it is authentically "Christologically oriented proclamation" (*Theology and Proclamation,* 36). And Fuchs contends preaching requires a text, since in it the text "interprets us" by means of the Christological language of the gospel (*Studies,* 204f.; see also Robinson, *The New Hermeneutic,* 52ff.).

might be influenced by what we have learned. What does Paul's theology of preaching have to contribute to contemporary preachers and current preaching?

In some respects it is tempting to lay hold of Paul's theology of preaching as a norm. For Paul's theology of preaching is certainly attractive in its clarity, vitality, breadth, and sense of direction. It could easily serve as the measure of the preaching task. But that would be too facile. Paul's theology of preaching is not the last word on the subject. Many questions of concern to contemporary preaching, such as the relationship of preaching to liturgy or to the sacraments, are not treated by Paul. Nor is Paul the only Christian theologian in the early church to have wrestled with the nature of the preaching task. To the degree that they could be identified, one could profitably investigate the theologies of preaching embedded in the Synoptic Gospels, the Johannine materials, the deutero-Pauline letters, or even the Q source. All this suggests that preaching has evolved in the cross-fertilization of theological perspectives within Christian history. To elevate Paul as the supreme arbiter of preaching would be not only unwise, but unconscious of the Spirit's movement across the breadth of early Christianity and down through the centuries of Christian history.

Paul is not the last word on preaching, but he is the first word. And that perhaps suggests the way in which the great apostle to the gentiles should be understood. Paul's theology of preaching provides a solid point of departure for the thinking and rethinking of the preaching task. His conception of preaching provides an important and useful framework from which one can work out a theology of preaching appropriate for today. And it should be clear by now that such a theological undertaking is not only vital for every preacher, but is the *sine qua non* of any genuine proclamation. If the preacher cannot clearly articulate where in the economy of God preaching originates, what it is, how it functions, what its nature and character are, and what it is supposed to accomplish, it is difficult to see how that person's preaching can be beneficial or satisfying to anyone. Yet it appears, if Clement Welsh's experience is any indication to go by, that many preachers today are unable to express clearly their own theology of preaching.[43] If that continues to be the case, such preachers now have even less excuse than before. For Paul's theology of preaching, together with the insights of the modern scholars we have examined, provides some important building blocks and vital emphases from which to work. We now turn to specify what some of those are.

Perhaps the most important thing of which modern preachers should be conscious proceeds from a central insight revealed in our exegetical study, namely, that preaching is the mediating term between the word of God and

---

[43]Nichols, *Building the Word*, 1.

the gospel. Preaching, as the instrument of the creative activity of God, functions by proclaiming the gospel, the gospel which is at one and the same time the rehearsal of God's historical saving act in Christ and also the sphere of God's continuing saving activity. It is the heralding of God's new creation, and it has nothing to stand on except God's own authority. This places the act of preaching in a vulnerable position, as we saw clearly in our study of the Corinthian letters. As a result, it must be said emphatically that preaching is not for the faint of heart! Preaching is a risky business, for in and of itself the act of preaching does not have the wherewithal to demonstrate the power of God it comes to announce. And in the contemporary world, so accustomed to relying on empirical demonstration as the litmus test of all truth, this makes preaching in our time not only more difficult, but makes it appear all the weaker. Perhaps this suggests why many listeners, as well as preachers, are attracted to the performer-preachers of radio and television. For their preaching sounds and appears so much more potent, because it is dressed up in demonstrable symbols of power derived from contemporary western culture. But for all its attractiveness, that approach cannot be squared with Paul's theology of preaching. From Paul's point of view, authentic preaching does not draw its strength from itself, nor does it draw attention to itself, but it operates exclusively from the strength of God. If the gospel is true, as God is true, then preaching is true, and its power is unimpeachable. For preaching the gospel means announcing the reality that undergirds the universe. It needs no other signs of authentication.

If our analysis is accurate, then it may be safe to say that the besetting sin of many contemporary preachers is simply a loss of nerve. Or, as Paul would doubtless say it, a loss of faith. Perhaps the most important first step for rethinking the theology of preaching is to ask, "Do I really believe the gospel? Is the gospel of Christ really the locus of the saving act of God in human history for me? Does it create for me a saving universe of meaning?" For as we have learned from Paul, there is no preaching without the gospel. The gospel is the norm by which all preaching must be tested. If I really believe that, then I am ready to be the authentic voice of the new creation of God as I announce the gospel to all who will hear. For in proclaiming the gospel, I announce what is! And that makes all the difference.

Armed with this fundamental perspective from Paul, we are now in a position to assimilate several of the important accents that surfaced in our study of the apostle's letters. The first is that preaching the gospel creates a power sphere. One suspects that insight, so important to Paul, may take some getting used to on the part of modern preachers, for it requires us to think of the language medium and of the gospel as a spatial concept. It is probably safe to say that for most people the gospel, and the language of preaching that delivers it, is conceived of in ideational or experiential terms. That is to say,

preaching the gospel is thought of both by preachers and hearers as the trans-
mitting of ideas or of emotional experience. But for Paul the gospel is spatial,
meaning that it gathers and sustains a circle of hearers, a company of people.
Preaching the gospel means establishing and maintaining a saving linguistic
environment, an atmosphere in which people can draw the breath of authentic
life.

At this juncture the insights of Nichols may prove helpful in understanding the point we have just made. Nichols reminds us that language by its very
nature creates a group, a community, which modern communications re-
searchers and theorists refer to as "publics."[44] These "publics" are groups
of people who are gathered around common interests and values, and they are
maintained as an identifiable group by communication which focuses on specific topics and chooses appropriate words and emphases.[45] This means for
preachers that preaching the gospel is a creative enterprise. For those believers who gather around the gospel of Christ are taking their cues for existence
from that "shared meaning."[46] Or, as Harry Emerson Fosdick so aptly phrased
it, "Life is largely made by what people habitually say to themselves."[47]

This emphasis on the spatial nature of the preaching of the gospel should
be particularly welcome to those who often lament the lack of community on
the American scene. If it is true, as Charles Rice persuasively maintains, that
one of the problems of modern life is that we do not have a common "story"
that serves as the cohesive center for our life together, then the preaching of
the gospel as a spatial entity, as creating a "public," offers a rich resource
ready to hand.[48] If contemporary preachers will have the courage of the gospel they proclaim, then they will reap the satisfaction of being the instrument
of God's "public." Or, as Nichols points out, if language always creates a
community, then for Christian preachers the central question becomes, What
kind of community?[49] By the preaching of the gospel the "public" of God is
that gathering of believers which is created and sustained within the orbit of
the gospel's power. Thus, Christians, by means of preaching, live out of the
interpretation of life that comes when one lives within the sphere of influence
that is God's gospel, the gospel of life and salvation focused in the death and
resurrection of Christ. Preaching the gospel is, therefore, the means of a new
sense of community, of social unity and coherence.

---

[44]Ibid., 107.

[45]Ibid.

[46]Farmer, *The Servant of the Word,* 28.

[47]Quoted in E. H. Linn, *Preaching As Counselling; The Unique Method of Harry Emerson
Fosdick* (Valley Forge: Judson, 1966), 112.

[48]Steimle, Niedenthal and Rice, *Preaching the Story,* 56ff.

[49]Nichols, *Building the Word,* 107.

But we can take this one step further. If the gospel is the truth of God in Christ, the sphere in which we exist, and the basis for a new social order, then preaching the gospel is definitively interpretive. On the basis of the gospel the preacher interprets life under God for herself/himself and fellow believers. Negatively this means exposing the sordid values, unworthy attitudes, and faulty presuppositions about life that are generated by the dominant culture and which play upon the human vulnerability that is "sin at work in the flesh," to use Paul's way of saying it (Rom. 7:5, 21-25). This is the destructive application of the preaching task. Positively, preaching interprets life by defining reality on the basis of the love and power of God. And given the fact that there is no lack of those who, for their own ends, are only too eager to define reality for us, the preaching task becomes all the more urgent in our time. In fact, one can easily say that the burgeoning of mass media has brought to hearers and viewers in the western world such a clash of competing definitions of reality that most people, especially young people, are left hopelessly confused. Preaching the gospel is the opportunity every preacher has to bring order out of chaos on the basis of the word of God, which speaks into existence the new creation in Christ. Paul's emphasis on the interpretive function of preaching is to be welcomed anew.

Another aspect of Paul's theology of preaching which should give pause to modern preachers is his accent on the orality of preaching. Preaching requires the living voice. Paul does not even regard his letters as a sufficient replacement for his own voice in the living present. Preaching is by its very commission a direct, dialogical form of address. Its orality means it has an immediacy which calls hearers into a living moment, a reponse. For preachers of the gospel that should be significant, for it means, above all, that preaching the gospel involves a personal gospel. The gospel of God lives within every authentic preacher, is in a certain sense incarnated in her/him. It is the gospel "according to" Jim or Nancy or Dorothy or Jack. And this fact suggests two important spin-offs. The first is that if the gospel is personal, then it is unique, and the preacher does himself/herself a disservice by continually casting about for "what works" in another congregation or in another's preaching. That is not to be misunderstood, of course, to mean we cannot learn from each other. But it simply asserts that being a preacher first means being one's self, as each of us has been uniquely created by God and shaped by his gospel at work in us. Secondly, it means that those scholars and students of preaching who have warned us that preparing to preach is not a matter of coming up with a document or a manuscript are exactly right.[50] It can hardly be better said than in the words of Ronald Allen and Thomas Herin,

---

[50]Among others, Caemmerer makes much of this point. He argues that the writing of the sermon must be done with the hearer constantly in mind (*Preaching for the Church*, 93-110).

who say of the process of sermon preparation, " . . . I am ultimately preparing a person rather than a product."[51]

If the gospel requires the direct immediacy of the oral voice, of a human being, then it is an experiential realm between preacher and hearers. That is precisely how Paul conceives of it. And as we have noted, the experiences of Paul and his congregations in the power sphere of the gospel become themselves part of the gospel. The gospel of Christ incorporates into its structure all who hear and believe as well as all that happens as a result of their hearing and believing. This means, if contemporary preachers will take it seriously, that the ongoing mutual experiences of preachers and hearers within the framework of preaching become part of the proclamation. It means lifting up those experiences in which preacher and congregation have identified certain realities and the specific call of God to service, and then, acting on the basis of their common faith, they have carried out the will of God. Parish consultant Lyle Schaller is close to Paul's viewpoint when he urges preachers to lead congregations in celebrating those works of ministry which they are able to accomplish together.[52] It must be added immediately, however, that this is not to be confused with the "success story" model so rampant among the mass media preachers of our time. Paul is never afraid to acknowledge the good things that have happened in his exercise of the gospel, but it is always the strength *out of weakness* that he boasts about! It is at those points where, humanly speaking, there is nothing to be expected, where if anything is to happen it can happen only on the strength of the gospel, that Paul "boasts." The "boast" which is ours in the preaching of the gospel is always a boast "in the Lord" (1 Cor. 1:31). But it is, for all that, no less a "boast," a reason to celebrate the experience of the power of God at work among us. The preacher, as interpreter of life within the gospel's "magnetic" field, draws together all the slivers of experience to form the unique character of the gospel "according to" a specific group of Christian people. In a world of people who long to know that their lives count, the preaching of the gospel, understood in terms of the experience in the gospel, ought to be a source of special joy to modern Christians.

From the results of our study there can be little question that Paul has a lofty view of the potential of preaching the gospel. He expected the obedience of faith to come about on the basis of the simple speaking of the truth, the gospel of Christ. And he expected whole communities of the faithful to be formed and sustained on the basis of the gospel's sphere of influence, ex-

---

[51]Steimle, Niedenthal and Rice, *Preaching the Story,* 161. They point particularly to 1 Thess. 2:8.

[52]This point was made by Schaller in a lecture delivered during a continuing education program for pastors held at Concordia Seminary, St. Louis, in June, 1973.

ercised in preaching. For Paul, to preach the gospel was to exercise the very authoritative power of God. So bold was his view of preaching that every other aspect of his apostolic ministry flowed from that one single call to ''preach the gospel to the Gentiles.'' It is for this reason that Paul's theology of preaching is inspiring. No preacher who pays attention to Paul's theology of preaching has to step into the pulpit uncertain about what he/she is doing or what is to be accomplished. And if the reader has caught nothing more than Paul's spirit, then we have come a long way in rectifying the lack of certainty which Ebeling identified as the chief obstacle for preaching the gospel today.[53]

---

[53]Ebeling, *Theology and Proclamation*, 13.

BIBLIOGRAPHY

PRIMARY SOURCES

Bible, Holy. Revised Standard Version. New York: Thomas Nelson, 1952.

The Greek New Testament. Edited by Kurt Aland, *et al.* Third edition. New York: United Bible Societies, 1975.

REFERENCE WORKS

Bauer, Walter. *A Greek-English Lexicon of the New Testament and Other Early Christian Literature.* Translated and adapted by William F. Arndt and F. Wilbur Gingrich. Chicago: University of Chicago Press, 1957.

Blass, F., and DeBrunner, A. *A Greek Grammar of the New Testament and Other Early Christian Literature.* Translation of the 9-10th German edition by Robert W. Funk. Chicago: University of Chicago Press, 1961.

Crim, Keith, ed. *The Interpreter's Dictionary of the Bible,* Supplementary Volume. Nashville: Abingdon, 1976.

Kittel, Gerhard, ed. *Theological Dictionary of the New Testament.* Translated and edited by Geoffrey W. Bromiley. Ten volumes. Grand Rapids: Eerdmans, 1964-76.

Metzger, Bruce. *A Textual Commentary on the Greek New Testament.* New York: United Bible Societies, 1971.

Moulton, W. F., and Geden, A. S. *A Concordance to the Greek New Testament.* Fifth edition, revised by H. K. Moulton. Edinburgh: Clark, 1978.

COMMENTARIES, BOOKS AND ARTICLES

Achtemeier, Elizabeth. *Creative Preaching.* Nashville: Abingdon, 1981.

Achtemeier, Paul. *An Introduction to the New Hermeneutic.* Philadelphia: Westminster, 1969.

Achtemeier, Paul. *Romans.* Atlanta: John Knox, 1985.

Barrett, C. K. *A Commentary on the Epistle to the Romans.* New York: Harper, 1957.

Barrett, C. K. *A Commentary on the First Epistle to the Corinthians*. New York: Harper, 1968.

Barrett, C. K. *A Commentary on the Second Epistle to the Corinthians*. New York: Harper, 1973.

Barrett, C. K. "Paul's Opponents in II Corinthians." *New Testament Studies* 17 (3, 1971): 233-254.

Barth, Karl. *Church Dogmatics*. Volume I, Parts One and Two. Second edition, edited by G. W. Bromiley and T. F. Torrance. Translated by G. W. Bromiley. Edinburgh: Clark, 1975.

Barth, Karl. *The Preaching of the Gospel*. Translated by B. E. Hooke. Philadelphia: Westminster, 1963.

Barth, Karl. *The Resurrection of the Dead*. Translated by H. J. Stenning. New York: Revell, 1933.

Barth, Karl. *The Word of God and the Word of Man*. Translated by Douglas Horton. New York: Harper, 1957.

Barbour, Robin S. "Wisdom and the Cross in I Corinthians 1 and 2." In *Theologia Crucis—Signum Crucis,* edited by C. Andresen. 1979, 57-71.

Bartsch, Hans-Werner. "Die Argumentation des Paulus in I Cor. 15:3-11." *Zeitschrift für die neutestamentliche Wissenschaft* 55 (3-4, 1964): 261-74.

Bartsch, Hans-Werner. "The Historical Situation of Romans." *Encounter* 33 (1972): 329-339.

Batey, R. A. "Paul's Interaction with the Corinthians." *Journal of Biblical Literature* 84 (June, 1965): 139-46.

Becker, Jürgen, Hans Conzelmann and Gerhard Friedrich. *Die Briefe an die Galater, Epheser, Philipper, Kolosser, Thessalonicher, und Philemon*. Göttingen: Vandenhoeck & Rupprecht, 1976.

Beker, J. Christiaan. *Paul The Apostle*. Philadelphia: Fortress, 1980.

Best, Ernest. *A Commentary on the First and Second Epistles to the Thessalonians*. New York: Harper and Row, 1972.

Betz, Hans Dieter. *Galatians*. Philadelphia: Fortress, 1979.

Betz, Hans Dieter. *Nachfolge und Nachahmung Jesu Christi im Neuen Testament*. Tübingen: Mohr, 1967.

Betz, Hans Dieter. *Paul's Apology in II Corinthians 10-13 and the Socratic Tradition*. Berkeley: Center for Hermeneutical Studies, 1975.

Bligh, John. *Galatians: A Discussion of St. Paul's Epistle*. London: St. Paul, 1969.

Boers, Hendrikus. "The Form-Critical Study of Paul's Letters. 1 Thessalonians as a Case Study." *New Testament Studies* 22 (1975/76): 140-158.

Bormann, Paul. *Die Heilswirksamkeit der Verkündigung nach dem Apostel Paulus; Ein Beitrag zur Theologie der Verkündigung*. Paderborn: Bonfacius Druckerei, 1965.

Bornkamm, Günther. *Paul*. Translated by D. M. G. Stalker. New York: Harper, 1971.

Braumann, Georg. *Vorpaulinische christliche Taufverkündigung bei Paulus*. Stuttgart, 1962.

Browne, Robert E. C. *The Ministry of the Word*. London: S. C. M., 1958.

Brox, Norbert. *Understanding the Message of Paul*. Translated by J. Blenkinsopp. Notre Dame, Ind.: University of Notre Dame Press, 1968.

Buechner, Frederick. *Telling the Truth: The Gospel as Tragedy, Comedy and Fairy Tale*. San Francisco: Harper, 1977.

Bultmann, Rudolf. *Der zweite Brief an die Korinther*. Göttingen: Vandenhoeck & Rupprecht, 1976.

Bultmann, Rudolf. *Faith and Understanding*. Volume I, edited by Robert Funk. Translated by Louise Smith. New York: Harper, 1969.

Bultmann, Rudolf. *Jesus Christ and Mythology.* New York: Scribner's, 1958.

Bultmann, Rudolf. *Theology of the New Testament.* Two volumes. Translated by Kendrick Grobel. New York: Scribner, 1951-55.

Burton, Ernest de Witt. *A Critical and Exegetical Commentary on the Epistle to the Galatians.* The International Critical Commentary. New York: Scribner's, 1920.

Bussmann, Claus. *Themen der paulinischen Missionspredigt auf dem Hintergrund der spätjüdischen-hellenistischen Missionsliteratur.* Bern: Herbert Lang, 1971.

Caemmerer, Richard. "In Many, Much." *Concordia Theological Monthly* (November, 1968): 653-669.

Caemmerer, Richard. *Preaching for the Church.* St. Louis: Concordia, 1959.

Chamberlin, Charles A. "The Preaching of the Apostle Paul, Based on a Study of Acts of the Apostles and Paul's Letters, with Special Reference to the First and Second Corinthians." Ph. D. Dissertation, Temple University, 1959.

Conzelmann, Hans. *An Outline of the Theology of the New Testament.* Translated by John Bowden. London: S. C. M., 1969.

Conzelmann, Hans. *First Corinthians.* Translated by J. W. Leitch. Hermeneia Commentary Series. Philadelphia: Fortress, 1975.

Craddock, Fred B. *As One Without Authority.* Enid, Oklahoma: Phillips University Press, 1971.

Cranfield, C. E. B. *A Critical and Exegetical Commentary on the Epistle to the Romans.* Two volumes. The International Critical Commentary, 6th edition. Edinburgh: Clark, 1975-79.

Delling, Gerhard. *Studien zum Neuen Testament und zum hellenistischen Judentum.* Göttingen: Vandenhoeck & Rupprecht, 1970.

Dibelius, Martin, and Werner Georg Kümmel. *Paul.* London: Longmans, Green, 1953.

Dinkler, Erich. "Die Verkündigung als eschatologisch- sakramentales Geschehen: Auslegung von 2 Kor. 5:14-6:2." In *Die Zeit Jesu,* edited by Günther Bornkamm and Karl Rahner. Freiburg: Herder, 1970: 169-189.

Dodd, Charles H. *The Apostolic Preaching and Its Developments.* Second edition. New York: Harper, 1954.

Donfried, Karl. "Paul and Judaism: 1 Thessalonians 2:13-16 as a Test Case." *Interpretation* 38 (July, 1984): 242-253.

Donfried, Karl. *The Romans Debate.* Minneapolis: Augsburg, 1977.

Duke, Robert. *The Sermon as God's Word.* Nashville: Abingdon, 1980.

Ebeling, Gerhard. *Theology and Proclamation.* Translated by John Riches. Philadelphia: Fortress, 1966.

Ebeling, Gerhard. *Word and Faith.* Translated by James W. Leitsch. London: S. C. M., 1963.

Eichholz, Georg. *Die Theologie des Paulus im Umriss.* Vluyn: Neukirchener Verlag, 1977.

Fant, Clyde. *Preaching for Today.* New York: Harper, 1975.

Fitzmyer, Joseph A. "The Gospel in the Theology of Paul." *Interpretation* 33 (4, 1979): 339-350.

Farmer, Herbert H. *The Servant of the Word.* Philadelphia: Fortress, 1974.

Fuchs, Ernst. *Studies of the Historical Jesus.* Translated by Andrew Scobie. London: S. C. M., 1964.

Furnish, Victor. *Theology and Ethics in Paul.* Nashville: Abingdon, 1968.

Furnish, Victor. "Ministry of Reconciliation." *Currents in Theology and Mission* 4 (August, 1977): 204-18.

Georgi, Dieter. "Corinthians. Second." In *Interpreter's Dictionary of the Bible*, Supplement. Nashville: Abingdon, 1976.

Georgi, Dieter. *Die Gegner des Paulus im zweite Korintherbrief*. Neukirchen-Vluyn: Verlag des Erziehungsverein, 1964.

Grässer, Erich. "Das eine Evangelium. Hermeneutische Erwägungen zu Gal. 1:6-10." *Zeitschrift für Theologie und Kirche* 66 (1969): 306-344.

Grayston, Kenneth. *The Letters of Paul to the Philippians and to the Thessalonians*. Cambridge, 1967.

Güttgemanns, E. *Der Leidende Apostel und sein Herr. Studien zur paulinischen Christologie*. Göttingen: Vandenhoeck & Rupprecht, 1966.

Henneken, Bartholomäus. *Verkündigung und Prophetie in I. Thessalonicherbrief*. Stuttgart: Katholisches Bibelwerk, 1969.

Hering, Jean. *The First Epistle of St. Paul to the Corinthians*. Translated by A. W. Heathcote and P. J. Allcock. London: Epworth, 1962.

Hering, Jean. *The Second Epistle of St. Paul to the Corinthians*. Translated by A. W. Heathcote and P. J. Allcock. London: Epworth, 1967.

Hock, R. F. *The Social Context of Paul's Ministry. Tentmaking and Apostleship*. Philadelphia: Fortress, 1980.

Holmberg, Bengt. *Paul and Power*. Lund: C. W. K. Gleerup, 1978.

Horsley, Richard A. "Wisdom of Word and Words of Wisdom in Corinth (I Cor. 1-4)." *Catholic Biblical Quarterly* 39 (April, 1977): 224-39.

Howard, George. *Paul: Crisis in Galatia*. Cambridge: Cambridge University Press, 1979.

Jewett, Robert. "The Agitators and the Galatian Congregation." *New Testament Studies* 17 (1971): 198-212.

Käsemann, Ernst. *Commentary on Romans*. Translated and edited by Geoffrey W. Bromiley. Translated from the fourth German edition (Tübingen, 1980). Grand Rapids: Eerdmans, 1980.

Käsemann, Ernst. *Essays on New Testament Themes*. Translated by J. W. Montague. London: S. C. M., 1964.

Käsemann, Ernst. *New Testament Questions of Today*. Translated by J. W. Montague. Philadelphia: Fortress, 1969.

Käsemann, Ernst. *Perspectives on Paul*. Translated by M. Kohl. Philadelphia: Fortress, 1971.

Keck, Leander. *Paul and His Letters*. Philadelphia: Fortress, 1979.

Keck, Leander, *The Bible in the Pulpit*. Nashville: Abingdon, 1978.

Kertelge, Karl. "Apokalypsis Jesou Christou (Gal. 1:12)." In *Neues Testament und Kirche*, edited by Joachim Gnilka. Freiburg/Basel: Herder, 1974.

Kertelge, Karl. "Das Apostelamt des Paulus, sein Ursprung und seine Bedeutung." *Biblische Zeitschrift* 14 (2, 1970): 161-81.

Kümmel, Werner G. *Introduction to the New Testament*. Revised edition. Translated by H. C. Kee. Nashville: Abingdon, 1975.

Linn, E. H. *Preaching as Counselling; The Unique Method of Harry Emerson Fosdick*. Valley Forge: Judson, 1966.

Lischer, Richard. *A Theology of Preaching: The Dynamic of the Gospel*. Nashville: Abingdon, 1981.

Malherbe, Abraham. "Gentle as a Nurse." *Novum Testamentum* 12 (1970): 203-217.

Marxsen, Willi. *Der erste Brief an die Thessalonicher*. Zürich: Theologischer Verlag Zürich, 1979.

Marxsen, Willi. *Introduction to the New Testament.* Translated by G. Buswell. Philadelphia: Fortress, 1968.

McMillan, E. "An Aspect of Recent Wisdom Studies in the New Testament." *Restoration Quarterly* 10 (4, 1967): 201-210.

Meeks, Wayne. *The First Urban Christians. The Social World of the Apostle Paul.* New Haven: Yale University Press, 1983.

Meeks, Wayne. "The Social Context of Pauline Theology." *Interpretation* 37 (July, 1982): 266-277.

Moore, A. L. *1 and 2 Thessalonians.* London: Nelson, 1969.

Morris, L. *The First and Second Epistles to the Thessalonians.* Grand Rapids, 1959.

Munck, Johannes. *Paul and the Salvation of Mankind.* Translated by F. Clarke. Atlanta: John Knox, 1977.

Murphy-O'Connor, Jerome. *Paul on Preaching.* New York: Sheed & Ward, 1963.

Murphy-O'Connor, Jerome. "Tradition and Redaction in I Cor. 15:3-7." *Catholic Biblical Quarterly* 43 (4, 1981): 582-89.

Neill, Stephen. *The Interpretation of the New Testament 1861-1961.* New York: Oxford University Press, 1966.

Nichols, J. Randall. *Building the Word.* San Francisco: Harper, 1980.

Oepke, Albrecht. *Der Brief an die Galater.* Edited by Joachim Rohde. Berlin: Evangelische Verlagsanstalt, 1973.

Oepke, Albrecht. *Der Briefe an die Thessalonicher.* Göttingen: Vandenhoeck & Rupprecht, 1953.

Oepke, Albrecht. *Die Missionspredigt des Apostels Paulus.* Leipzig, 1920.

Palmer, Richard E. *Hermeneutics.* Evanston, Illinois: Northwestern University Press, 1969.

Pearson, Birger A. "Hellenistic-Jewish Wisdom Speculation and Paul." In *Aspects of Wisdom in Judaism and Christianity;* edited by R. Wilken. 1975: 43-66.

Perrin, Norman. *The New Testament, An Introduction.* New York: Harcourt, Brace, Jovanovich, 1974.

Perrin, Norman. *The Promise of Bultmann.* Philadelphia: Lippincott, 1969.

Robinson, James M., and John Cobb, eds. *The New Hermeneutic.* New York: Harper, 1964.

Robinson, William C., Jr. "Word and Power (I Cor. 1: 17-25)." In *Soli Deo Gloria; W. C. Robinson,* edited by J. M. Richards. Richmond: John Knox, 1968: 68-82.

Rice, Charles L. *Interpretation and Imagination: The Preacher and Contemporary Literature.* Philadelphia: Fortress Press, 1980.

Rice, Charles L. "Just Church Bells? One Man's View of Preaching Today." *Drew Gateway* (Spring, 1979): 21-27.

Richard, E. "Polemics, Old Testament, and Theology. A Study of II Cor. 3:1-4:6." *Revue Biblique* 88 (3, 1981): 340-367.

Ridderbos, H. *Paul. An Outline of His Theology.* Translated by J. R. DeWitt. Grand Rapids: Eerdmanns, 1975.

Ritschl, Dietrich. *A Theology of Proclamation.* Richmond: John Knox, 1960.

Robertson, Archibald, and Plummer, Alfred. *A Critical and Exegetical Commentary on the First Epistle of St. Paul to the Corinthians.* The International Critical Commentary. Edinburgh: Clark, 1914.

Robinson, James M. and Koester, Helmut. *Trajectories through Early Christianity.* Philadelphia: Fortress, 1971.

Sanders, E. P. *Paul and Palestinian Judaism.* London: S. C. M., 1977.

Scherer, Paul. *The Word God Sent.* Grand Rapids: Baker, 1977.

Schlier, Heinrich. *Der Brief an die Galater.* Göttingen: Vandenhoeck & Rupprecht, 1951.

Schmithals, Walter. *An Introduction to the Theology of Rudolf Bultmann.* Translated by John Bowden. Minneapolis: Augsburg, 1968.

Schmithals, Walter. *Paul and the Gnostics.* Translated by John E. Steely. Nashville: Abingdon, 1972.

Schmithals, Walter. *Gnosticism in Corinth.* Translated by John E. Steely. Nashville: Abingdon, 1973.

Schütz, John H. *Paul and the Anatomy of Apostolic Authority.* New York: Cambridge University Press, 1975.

Schweitzer, Albert. *Paul and His Interpreters.* London: Adam & Charles Black, 1912.

Schweitzer, Albert. *The Mysticim of Paul the Apostle.* Translated by W. Montgomery. New York: Seabury, 1968.

Steimle, Edmund. "Preaching the Biblical Story of Good and Evil." *Union Seminary Quarterly Review* 31 (Spring, 1976): 198-211.

Steimle, Edmund, Morris J. Niedenthal, and Charles L. Rice. *Preaching the Story.* Philadelphia: Fortress, 1980.

Stuhlmacher, Peter. *Das paulinische Evangelium. I. Vorgeschichte.* Göttingen: Vandenhoeck & Rupprecht, 1968.

Stuhlmacher, Peter. *Gerechtigkeit Gottes bei Paulus.* Göttingen: Vandenhoeck & Rupprecht, 1965.

Suggs, M. Jack. "The Word is Near You: Rom. 10:6-10 within the Purpose of the Letter." In *Christian History and Interpretation: Studies Presented to John Knox,* edited by W. Farmer, *et al.* Cambridge: Cambridge University Press, 1967: 289-312.

Theissen, Gerd. "Soteriologische Symbolik in den paulinischen Schriften." *Kerygma und Dogma* 20 (1974): 282-304.

Theissen, Gerd. *The Social Setting of Pauline Christianity.* Translated by J. Schütz. Philadelphia: Fortress, 1981.

Thielecke, Helmut. *The Trouble with the Church; A Call for Renewal.* Translated and edited by John W. Doberstein. New York: Harper, 1965.

Ward, Roy Bowen. "The Opponents of Paul." *Restoration Quarterly* 10 (1967): 185-195.

Wilckens, Ulrich. *Der Brief an die Römer.* Three volumes. Zürich, Einsiedeln, Köln: Benziger/Neukirchener Verlag, 1978-82.

Wilckens, Ulrich. *Weisheit und Torheit. Eine exegetisch-religionsgeschichtliche Untersuchung zu I Kor. 1 und 2.* Tübingen: Mohr-Siebeck, 1959.

Williams, Sam K. "The 'Righteousness of God' in Romans." *Journal of Biblical Literature* 99 (1980): 241-290.

Willimon, William H. *Worship as Pastoral Care.* Nashville: Abingdon, 1979.